# Destination B2

## Grammar & Vocabulary



Malcolm Mann
Steve Taylore-Knowles

MACMILLAN

Macmillan Education
4 Crinan Street
London N1 9XW
A division of Macmillan Publishers Limited
Companies and representatives throughout the world

ISBN 978-0-230-03539-3



First published 2006



Original design by Antony Kleidouchakis
Page make-up by Anne Sherlock
Cover design by Macmillan Publishers Limited
Cover photograph by Bananastock

Authors' acknowledgements
The authors would like to thank Rachel Finnie and Ruth Jimack for their valuable contributions to the planning, writing and editing of this book.



Printed and bound in Thailand
2018 2017 2016
15 14 13

# Introduction

## Overview

***Destination B2: Grammar and Vocabulary*** has been designed for students preparing to take any examination at B2 (Vantage) level on the Council of Europe's Common European Framework scale.
The book provides presentation and practice of all the key grammar, vocabulary and lexico-grammatical areas required for all main B2 level exams, eg Cambridge First.
There are 28 units in the book, with alternating grammar and vocabulary units.

## Grammar

Each grammar unit begins with a clear two-page presentation of grammar rules and examples in table form. Important points are highlighted in Watch out! boxes and US/UK differences are explained.
The grammar practice exercises follow the order of the grammar presentation on a point-by-point basis, and are graded in difficulty through the unit. Exercise types found in all main B2 level exams are included.
In each grammar unit, the vocabulary focus of the following unit is used as a context for presentation and text based exercises.

## Vocabulary

The vocabulary units are topic based, covering all the topics appropriate to exams at B2 level. Each vocabulary unit begins with a clear presentation table comprising five sections: topic vocabulary in contrast, phrasal verbs, phrases and collocations, word patterns and word formation.
The vocabulary exercises are organised according to these sections, and provide systematic practice of the vocabulary presented. Exercise types found in all major B2 examinations are included.
The grammar focus of the preceding unit is consolidated within these exercises.

## Revision and consolidation

Strong emphasis is placed on revision and consolidation. The book includes:

- fourteen two-page reviews (after every two units)
- two four-page progress tests (after units 14 and 28)

## Additional material

Additional reference material is provided at the back of the book. This includes:

- a list of all key irregular verbs
- a unit-by-unit glossary of all contrastive topic vocabulary with definitions and example sentences from the Macmillan Essential Dictionary
- a phrasal verbs database, with definitions and example sentences
- a phrases and collocations database
- a word patterns database
- a word formation database
- a guide to the major differences in vocabulary and spelling between US English and UK English

# Contents

# Unit 1 Grammar

## Present time: present simple, present continuous, present perfect simple, present perfect continuous, stative verbs

### Present simple

| | | | |
|---|---|---|---|
| **Form** | *statement:* | *I/you/we/they* ***travel*** *...* | *He/she/it* ***travels*** *...* |
| | *negative:* | *I/you/we/they* ***don't travel*** *...* | *He/she/it* ***doesn't travel*** *...* |
| | *question:* | ***Do*** *I/you/we/they* ***travel*** *... ?* | ***Does*** *he/she/it* ***travel*** *... ?* |

| Use | Example |
|---|---|
| Current habits | *Toby* ***walks*** *to work.* |
| To talk about how often things happen | *Angela* ***doesn't visit*** *us very often.* |
| Permanent situations | *Carlo* ***works*** *in a travel agent's.* |
| States | ***Do*** *you* ***have*** *an up-to-date passport?* |
| General truths and facts | *Poland* ***is*** *in the European Union.* |

**Watch out!**

- We can also use *do/does* in present simple statements for emphasis.
  *'You don't like going by bus, do you?' 'Actually, I* ***do like*** *going by bus for short distances.'*
  *The bus isn't quicker than the train but it* ***does stop*** *right outside the factory.*

### Present continuous

| | | |
|---|---|---|
| **Form** | *statement:* | *I* ***am driving*** *... You/we/they* ***are driving*** *... He/she/it* ***is driving*** *...* |
| | *negative:* | *I'****m not driving*** *... You/we/they* ***aren't driving*** *... or You'****re****/we'****re****/they'****re not driving*** *... He/she/it* ***isn't driving*** *... or He'****s****/she'****s****/it'****s not driving*** *...* |
| | *question:* | ***Am*** *I* ***driving*** *... ?* ***Are*** *you/we/they* ***driving*** *... ?* ***Is*** *he/she/it* ***driving*** *... ?* |

| Use | Example |
|---|---|
| Actions happening now | *Mike* ***is driving*** *to work at the moment.* |
| Temporary series of actions | *Taxi drivers* ***aren't stopping*** *at the train station because of the roadworks.* |
| Temporary situations | ***Are*** *they* ***staying*** *in a hotel near the Olympic stadium?* |
| Changing and developing situations | *Holidays abroad* ***are becoming*** *increasingly popular.* |
| Annoying habits (usually with *always*) | *Dad* ***is always cleaning*** *the car when I want to use it!* |

### Present perfect simple

| | | | |
|---|---|---|---|
| **Form** | *have/has* + past participle | | |
| | *statement:* | *I/you/we/they* ***have flown*** *...* | *He/she/it* ***has flown*** *...* |
| | *negative:* | *I/you/we/they* ***haven't flown*** *...* | *He/she/it* ***hasn't flown*** *...* |
| | *question:* | ***Have*** *I/you/we/they* ***flown*** *... ?* | ***Has*** *he/she/it* ***flown*** *... ?* |

| Use | Example |
|---|---|
| Situations and states that started in the past and are still true | *She'****s had*** *her motorbike for over six years.* |
| A series of actions continuing up to now | *We'****ve travelled*** *by taxi, bus, plane and train – all in the last twenty-four hours!* |
| Completed actions at a time in the past which is not mentioned | ***Have*** *you ever* ***flown*** *in a helicopter?* |
| Completed actions where the important thing is the present result | *I'****ve booked*** *the coach tickets.* |

**Watch out!**

- Phrases such as *It's the first/second/etc time ...* are followed by the present perfect simple.
  ✓ *It's the second time **I've been** on a plane.*

**US vs UK Grammar**

- Speakers of American English often use the past simple in situations where speakers of British English would use the present perfect simple.
  **US:** *We already **saw** the Sphinx.*
  **UK:** *We**'ve** already **seen** the Sphinx.*
- Speakers of American English use *gotten* as the past participle of the verb 'get', except when 'get' means 'have' or 'possess'. Speakers of British English only ever use *got.*
  **US:** *We've already **gotten** Dan a new backpack for his summer vacation.*
  **UK:** *We've already **got** Dan a new rucksack for his summer holiday.*

## Present perfect continuous

| **Form** | | | |
|---|---|---|---|
| | *statement:* | I/you/we/they **have been travelling** ... | He/she/it **has been travelling** ... |
| | *negative:* | I/you/we/they **haven't been travelling** ... | He/she/it **hasn't been travelling** ... |
| | *question:* | **Have** I/you/we/they **been travelling** ... ? | **Has** he/she/it **been travelling** ... ? |

| Use | Example |
|---|---|
| Actions continuing up to the present moment | *We **have been driving** for hours. Can't we have a break soon?* |
| Actions stopping just before the present moment | *I'm out of breath because I**'ve been running** to get here in time.* |

**Watch out!**

- The present perfect continuous is often used with words and phrases like *all day/week/year/etc, for, since, just,* etc.
  ✓ *We**'ve been walking** for hours and I need a rest.*
- The present perfect continuous is **not** normally used with the words *ever* and *never.*
  ✓ ***Have** you **ever flown** in a helicopter before?*
  ✗ ~~***Have** you **ever been flying** in a helicopter before?*~~
- Sometimes there is very little difference in meaning between the present perfect simple and the present perfect continuous and sometimes there is a difference in meaning.
  ✓ *I **have worked** at the airport for four years.* = *I **have been working** at the airport for four years.*
  ✓ *I **have read** that book about cruise ships.* (I have finished it.) *I **have been reading** that book about cruise ships.* (I have not finished it.)

## Stative verbs

Stative verbs are not normally used in continuous tenses because they don't describe actions.
✓ *I **see** what you mean.*
✗ ~~*I **am seeing** what you mean.*~~

| Use<br>Stative verbs often refer to: | Example |
|---|---|
| thinking | ***believe**, **imagine**, **know**, **mean**, **think**, **understand*** |
| existence | ***be**, **exist*** |
| emotions | ***hate**, **like**, **love**, **need**, **prefer**, **satisfy**, **want*** |
| the human senses | ***hear**, **see**, **smell**, **sound**, **taste*** |
| appearance | ***appear**, **look**, **resemble**, **seem*** |
| possession and relationships between things | ***belong to**, **consist of**, **have**, **include**, **involve**, **own*** |

**Watch out!**

- Some verbs (such as *be, have, imagine, look, see, smell, taste, think*) are stative with one meaning and non-stative with another meaning.
  ✓ ***Do** you **have** your plane ticket with you?* (state: possession)
  ✓ ***Are** you **having** lunch at the moment?* (action: eating)

## A Circle the correct word or phrase.

1 Elizabeth **usually goes / is usually going** to bed at around eleven o'clock.
2 Dan **talks / is talking** on the other phone right now.
3 We **don't eat / aren't eating** any meat at the moment as we're both on a diet.
4 **Does air travel get / Is air travel getting** increasingly safe?
5 My mum **calls / is calling** me every weekend without fail.
6 How much **do babysitters generally earn / are babysitters generally earning**?
7 **You always come / You're always coming** up with excuses for not having done your homework. It's so annoying!
8 **I don't go / I'm not going** out much during the week but **I always try / I'm always trying** to go out somewhere on Saturday night.
9 No, the train **does stop / is stopping** at Cirencester on Saturdays.
10 My mum **takes / is taking** part in ice-skating competitions almost every weekend.

## B Rewrite correctly. Change the words or phrases in bold.

1 My dad **is often getting up** late on Saturday mornings.

..........................................................................................................................................

2 **Are you speaking** any other languages apart from English?

..........................................................................................................................................

3 **I already buy** all my Christmas presents and it's only October!

..........................................................................................................................................

4 It's the first time **I'm ever having** a party at home.

..........................................................................................................................................

5 Actually, I think Darren **does works** quite hard sometimes.

..........................................................................................................................................

6 Carlo **is never eating** Chinese food before.

..........................................................................................................................................

7 Sean **already books** a table for tonight.

..........................................................................................................................................

8 **Needs Melanie** any help painting her new flat?

..........................................................................................................................................

## C Complete using the correct form of the verb in brackets.

1 It's the first time ........................................ (**I** / **ever** / **eat**) octopus!
2 Sandy ........................................ (**not** / **see**) his sister since she went to university.
3 They ........................................ (**go**) on holiday to Spain and won't be back until the end of the month.
4 Poor Tracy! She ........................................ (**write**) that essay for hours now and she still hasn't finished!
5 ........................................ (**you** / **ever** / **meet**) anyone famous?
6 ........................................ (**I** / **try**) to get in touch with Jenny all morning but I can't find her anywhere.
7 ........................................ (**I** / **not finish**) the book yet so I can't tell you what happens.
8 ........................................ (**you** / **already** / **decide**) where you're going this summer?
9 ........................................ (**We** / **live**) here for the last six years.
10 ........................................ (**I** / **never** / **hear**) such nonsense!

## D Complete using the words in the box.

**already • before • ever • for • just • rarely • since • so • still • yet**

1 Have you ...................... dreamt of winning the lottery?
2 I haven't worked out how to set the timer on the video ...................... .
3 My dad's lived in the same house ...................... he was born.
4 The film's only been on ...................... a couple of minutes.
5 Bruce has knocked three men out of the competition ...................... far.
6 I ...................... get the chance to get any exercise – I'm just too busy.
7 He's only ...................... got home.
8 It's eleven o'clock and Todd ...................... hasn't come home. Where could he be?
9 I've never met Ruth ...................... . What's she like?
10 Have you finished ...................... ? That was quick!

## E Choose the correct answer.

1 Ian .......... a shower at the moment, so could you call back in about half an hour?
A takes
B is taking
C has taken
D has been taking

2 .......... to Ipswich before?
A Do you ever go
B Are you ever going
C Have you ever been
D Have you ever been going

3 I .......... to all the local newspapers and TV stations to complain.
A already write
B already writing
C have already written
D have already been writing

4 .......... TV for the last four hours? Turn it off and get some exercise!
A Do you watch
B Are you watching
C Watched you
D Have you been watching

5 Eric, .......... hockey competitively or just for fun?
A do you usually play
B are you usually playing
C have you usually played
D have you usually been playing

6 That's the first time .......... an answer right today!
A I get
B I am getting
C I have got
D I have been getting

7 Jessica has .......... left, I'm afraid.
A already
B yet
C still
D so far

8 Dan .......... in the living room while we redecorate his bedroom.
A sleeps
B is sleeping
C has slept
D does sleep

9 Unfortunately, Simone .......... a day off very often.
A doesn't get
B isn't getting
C hasn't got
D hasn't been getting

10 Actually, I .......... a cup of tea first thing every morning but then I switch to coffee.
A do drink
B am drinking
C have drunk
D have been drinking

## F Complete using the correct form of the words in the box.

**be • disagree • do • include • know • look • see • seem • understand**

### *Ancient aviators?*

Everyone (**1**) ........................ that humans have been flying for only a few hundred years. But (**2**) ........................ it possible that ancient civilizations also had the ability and technology to fly?

In the Nazcan Desert in southern Peru, there are hundreds of lines which an ancient culture drew in the dust. On the ground, they just (**3**) ........................ like straight lines. But when you (**4**) ........................ them from the air, you (**5**) ........................ exactly what they are. They are incredible and enormous pictures. The pictures (**6**) ........................ animals, birds and symbols.

One bizarre theory, which most mainstream scientists (**7**) ........................ with, is that the people who made the lines thousands and thousands of years ago flew above the lines in balloons. It (**8**) ........................ incredible, but a few people (**9**) ........................ believe it's possible.

## G Match to make sentences.

| | | | |
|---|---|---|---|
| **1** | I think ............ | **A** | darker hair than her sister. |
| **2** | I'm thinking ............ | **B** | I'm going to buy the new Racetrack CD. |
| **3** | Phil's looking ............ | **C** | a haircut at the moment. |
| **4** | Phil looks ............ | **D** | for his glasses. Have you seen them? |
| **5** | Claire has ............ | **E** | not old enough to drive a car. |
| **6** | Claire is having ............ | **F** | of getting Dad a CD for his birthday. |
| **7** | Andy is ............ | **G** | very annoying at the moment! |
| **8** | Andy is being ............ | **H** | like he needs a holiday! |

## H Find the extra word in each line.

### International friends

| | | |
|---|---|---|
| **1** | ........................ | I've been to travelling round Europe all summer. It's the first time I've |
| **2** | ........................ | ever been going abroad, and I've had a fantastic time! I've seen |
| **3** | ........................ | loads of interesting places and I have to also made loads of new friends. |
| **4** | ........................ | I've been decided to stay in touch with them now I'm back. One of |
| **5** | ........................ | them, Giselle, is French. She was making on holiday too. We now send |
| **6** | ........................ | text messages are to each other all the time. They're usually in English |
| **7** | ........................ | because my French isn't very good! I'm planning to have visit her in |
| **8** | ........................ | France next year sometime. I hope I can. I am love meeting people from |
| **9** | ........................ | other countries! I want to have had lots of friends from all over the world! |
| **10** | ........................ | Travelling certainly broadens the mind but it also is broadens your circle of friends! |

## I Write one word in each gap.

### Holiday Blues

'You've (**1**) ........................ looking at that timetable for the last ten minutes. It can't be that confusing!' said Sheila angrily.
'I (**2**) ........................ wish you'd be quiet! I've (**3**) ........................ a splitting headache thanks to you!' replied Matt.
'Mum! Dad! Please!' said Alison. 'You're both (**4**) ........................ very silly. (**5**) ........................ is no point at all in blaming each other. That's not going to help us find out what time the next train to Budapest is due to leave.'
'You (**6**) ........................ quite right, darling. I (**7**) ........................ sorry,' said Sheila.
'Me too,' mumbled Matt. 'Now, let's have another look at this timetable. Well, it (**8**) ........................ like we (**9**) ........................ definitely missed the last train today. That was the 18.20 we just missed, wasn't it?'
'I (**10**) ........................ so,' said Sheila. 'I mean, it did leave at 18.20. Whether it's actually going to Budapest or not is another question.'
'Well, one thing is (**11**) ........................ in doubt,' said Matt.
'What's that?' asked Sheila and Alison together.
'This is the worst holiday we've (**12**) ........................ been on,' said Matt. 'Next year, we're going to try something far less adventurous.'
'Agreed!' said Sheila and Alison.

## J Complete each second sentence using the word given, so that it has a similar meaning to the first sentence. Write between two and five words in each gap.

**1** What's the price of the tickets, Jimmy? **much**
How ........................................................................ , Jimmy?

**2** Are these your trainers? **to**
Do ........................................................................ you?

**3** Sasha's not keen on team sports at all. **like**
Sasha ........................................................................ team sports at all.

**4** It's only her second time in a recording studio. **been**
She ........................................................................ in a recording studio once before.

**5** We got here three hours ago. **have**
We ........................................................................ three hours.

**6** I started writing this hours ago and it's still not right. **writing**
I ........................................................................ hours and it's still not right.

**7** This is my first experience of flying alone. **time**
It is the first ........................................................................ alone.

**8** Sharon's in the bath at the moment. **a**
Sharon ........................................................................ at the moment.

**9** Paul enjoys surprises apart from on his birthday. **does**
Paul ........................................................................ surprises, just not on his birthday!

## Travel and transport

### Topic vocabulary in contrast

see page 186 for definitions

| | | |
|---|---|---|
| voyage / journey / trip / travel / excursion | fare / ticket / fee | live / stay |
| view / sight | miss / lose | border / edge / line |
| world / earth | take / bring / go | length / distance |
| area / territory | book / keep | guide / lead |
| season / period | arrive / reach | native / home |

### Phrasal verbs

| | |
|---|---|
| **catch up with** reach the same point/level as | **pick up** stop in a vehicle to give someone a lift |
| **check in** register at a hotel or an airport | **pull in** stop by the side of the road in a car |
| **check out** leave a hotel; investigate | **run over** hit with a car |
| **drop off** let someone get out of a vehicle; fall asleep | **see off** go to a train station, etc, to see someone leave |
| **get back** return from a place | **set out/off** start a journey |
| **go away** go on holiday | **take off** leave the ground |
| **keep up with** stay at the same point/level as | **turn round** go back in the opposite direction |
| **make for** go in the direction of | |

### Phrases and collocations

| | |
|---|---|
| **accident** | have an accident; be (involved) in an accident; do sth by accident |
| **advance** | in advance; advance to/towards a place |
| **ahead** | go straight ahead; go ahead; be ahead of sth/sb |
| **direction** | a change of direction; in the direction of sth; in this/that direction |
| **head** | off the top of your head; head for/towards a place; head over heels (in love) |
| **holiday** | go/be on holiday; have/take a holiday; bank holiday |
| **left** | go/turn/etc left; on the left; on the left-hand side; in the left-hand corner; left-handed |
| **route** | plan your/a route; take a route |
| **sights** | see the sights |
| **sightseeing** | go sightseeing |
| **speed** | at (high/full/etc) speed; a burst of speed; speed limit |
| **tour** | go on/take a tour of/(a)round somewhere; tour a place; tour guide |
| **trip** | business trip; school trip; go on a trip; take a trip (to a place) |
| **way** | lose/make/find your way; in a way; on the way; go all the way (to sth/swh) |

### Word patterns

| | |
|---|---|
| **afraid** of sth/sb/doing; afraid to do | **invite** sb to do |
| **appear** to be | **keen** to do; keen on sth/sb/doing |
| **arrange** sth (with sb); arrange for sb to do | **live** in/at a place; live on/for sth; live here/there |
| **arrive** in/at a place; arrive here/there | **regret** (not) doing; regret sth; regret to tell/inform you |
| **continue** sth/doing; continue to do; continue with sth | **think** of/about sth/sb/doing |
| **differ** from sth/sb | **write** about sth/sb/doing; write (sth) (to sb); write sb sth; write sth down |
| **dream** about/of sth/sb/doing | |

### Word formation

| | | |
|---|---|---|
| **arrange** rearrange, arrangement | **direct** indirect, direction, director, (in)directly | **recognise** (un)recognisable, recognition |
| **arrive** arrival | **distant** distantly, distance | **time** timetable |
| **broad** breadth, broaden | **enter** entrance | **tour** tourism, tourist |
| **culture** cultural(ly), (un)cultured | **inhabit** inhabitant | **world** worldwide |
| **differ** different(ly), difference | **photograph** photography, photographer, photographic | |

### Topic vocabulary in contrast

## A Choose the correct answer.

1 You need a passport to cross the ........... between Mexico and the United States.
A edge C border
B line D rim

2 The hotel where we are ........... is quite luxurious.
A living C existing
B remaining D staying

3 When you ........... your destination, your tour guide will meet you at the airport.
A arrive C reach
B get D achieve

4 It can be quite busy here during the tourist ........... .
A season C phase
B period D stage

5 David ........... me to the train station every morning.
A goes C has
B takes D makes

6 I always enjoy our school ........... to France.
A excursion C trip
B journey D travel

7 Hurry up, or we'll ........... the bus!
A avoid C drop
B miss D lose

8 The brochure says that the hotel has a great ........... of the sea.
A appearance C sight
B look D view

9 I must remember to ........... a souvenir back from Spain for my grandmother.
A go C bring
B take D keep

10 The ........... from London to Berlin is about 919 kilometres.
A measure C gap
B length D distance

11 Make sure you ........... a hotel before you come to our island, especially in the summer.
A book C put
B keep D take

12 I live in Barcelona, but my ........... town is Madrid.
A birth C native
B home D origin

## B Circle the correct word.

1 I hope to go on a trip round the **world / earth** one day.
2 You learn a lot about the local **territory / area** by speaking to local people.
3 It's good to have someone to **lead / guide** you when you are on holiday.
4 I get the train to work every day and the **fare / fee** is quite expensive.
5 Captain Cook discovered Australia on a **voyage / travel** to the Pacific.
6 Most tourist attractions in London charge an admission **fee / ticket**.
7 The sunset over Niagara Falls really is a magnificent **look / sight**.

### Phrasal verbs

## C Complete using the correct form of the words in the box.

| |
|---|
| **catch • check • get • go • make • pick • pull • see** |

1 Let's go to the airport to .................................. Grandpa off when he flies back home.
2 If it starts to rain, .................................. for a nearby cave to wait for it to pass.
3 We would like to remind all guests that they must .................................. out before midday.
4 Please .................................. in and stop so that I can buy something to drink.
5 Every Saturday night my dad .................................. us up outside the cinema.
6 I think the neighbours have .................................. away for the weekend.
7 John's up ahead so Greg is pedalling fast to .................................. up with him.
8 We're going on holiday tomorrow, but we'll call you when we .................................. back.

**D** Write a phrasal verb in the correct form to replace the words in italics. Add any other words you need.

1 We can *start our journey* .............................................. towards the mountains at dawn.
2 Dad fetched the luggage while Mum *registered* .............................................. at the hotel.
3 I asked the taxi driver to *let me get out* .............................................. outside the train station.
4 Oh, no! I've forgotten my passport! We'll have to *go back* .............................................. and get it!
5 The most exciting moment is when the plane *leaves the ground* .............................................. .
6 Stop the car! I think we've *hit* .............................................. a dog.
7 I don't think a horse can ever *stay at the same speed as* .............................................. a car.

### Phrases and collocations

**E** Write one word in each gap.

1 The speed ....................... in towns is 50 km/h and you shouldn't go faster than that.
2 Why don't we ....................... the scenic route along the coast?
3 If you buy your plane ticket ....................... advance, it's often cheaper than if you wait.
4 I can't remember the name of the hotel we stayed at off the ....................... of my head.
5 I'm sorry I'm late! I ....................... my way and had to ask for directions.
6 My mum's away in Germany on a business ....................... at the moment.
7 The bank? Well, turn left here, then go ....................... ahead for a kilometre and it's on the left.
8 If you look on your left-hand ....................... as we turn this corner, you'll see Big Ben.
9 I'll look round the shops in the morning and then ....................... sightseeing in the afternoon.
10 My grandma hasn't driven since she ....................... an accident last year.
11 I love visiting foreign places, ....................... the sights and learning about other cultures.
12 During the 70s, many British people started to go ....................... holiday to Spain.
13 While you're in London, you should take a tour ....................... the Houses of Parliament.

### Word patterns

**F** Choose the correct answer.

1 I've always dreamt ........... China.
A to visit B of visiting C I visit D visit
2 The travel agency is arranging for us ........... at a really nice hotel.
A stay B of staying C to stay D staying
3 My dad says he always regrets ........... more.
A to not travel B not travelling C he not travel D of not travelling
4 John seems keen ........... how to drive as soon as he can.
A of learning B he learn C for learn D to learn
5 Now, class, I'd like you all to write ........... a description of your last holiday.
A me B to me C it me D about me
6 When you arrive ..........., have your passport ready.
A to the airport B in the airport C on the airport D at the airport
7 The Joneses have invited us ........... to Australia with them this summer.
A going B for going C about going D to go
8 The in-flight entertainment may differ ........... that advertised.
A to B from C in D at

## G Find the extra word in each line.

### The cancelled trip

1 ........................ Oh, let me tell you about our trip. Did you know that Sara is afraid of be
2 ........................ flying? We had arranged it with her family to go to France for a few days.
3 ........................ I have always wanted to see Paris and would love to live in there one day.
4 ........................ Well, we got to the airport and Sara appeared being nervous. I asked her if
5 ........................ she was okay and she said she was fine, so we continued on to our way.
6 ........................ We went through passport control and I could see so that Sara wasn't
7 ........................ keen on going any further. Just then, a voice announced: 'We regret it to
8 ........................ inform passengers that Flight 114 to France is been cancelled.' That was
9 ........................ our flight! Sarah said she was glad because of she was too frightened to
10 ........................ fly anyway! So, we all went to home. That was the end of *that* trip!

**Word formation**

## H Use the word given in capitals at the end of each line to form a word that fits in the gap in the same line.

It's not always easy being a (**1**) .............................. . You spend half your — **TOUR**
time making (**2**) .............................. for your holiday and the other half — **ARRANGE**
worrying about sticking to the (**3**) .............................. . I think it's relaxing — **TIME**
sometimes to spend a holiday at home. There are no (**4**) .............................. — **CULTURE**
problems, you don't need someone to be the (**5**) .............................. and — **PHOTOGRAPH**
you know that the local (**6**) .............................. are always friendly! — **INHABIT**

## I Complete the sentences by changing the form of the word in capitals when this is necessary.

1 Beijing has changed so much in the last few years that it's almost .............................. . (**RECOGNISE**).
2 The number of cars .............................. (**WORLD**) is about a billion and is increasing all the time.
3 The new maglev trains run on a completely .............................. (**DIFFER**) system from ordinary trains.
4 Living in a foreign country really does .............................. (**BROAD**) your horizons.
5 I can't find a .............................. (**DIRECT**) flight from London to Delhi so I've booked one that changes in Frankfurt.
6 All passengers must complete a visa form upon .............................. (**ARRIVE**) at Singapore airport.
7 You can still see old milestones by the side of the road in England, showing the .............................. (**DISTANT**) to the nearest town.
8 The Museum of Transport has a full-sized jet plane next to the .............................. (**ENTER**).

## A Write one word in each gap

### THE GREAT BRITISH SEASIDE

What (1) ........................ the phrase 'the great British seaside' bring to mind? Most people, if asked to respond (2) ........................ the top of their heads, associate (3) ........................ on holiday to places such as Blackpool or Torquay with poor weather, old, faded attractions and a low standard of accommodation. These days, when people are more likely to go abroad to (4) ........................ the sights, traditional British seaside towns (5) ........................ suffering from an image problem. Now, finally, some of the resorts (6) ........................ decided to bring their images up to date in the hope that a (7) ........................ of direction will bring back the tourists. Many will need a lot of convincing, but those that (8) ........................ come will find that today's Blackpool differs quite a bit (9) ........................ the picture postcard past.

After years of neglect, Blackpool has to work hard to catch (10) ........................ with foreign destinations but that's precisely what it (11) ........................ doing. It's the first time so much (12) ........................ happened to improve the place in such a short time. A massive building project, including a new casino and indoor entertainment centre, (13) ........................ that rainy days are no longer a problem. And it appears (14) ........................ be working. As the tourists start to make (15) ........................ the bright lights of Blackpool once again, it seems that the great British seaside has a bright future ahead.

(1 mark per answer)

## B Complete the sentences by changing the form of the word in capitals when this is necessary.

**16** I've always wanted to be a travel .............................. (**PHOTOGRAPH**) and take pictures of exotic places.

**17** None of us were sure which .............................. (**DIRECT**) to go in, so we got out the map.

**18** Since I was here five years ago, Delhi has changed so much that it's practically .............................. (**RECOGNISE**).

**19** Once we got to the station, I quickly looked through the .............................. (**TIME**) to see when the next train was.

**20** I've got a cousin at university who is studying .............................. (**TOUR**) and hopes to open a hotel.

**21** As we got closer to the Amazonian village, the .............................. (**INHABIT**) came out to meet us.

**22** The .............................. (**ARRIVE**) of Flight 472 from Amsterdam has been delayed by one hour.

(1 mark per answer)

## C Complete each second sentence using the word given, so that it has a similar meaning to the first sentence. Write between two and five words in each gap.

**23** As soon as we got on the plane, the pilot told us to get off again. **just**
We ........................................................................ the plane when the pilot told us to get off again.

**24** We arrived in Budapest two days ago. **for**
We ........................................................................ two days.

**25** I visited Paris once before. **second**
This is the ........................................................................ Paris.

**26** I find it hard to go at the same speed as my husband on walking holidays. **up**
I find it hard to ........................................................................ my husband on walking holidays.

27 Joan has always been very fond of travelling and has been everywhere. **keen**
Joan has always been very ............................................................................................ and has been everywhere.

28 We drove away as fast as we could, ready to begin our adventure. **full**
We drove away ............................................................................................ , ready to begin our adventure.

29 As the storm started, we went towards the old house. **direction**
As the storm started, we went ............................................................................................ the old house.

30 I'm sorry I didn't look at the hotel room before I booked it. **regret**
I ............................................................................................ the hotel room before I booked it.

(2 marks per answer)

## D Choose the correct answer.

31 Our next door neighbour ........... his car every Sunday.
A is washing
B washes
C has washed
D is wash

32 Last summer, I ........... to the beach almost every day.
A went
B was going
C have been
D have been going

33 'Whose is this plane ticket on the floor?'
'Oh, it ........... to me. Thank you.'
A is belonging
B belongs
C has belonged
D belonged

34 'I'm really tired of travelling so much.'
'I thought you ........... a bit quiet.'
A were seeming
B have seemed
C have been seeming
D seemed

35 'You look thoughtful.'
'I ........... about our holiday last year.'
A just think
B had just thought
C am just think
D was just thinking

36 'You went to Chile, didn't you?'
'No, but I ........... to Peru, which is right next door.'
A had gone
B was gone
C did go
D was going

(1 mark per answer)

## E Choose the correct answer.

37 Three people were captured at the ........... today trying to get into the country.
A line C border
B equator D edge

38 There's a fantastic ........... from the top of the Empire State Building!
A view C appearance
B sight D look

39 Once we get to the hotel, let's just ........... quickly and then do a bit of sightseeing.
A set down C check in
B make up D turn up

40 I'm going to ask for directions because I think we've ........... our way.
A missed C mistaken
B misplaced D lost

41 We usually do go by train, even though the car ........... is a lot quicker.
A travel C trip
B journey D voyage

42 Passengers requiring a special meal during the flight should inform the airline in ........... .
A ahead C advance
B front D forward

(1 mark per answer)

**Total mark: ...... / 50**

## Past time: past simple, past continuous, past perfect simple, past perfect continuous, would, used to / be/get used to

### Past simple

**Form** statement: *I/you/he/she/it/we/they* ***played*** *...*
negative: *I/you/he/she/it/we/they* ***didn't play*** *...*
question: ***Did*** *I/you/he/she/it/we/they* ***play*** *... ?*

Note: Irregular verbs do not take 'ed' in the past simple. Learn the past simple form of irregular verbs. See page 194.

| Use | Example |
|---|---|
| Single completed actions | *Tom and I* ***played*** *a game of chess and he* ***won****.* |
| Habits in the past | ***Did*** *you* ***collect*** *stamps when you were younger?* |
| Permanent situations in the past | *A famous footballer* ***lived*** *in our house before we bought it.* |
| General truths and facts about the past | *Crosswords* ***didn't become*** *popular until the 1930s.* |
| The main events in a story | *The referee* ***blew*** *the whistle and Simon* ***passed*** *the ball to James, who* ***ran*** *towards the goal.* |

**Watch out!**

- We can also use *did* in past simple statements for emphasis.
  ✓ *'Why didn't you win your match yesterday?' 'I* ***did win****. Who told you I didn't?'*
  ✓ *We lost 5-0 but at least we* ***did get*** *into the final.*

### Past continuous

**Form** statement: *I/he/she/it* ***was playing*** *...* — *You/we/they* ***were playing*** *...*
negative: *I/he/she/it* ***wasn't playing*** *...* — *You/we/they* ***weren't playing*** *...*
question: ***Was*** *I/he/she/it* ***playing*** *... ?* — ***Were*** *you/we/they* ***playing*** *... ?*

| Use | Example |
|---|---|
| Actions happening at a particular moment in the past | *At five o'clock, I* ***was reading*** *my new book.* |
| Temporary situations in the past | *Greg* ***was living*** *in London at the time.* |
| Annoying past habits (usually with *always*) | *When we were young, my brother* ***was always borrowing*** *my toys.* |
| Actions in progress over a period of time | *Daniel* ***was playing*** *video games all morning yesterday.* |
| Two actions in progress at the same time | ***Were*** *Ulla and her friends* ***playing*** *Monopoly while we* ***were playing*** *Draughts?* |
| Background information in a story | *The sun* ***was shining*** *and the birds* ***were singing****. Lisa opened the window and looked out.* |

**Watch out!**

- When one action in the past interrupts another action in progress, we use the past simple and the past continuous together.
  ✓ *I* ***was playing*** *on my computer when it suddenly* ***crashed****.*
- We do **not** use the past continuous for regular or repeated actions in the past.
  ✓ *When we were on holiday, we* ***played*** *volleyball every day.*
  ✗ ~~*When we were on holiday, we* ***were playing*** *volleyball every day.*~~
- We do not usually use stative verbs in continuous tenses. See Unit 1, page 7.

### Past perfect simple

**Form** *had* + past participle

| Use | Example |
|---|---|
| Situations and states before the past | *We****'d lived*** *next to the gym for a couple of months before I decided to join.* |
| Completed actions before a moment in the past | *I****'d*** *already* ***bought*** *the computer game when I saw it was cheaper in another shop.* |
| Completed actions where the important thing is the result at a moment in the past | *We didn't feel like playing Scrabble because we* ***had*** *just* ***finished*** *a long game of Monopoly.* |

**Watch out!**

- There is often little or no difference in meaning between the past perfect simple and the past simple.
  ✓ *We'**d lived** next to the gym for a couple of months before I decided to join.*
  ✓ *We **lived** next to the gym for a couple of months before I decided to join.*
- After we have used the past perfect simple once, we often then use the past simple instead of continuing to use the past perfect. *I **had** already **had** one flying lesson, which **was** great fun, and I **knew** immediately that I **wanted** to get my pilot's licence.*
- Phrases such as *It was the first/second/etc time …* are followed by the past perfect simple.
  ✓ *It was the second time **I'd been** on a plane.*

## Past perfect continuous

**Form**
statement: *I/you/he/she/it/we/they **had been playing** …*
negative: *I/you/he/she/it/we/they **hadn't been playing** …*
question: ***Had** I/you/he/she/it/we/they **been playing** … ?*

| Use | Example |
|---|---|
| Actions continuing up to a moment in the past | *When you saw us, we **had been running** for six miles – and we still had a mile to go!* |
| Actions stopping just before a moment in the past | *Sarah looked tired because she **had been exercising** all morning.* |

## would

**Form** *would* + bare infinitive

| Use | Example |
|---|---|
| Past habits, particularly for the distant past | *When I was very young, my grandfather **would** take me to the park to play.* |

**Watch out!**

- We don't often use *would* in questions or negative statements with this meaning. In negative statements, we can use *would never*.
  ✓ *We **would never** play games together as a family when I was growing up.*

## used to

**Form** *used to* + bare infinitive
statement: *I/you/he/she/it/we/they **used to** train three times a week.*
negative: *I/you/he/she/it/we/they **didn't use to** be good at football.*
*I/you/he/she/it/we/they **never used to** be so good at football.*
*I/you/he/she/it/we/they **used not to** be good at football.*
question: ***Did** I/you/he/she/it/we/they **use to** play hockey here?*

| Use | Example |
|---|---|
| Past habits and states, particularly for the distant past | *My mother **used to** play a lot of squash before I was born.* |

**Watch out!**

- To talk about a past state, we can use *used to*, but **not** *would*.
  ✓ *We **used to** have a house that was right next to the park.*
  ✗ ~~*We **would** have a house that was right next to the park.*~~

## be/get used to

**Form** *be/get used to* + *-ing* form / noun

| Use | Example |
|---|---|
| A situation that is familiar or no longer strange | *I didn't like being the goalkeeper at first but now I'**m used to** it.* |

**Watch out!**

- When we want to talk about the process of becoming familiar with something, we use *get used to*.
  ✓ *I'**m** gradually **getting used to** being in a new team.*

## A Circle the correct word or phrase.

1 I **saw / was seeing** Maria for the first time at Ray's birthday party.
2 Richard **watched / was watching** TV when the phone rang.
3 When we were on holiday, we **went / were going** to the café almost every day.
4 Denise **practised / was practising** the song every day until she could sing it perfectly.
5 The phone was engaged when I called. Who **did you talk / were you talking** to?
6 Mr Connors **owned / was owning** two houses and a villa in the south of France.
7 I **did / was doing** my homework as soon as I got home from school.
8 A car came round the corner and I **jumped / was jumping** out of the way.
9 When my dad met my mum, he **worked / was working** as a bus driver.
10 I **got / was getting** up at six o'clock every morning last week!
11 My cousin and I **played / were playing** on the computer when there was a power cut.
12 No, that's not right. I **did pass / was passing** the test. I got a B.

## B Complete using the correct form of the verb in brackets.

1 Where ............................................ (**you / go**) when I saw you on the bus last night?
2 ............................................ (**you / enjoy**) the film?
3 When we shared a room, Zoë ............................................ (**always / take**) my things. It was so annoying!
4 When I went to get the tickets, I realised I ............................................ (**not / have**) any money.
5 When I was young, we ............................................ (**go**) to France every year on holiday.
6 Elvis ............................................ (**become**) famous for the song *Blue Suede Shoes*.
7 When you rang last night, I ............................................ (**work**) in the garden so I didn't hear the phone.
8 I ............................................ (**hear**) from Davina last night. She says hello.
9 The old man ............................................ (**appear**) to be very tired and he slowly sat down.
10 We ............................................ (**throw**) a surprise party for my brother last Saturday.

## C Circle the correct word or phrase.

Dear Lisa,

Thanks for your letter. I (**1**) **just left / had just left** for school when I saw the postman and he (**2**) **gave / had given** it to me. It was really funny! I (**3**) **read / had read** it during maths and it (**4**) **made / had made** me laugh. I almost (**5**) **got / had got** in trouble!

Anyway, I'm excited because I (**6**) **had / had had** my first judo lesson yesterday. I (**7**) **was / had been** late for the lesson because when I (**8**) **got / had got** there, I suddenly realised I (**9**) **left / had left** my judo suit at home! So I (**10**) **went / had gone** all the way home and when I (**11**) **got / had got** back, the lesson (**12**) **already began / had already begun**. The instructor was really nice, though, and I (**13**) **learned / had learned** how to do some basic throws. Can't wait till next time!

What about you and your taekwondo? The last time I (**14**) **spoke / had spoken** to you, you (**15**) **talked / had talked** about giving it up. What (**16**) **did you decide / had you decided**?

I think that's all for now. My mum and I are going shopping shortly, so I'd better post this.

Speak to you soon.

Love,

Charlotte

## D Complete using the past perfect simple or past perfect continuous of the verbs in the box. You may need to use a negative form.

| **eat • stay • wait • know • write • see • listen • get • have • run** |
|---|

1. By the time he died, Beethoven ............................................ nine symphonies.
2. We chose the Hotel Rio because we ............................................ there before.
3. We ............................................ for over an hour when the train finally arrived.
4. I was completely out of breath because I ............................................ .
5. I ............................................ the film before, so I knew how it ended.
6. When he got married, I ............................................ Chris for about two years.
7. Johnson ............................................ ready for the race for six months and finally the big moment came.
8. Vivian ............................................ computer lessons for very long so she wasn't sure how to use the Internet.
9. Holly ............................................ oysters before, so she wasn't sure what to do with them.
10. I ............................................ to my new CD for a few minutes when the CD player started making a funny noise.

## E Choose the correct answer.

1. My brother and I ........... swimming almost every day last summer.
   A went
   B had been going
   C were going
   D had gone

2. We ........... when someone knocked at the door.
   A talked
   B had talked
   C were talking
   D were talked

3. When the robbery happened, the security guard ........... !
   A slept
   B was sleeping
   C had slept
   D was slept

4. Jack ........... chess before so I showed him what to do.
   A hadn't been playing
   B didn't play
   C wasn't playing
   D hadn't played

5. I wasn't sure how Belinda would react because I ........... her long.
   A didn't know
   B wasn't knowing
   C hadn't been knowing
   D hadn't known

6. Ian ........... at the factory long when he was made a manager.
   A hadn't been working
   B wasn't working
   C didn't work
   D wasn't worked

7. I wanted to say goodbye to Jerry, but he ........... .
   A was already left
   B already left
   C had already been leaving
   D had already left

8. When we got to the airport, I realised I ........... my passport at home!
   A was left
   B had left
   C left
   D had been leaving

## F Circle the incorrect words or phrases and rewrite them correctly.

1 I had paint on my shoes because I'd painted my bedroom all morning.
..............................................
2 I missed the start of the film because I buy popcorn.
..............................................
3 It was obvious that Bill has worked because he was very tired when I saw him.
..............................................
4 We had been tidying the garden for hours and I was needing a rest.
..............................................
5 When the bus was arriving, we missed it because we were talking.
..............................................
6 During the Christmas holiday, I was eating too much and watching too much TV!
..............................................
7 Julian was learning all about computer games by the time he was six.
..............................................
8 My grandfather was owning a hotel by the beach until he sold it last year.
..............................................

## G Circle the correct word or phrase.

1 When she was a girl, my mum **would / used to** live in a village.
2 I really can't **be / get** used to having a new baby brother.
3 People **would** / **are used to** die of diseases in the past that we can cure today.
4 There **would / used to** be a cinema on this corner, but they knocked it down.
5 It was strange at first, but I'm used to **play / playing** the bagpipes now.
6 Didn't you **use to / be used to** have blonde hair?
7 Christopher was **being / getting** used to the idea of joining the army.
8 People never **would / used to** be so worried about crime in this area.

## H Complete each second sentence using the word given, so that it has a similar meaning to the first sentence. Write between two and five words in each gap.

1 People walked more fifty years ago than they do now. **would**
Fifty years ago, .................................................................................. than they do now.
2 My parents wouldn't let me stay out late when I was young. **used**
My parents .................................................................................. let me stay out late when I was young.
3 Did you know that Carol played basketball for her country? **to**
Did you know that Carol .................................................................................. basketball for her country?
4 Sending messages around the world instantly is no longer unusual. **got**
We .................................................................................. messages around the world instantly.
5 When he was a teacher, my dad often used to get home quite late. **would**
When he was a teacher, my dad .................................................................................. quite late.
6 Do you think you could learn to live without your mobile phone? **used**
Do you think you could .................................................................................. without your mobile phone?

**7** In the past, people wouldn't go as far away on holiday as they do today. **use**
In the past, people .......................................................................................... as far away on holiday as they do today.

**8** This town has a lot more cinemas than it had in the past. **used**
This town .......................................................................................... so many cinemas.

## I Find the extra word in each line.

### Childhood

**1** .......................... Childhood would used to be quite different from what it is today. Young
**2** .......................... people didn't use not to have so much leisure time. Today's children may
**3** .......................... complain about their schoolwork, but our great-grandparents would to go
**4** .......................... out to work at a very young age. They had often been left school by
**5** .......................... the time they were fourteen and were found a job. This meant that they
**6** .......................... have had little free time for hobbies or leisure activities, especially when
**7** .......................... they had been working hard all day. Of course, they got themselves used
**8** .......................... to working long hours eventually, but it would meant that they had to
**9** .......................... grow up very quickly. Today, we are got used to having some free time to
**10** .......................... do things we enjoy, a luxury people in the past rarely were had.

## J Write one word in each gap.

### The night before

Jane lay awake. She had (**1**) .......................... preparing for the next day (**2**) .......................... a long time and now she couldn't sleep. Her team (**3**) .......................... playing the local champions at water polo in the final and Jane was the captain. She (**4**) .......................... feeling the pressure.

She turned over and remembered how she (**5**) .......................... learned to swim. Her father had taught her. They (**6**) .......................... go to the local pool every day after school and her father (**7**) .......................... to show her what to do. She hadn't liked the water at first, but she soon (**8**) .......................... used to it. She learned quickly and joined the water polo team. She had (**9**) .......................... their youngest member!

She quickly got used to scoring goals and (**10**) .......................... under pressure, but tomorrow was different. It was the biggest match of her life. She closed her eyes again and tried to get to sleep. 'I (**11**) .......................... used to have problems sleeping,' she thought to herself. 'But then again, I didn't (**12**) .......................... to be the captain of the team.' She watched the clock change slowly and knew that it was going to be a long night.

# Hobbies, sport and games

## Topic vocabulary in contrast

see page 186 for definitions

| | | |
|---|---|---|
| pitch / track / court / course / ring / rink | umpire / referee | sport / athletics |
| win / beat / score | final / finale / end / ending | interval / half time |
| play / game | bat / stick / rod / racket | draw / equal |
| spectator / viewer | amateur / professional | competitor / opponent |

## Phrasal verbs

| | |
|---|---|
| **bring forward** change the date/time of an event so it happens earlier | **knock out** defeat and remove from a competition; make unconscious |
| **carry on** continue | **look out** be careful |
| **get round to** start (after planning to do sth for a long time) | **pull out** stop being involved in an activity |
| **get up to** do; do sth you should not do | **put off** delay, postpone |
| **go in for** enter (a competition, etc); like | **put up with** tolerate |
| **go off** stop liking | **take to** start (as a habit) |
| **join in** participate, take part | **take up** start (a hobby, sport, etc); fill an amount of space/time |

## Phrases and collocations

| | |
|---|---|
| **best** | make the best of sth; do your best; the best at sth/doing |
| **chance** | have/take/get a chance to do; have a chance of doing; some/little/etc chance of (your) doing; the chances of (your) doing; take a chance (on sth); chance of a lifetime |
| **go** | your go; have a go |
| **height** | in height; afraid of heights; height of sth |
| **mad** | mad about/on sth/sb/doing; go/become mad |
| **pleasure** | take pleasure in sth/doing; gain/get pleasure from sth/doing |
| **popular** | popular with/among |
| **side** | (on) the opposite side; (on) the far side; side with sb; on the winning/losing side |
| **talent** | have a talent (for sth/doing); talent contest |
| **time** | on time; (just) in time; the whole time; high/about time; take your time (doing); take time to do; sth takes up (your) time; spend time doing; spend time on; at/for a certain time; time passes; find time to do; make/find time for; for the time being; have a good/nice time (doing); tell the time; free/spare/leisure time |
| **turn** | turn (a)round/away; turn sth over; in turn; take turns; take it in turn(s) (to do); your turn (to do) |

## Word patterns

| | |
|---|---|
| **compete** against/with sb; compete for/in sth | **listen** to sth/sb |
| **concentrate** on sth/doing | **love** sth/sb/doing; love to do |
| **difficult** to do; find sth difficult; find it difficult to do | **mean** to do; it/this means that; it/this means sth/doing |
| **fond** of sth/sb/doing | **prefer** to do (rather than [to] do); prefer sth (rather than sth); prefer sth/doing (to sth/doing) |
| **free** to do; free from/of sth; free for sth | **stop** sth/doing; stop to do; stop sb from doing |
| **interested** in sth/doing | **sure/certain** make/be sure/certain that; sure/certain to do; be sure/certain of sth |
| **involve** sth/doing; involved in sth/doing | |

## Word formation

| | | |
|---|---|---|
| **allow** disallow, allowance, allowable | **fortune** misfortune, (un)fortunate(ly) | **medal** medallist, medallion |
| **associate** disassociate, association, (un)associated | **interest** (un)interesting(ly) | **oppose** opposition, opponent, opposite, opposing |
| **compete** competition, competitor, competitive(ly) | **know** knowledge, (un)knowledgeable | **practice** practise, (im)practical(ly) |
| **enjoy** enjoyment, enjoyable | **lose** lost, loss | **train** retrain, trainer |
| **equip** equipment, equipped | **maintain** maintenance | |

### Topic vocabulary in contrast

## A Complete using the correct form of the words in the box.

| course |
|---|
| court |
| pitch |
| ring |
| rink |
| track |

1 We used to go skating at the ice ........................ every Saturday.
2 Keith had never seen such a large golf ........................ until he went to Scotland.
3 We all met at the basketball ........................ at half past three.
4 It's called a boxing ........................ , but it's actually square!
5 For the 800 metres race, you have to run round the ........................ twice.
6 The football match had to be called off because the ........................ was flooded.

| beat |
|---|
| win |
| score |

7 Our team ........................ until half time, but in the second half the other team ........................ three goals, and so they ........................ us. But it was a great match!

| bat |
|---|
| stick |
| rod |
| racket |

8 Adrian got a new fishing ........................ for his birthday.
9 Can I borrow your tennis ........................ ?
10 Why are hockey ........................ such a strange shape?
11 I'd spend hours putting linseed oil on my cricket ........................ to keep the wood strong.

## B Circle the correct word or phrase.

1 The **umpire / referee** blew the whistle and the most important football match I've ever played began.
2 We used to play rugby in the winter term, football in the spring term, and we'd do **athletics / sport** and swimming in the summer term.
3 Do you fancy a **game / play** of cards?
4 I only do magic tricks for fun. I've never thought of becoming **an amateur / a professional** magician.
5 The play was so boring, we walked out during **half time / the interval**.
6 Coventry City **equalled / drew** 3-3 with Sunderland in the match last Saturday.
7 **Spectators / Viewers** who watched last week's programme will remember we were looking at the history of baseball.
8 We got through to the **final / finale**, but then lost to Cirencester.
9 Most people prefer films which have a happy **end / ending**.
10 Would all **opponents / competitors** please make their way to the starting line?

### Phrasal verbs

## C Complete each second sentence using the word given, so that it has a similar meaning to the first sentence. Write between two and five words in each gap.

1 I don't know how you can stand getting up so early to go to the pool. **put**
I don't know how you can ........................................................ up so early to go to the pool.
2 I've finally started sorting out my postcard collection. **round**
I've finally ........................................................ sorting out my postcard collection.
3 What did you do at the weekend? **get**
What did you ........................................................ at the weekend?
4 I'm not so keen on skiing now I've discovered snowboarding. **gone**
I've ........................................................ since I discovered snowboarding.
5 Why do you continue to have riding lessons if you can't afford them? **on**
Why do you ........................................................ riding lessons if you can't afford them?
6 We can't delay the match any longer. **put**
We can't ........................................................ any longer.

## D Write one word in each gap.

1 Tony never used to want to join ........................ with the other kids in the playground.
2 Look ........................ ! There's a car coming!
3 Simone's ........................ to wearing a helmet whenever she goes cycling.
4 I was thinking of taking ........................ scuba diving until I found out how expensive the equipment is.
5 They were knocked ........................ in the semi-final.
6 Maybe we should bring the meeting ........................ to this Tuesday instead of having it in two weeks' time.
7 Becca had to pull ........................ of the race when she sprained her ankle.
8 Melissa doesn't ........................ in for adventure sports.

### Phrases and collocations

## E Choose the correct answer.

1 Why don't you ........... a go? It's not difficult!
A make C do
B have D set

2 Carl wasn't very good at mountain climbing as he's afraid of ........... .
A highs C heights
B highness D height

3 There's little ........... of our getting into the final.
A opportunity C luck
B chance D fortune

4 Rachel is mad ........... the Eurovision Song Contest.
A from C for
B against D about

5 Just ........... your best – that's all anyone can ask of you.
A do C be
B make D have

6 It's ........... time you learned to swim.
A big C high
B tall D far

7 Grandma ........... a lot of pleasure from gardening.
A does C makes
B has D gets

8 ........... your time – don't rush.
A Tell C Spend
B Find D Take

9 Each player takes it ........... turn to roll the dice.
A on C at
B in D to

10 Time ........... so quickly when you're doing something enjoyable.
A takes C passes
B spends D finds

11 Our new coach is popular ........... the whole team.
A for C by
B to D with

12 She'd ........... hours lying on her bed, reading.
A spend C make
B take D pass

13 He'd been planning to leave the team the ........... time, and hadn't told anyone.
A complete C total
B whole D full

14 I'm not siding ........... her because she's my sister, but because she's right.
A from C to
B for D with

### Word patterns

## F Match to make sentences.

1 I'm not very fond ...........
2 She's interested ...........
3 You should concentrate ...........
4 I used to find it difficult ...........
5 Let's listen ...........
6 We stopped ...........
7 The bad weather stopped us ...........

A in playing for the school team.
B to find enough time to have any hobbies.
C to try to find the golf balls we'd lost.
D of playing in goal.
E from finishing the game.
F to what the coach thinks first.
G on getting fit.

**G** Water has damaged part of this text about sport at school. Read it and decide what you think each of the original words was. Write the words in the blank spaces.

### Sport at school

I used to wear glasses when I was at school, and so I sport 1 ........................
very difficult. I wanted to be involved school sports 2 ........................
competitions, and I loved the idea of teams competing each 3 ........................
other, but being on the rugby team, for example, having to 4 ........................
take off my glasses, and that meant I couldn't see! And it's 5 ........................
difficult catch a ball when you can't see it! So, I wasn't 6 ........................
very good and the captains always sure that I wasn't on 7 ........................
their team. This meant I free to do other activities, like being 8 ........................
on the debating team, and actually I preferred to things I 9 ........................
was good at doing than have everyone laugh at me. 10 ........................

**Word formation**

**H** Complete the sentences by changing the form of the word in capitals when this is necessary.

1 I need to buy a new pair of .............................. (**TRAIN**).
2 Ellie used to .............................. (**PRACTICE**) for hours to learn to juggle properly.
3 That was the most .............................. (**INTEREST**) book I've ever read. I can't wait for the sequel!
4 Would you describe yourself as a .............................. (**COMPETE**) person?
5 Many professional basketball players earn a .............................. (**FORTUNE**) these days.
6 F.A. stands for Football .............................. (**ASSOCIATE**).
7 The gold, silver and bronze .............................. (**MEDAL**) took their places on the podium for the presentation ceremony.
8 In Britain, the money parents give their children is often called pocket money. In America, it's often called an .............................. (**ALLOW**).
9 I'm afraid the swimming pool is closed at the moment as they're carrying out some essential .............................. (**MAINTAIN**).

**I** Use the word given in capitals at the end of each line to form a word that fits in the gap in the same line.

### *A snooker player speaks*

When I first started playing snooker, I had no real (**1**) .............................. of the **KNOW**
rules. I just thought it looked an (**2**) .............................. game. Also, I didn't need **ENJOY**
to buy any expensive (**3**) .............................. because the snooker hall near my **EQUIP**
house had tables and cues. I spent (**4**) .............................. all the free time I had **PRACTICAL**
practising, and then decided to enter a (**5**) .............................. . It was great fun! **COMPETE**
My (**6**) .............................. was someone who'd been playing for years. Of course, **OPPOSE**
he beat me, but the fact that I'd (**7**) .............................. didn't put me off at all. **LOSE**
And, (**8**) .............................. , my game improved enough for me to become a **FORTUNE**
professional snooker player three years ago.

**A** Use the word given in capitals at the end of each line to form a word that fits in the gap in the same line.

### A new hobby

| | |
|---|---|
| I saw some badminton on TV and found it quite (**1**) .............................. , so I | **INTEREST** |
| thought I'd see if there was a club or (**2**) .............................. in my area. I looked | **ASSOCIATE** |
| everywhere but, (**3**) .............................. , the nearest club was 80 kilometres | **FORTUNE** |
| away. So, without any (**4**) .............................. , I decided to form my own club. | **KNOW** |
| It was very hard in the beginning – I didn't have any (**5**) .............................. and I | **EQUIP** |
| had to convince a few people that it was an (**6**) .............................. way to keep | **ENJOY** |
| fit. I organised a small (**7**) .............................. , which was a lot of fun, and things | **COMPETE** |
| started to grow from there. Now we've got a full-time (**8**) .............................. and | **TRAIN** |
| our (**9**) .............................. come from all over the country. One of our members | **OPPOSE** |
| was even a bronze (**10**) .............................. in the national championship! | **MEDAL** |

(1 mark per answer)

**B** Match to make sentences.

**11** I refuse to put ............
**12** The current champion was knocked ............
**13** I used to love basketball, but I've gone ............
**14** The trainer asked us to carry ............
**15** The organisers had to bring ............
**16** You should think about taking ............
**17** Although she was very young, Olivia took ............
**18** Rob had to pull ............

**A** up a martial art, to defend yourself.
**B** to swimming as soon as she tried it.
**C** out in the second round of the competition.
**D** out of the race because of a last minute injury.
**E** on with the activity while he answered the phone.
**F** off team sports lately.
**G** the race forward by a week.
**H** up with people who cheat at games.

(1 mark per answer)

**C** Complete each second sentence using the word given, so that it has a similar meaning to the first sentence. Write between two and five words in each gap.

**19** Our tennis match started at one o'clock and we were still playing at four. **been**
At four o'clock, we .............................................................................. three hours.

**20** Terry never used to spend so much time playing on his computer. **use**
Terry .............................................................................. spend so much time playing on his computer.

**21** Before we play, check all the cards are there. **certain**
Before we play, .............................................................................. all the cards are there.

**22** Hang-gliding can be dangerous, but after a while you don't mind it. **used**
Hang-gliding can be dangerous, but after a while you .............................................................. it.

**23** I ran fifteen miles, and then my trainer told me to do fifty push-ups! **already**
When my trainer told me to do fifty push-ups, I .............................................................................. fifteen miles!

**24** We wouldn't spend so much time indoors when I was young. **used**
We .................................................................................. so much time indoors when I was young.

**25** I spend a lot of my time on my hobbies. **up**
My hobbies .................................................................................. a lot of my time.

**26** I would rather play ludo than snakes and ladders. **prefer**
I .................................................................................. ludo rather than snakes and ladders.

**27** I don't think it's likely that you'll win the competition. **chance**
I think there's .................................................................................. the competition.

(2 marks per answer)

## D Choose the correct answer.

**28** 'Why were you so tired yesterday?'
'Because I ....... all morning.'
A jog C had been jogging
B was jogged D had been jogged

**29** It was the first time I ....... a live match.
A was ever seeing C had ever seen
B had ever been seeing D was ever seen

**30** 'You live in a huge house, don't you?'
'Yes, but we ....... !'
A didn't use to C use not
B wouldn't D weren't used to

**31** I ....... the whole of *War and Peace* by the time I was seven years old.
A was reading C had read
B had been reading D had been read

**32** Karate hurt my hands at first, but I finally ....... it in the end.
A got used to C was used
B was used to D got use to

**33** I ....... for the match to begin when suddenly a dog ran onto the pitch.
A had waited C was waiting
B waited D wait

**34** Before she retired, my grandma ..... go for a run every morning before work.
A use to C got used to
B would D was used to

(1 mark per answer)

## E Choose the correct answer.

**35** The ....... in the stadium all cheered the athletes.
A viewers C spectators
B witnesses D onlookers

**36** I got a new baseball ....... yesterday.
A stick C racket
B club D bat

**37** After a hard match, United managed to ....... with City, 1-1.
A equal C draw
B exact D score

**38** In this game, the players ....... it in turns to throw the dice.
A take C make
B do D have

**39** It's nice to win, but the important thing is to ....... your best.
A make C have
B take D do

**40** Just ask them if you can play and I'm sure they'll let you ....... .
A take up C go off
B join in D take to

**41** Everyone expects Johnson to ....... Smith in today's final.
A beat C win
B score D champion

(1 mark per answer)

**Total mark: ...... / 50**

# Future time / present tenses in time clauses / prepositions of time and place

## Expressing the future: will/won't and be going to

There is sometimes little difference in meaning between **will** and ***be going to***. It is often just a matter of formality. ***Will*** is generally more formal than ***be going to***.

| Use | Example |
|---|---|
| Facts about the future | *The website* ***will*** *come online next week.* (more formal)<br>*The website****'s going to*** *come online next week.* (more informal) |
| Predictions not based on present evidence | *In the future, everyone* ***will*** *have their own flying car.* (more formal)<br>*In the future, everyone* ***is going to*** *have their own flying car.* (more informal) |
| Decisions made at the moment of speaking | *I've decided! I* ***won't*** *get a new DVD player just yet.* (emphasising the decision)<br>*I've decided!* ***I'm not going to*** *get a new DVD player just yet.* (emphasising the intention) |

Sometimes it is more appropriate to use ***will*** rather than ***be going to***.

| Use | Example |
|---|---|
| Offers and suggestions | *I****'ll*** *help you with your physics homework, if you like.* |
| Requests | ***Will*** *you help me with my physics homework?* |
| Most first conditional sentences | *If we get a computer, we****'ll*** *be able to surf the Internet.* |

**Watch out!**

- With offers and suggestions in the question form, we do not use ***will*** with *I* and *we*. We use ***shall***.

  ✓ ***Shall*** *I help you with your physics homework?*

  ✗ ~~***Will*** *I help you with your physics homework?*~~

Sometimes it is more appropriate to use ***be going to*** rather than ***will***.

| Use | Example |
|---|---|
| Plans and intentions (which you already have when you speak) | ***I'm going to*** *be a famous doctor one day!* |
| Predictions based on present evidence | *It sounds like the plane****'s going to*** *take off in a few minutes.* |

## Expressing the future: present continuous

| Use | Example |
|---|---|
| Arrangements made before the moment of speaking | ***Are*** *they* ***installing*** *the new computers next week?* |

## Expressing the future: present simple

| Use | Example |
|---|---|
| Timetables, arrangements and fixed events (which the speaker cannot change) | *The bus to the science museum* ***leaves*** *at 8 o'clock tomorrow morning.* |
| After *if* in first conditional and zero conditional sentences | *If technology* ***continues*** *to advance so quickly, what will life be like in a hundred years?* |
| After certain time expressions (see below) | *We'll find out as soon as we* ***get*** *to the lab.* |

## Expressing the future: future perfect simple

**Form** *will/won't* + *have* + past participle

| Use | Example |
|---|---|
| Actions which are completed some time between now and a point in the future | *I'**ll have finished** my chemistry homework by the time you come home.* |

## Expressing the future: future continuous

**Form** *will/won't* + *be* + *-ing* form

| Use | Example |
|---|---|
| Actions in progress at a point in the future | *This time next week, I'**ll be taking** my biology exam.* |
| Habits or repeated actions at a point in the future | *In the future, we'**ll** all **be flying** around using jet-packs.* |

## Expressing the future: future perfect continuous

**Form** *will/won't* + *have* + *been* + *-ing* form

| Use | Example |
|---|---|
| Actions in progress up to a point in the future | *At seven o'clock, I'**ll have been doing** my chemistry homework for three hours!* |

## Present tenses in time clauses

In time clauses, we do not use *will* or *be going to* immediately after some time words and phrases. We use a present tense (present simple, present continuous or present perfect) to talk about the future.

| Time words and phrases | Example |
|---|---|
| **when** | *It'll be wonderful **when** scientists **find** / **have found** a cure for cancer.* |
| **as soon as** | *Let me know **as soon as** your new computer **arrives** / **has arrived**.* |
| **before** | *It'll be several years **before** we **send** / we'**ve sent** a manned mission to Mars.* |
| **after** | *Let's go for a pizza **after** we **go** / **have been** to the natural history museum.* |
| **until / till** | *The rocket won't be launched **until** they **do** / **have done** a final check.* |
| **while** | *Think of me **while** you **travel** / **are travelling** to the Moon!* |
| **once** | *We'll stop for petrol **once** we **pass** / we'**ve passed** Cambridge.* |

## Prepositions of time and place

| | |
|---|---|
| **Key prepositions of time** | *(**from**) Monday **to** Friday, **on** Monday, **on** my birthday/Easter Sunday/etc, **in** July, **on** September 20th, **in** 2008, **in** (the) summer, **at** three o'clock, **in**/**for** an hour, **at** the moment, **in** the morning/afternoon/evening, **at** night, **in**/**on** time, just **in** time for, **in** the beginning/end, **at** the beginning/end of, **at** the age of, **at** the weekend, **next**/**last** week* |
| **Key prepositions of place** | *turn right **at** a place, sit **on** sth, go **in(to)** a building, wait **in(side)** a building, arrive **in** London/Greece, arrive **at** the stadium, **in**/**on**/**at** the corner (of), come/go/walk/etc **to** a place, **next to**/**beside**/**by** the building, **at**/**on** the front/back of, **in front of**/**behind** the station, go **out of** a building, go **towards** the station, **between** the two buildings, **opposite** the station* |

**US vs UK Grammar**

- Speakers of American English do not always use **on** before days of the week.
  **US**: *We've got a biology test Monday/on Monday.*
  **UK**: *We've got a biology test **on** Monday.*
- Speakers of American English often say 'Monday through Friday'.
  **US**: *I'm going to be on a field trip Monday **through** Friday.*
  **UK**: *I'm going to be on a field trip **from** Monday **to** Friday.*

## A If a word or phrase in bold is correct, put a tick (✓). If it is incorrect, rewrite it correctly on the line, including all possibilities.

1 The universe **is going to** continue to expand for billions of years. ..................................................
2 Look out! **You will** hit the car in front! ..................................................
3 **I'm going to** do the washing-up tonight, if you like. ..................................................
4 Do you think that, in the future, people **will** live to be hundreds of years old?
..................................................
5 **Will** I carry some of those bags for you, or can you manage? ..................................................
6 I know! **I'm going to** have a barbecue on my birthday! ..................................................
7 **Are you going to** just hold this door open for me for a minute? Thanks a lot!
..................................................
8 We've decided **we will try** that new restaurant after the play tomorrow night.
..................................................
9 **We're going to** fly to Jamaica in the summer. ..................................................
10 **Shall** we invite Tony and Tim round tonight? ..................................................
11 **Are we going to** invite Tony and Tim round tonight? ..................................................
12 **Will you go to** Jason's party next Saturday? ..................................................

## B Circle the correct word or phrase. If both options are correct, circle both.

1 **We aren't / We're not** going to miss the train, are we?
2 I think **I'm going to do / I'm doing** really badly in the English test tomorrow.
3 Josh **is going to sing / is singing** a song in the school talent contest next week.
4 I'm **going to buy / buying** a big yacht if I can when I'm older.
5 Sports Day is **going to be / being** held on the last day of term.
6 **Does / Will** the concert on Thursday last more than two hours?
7 **Are they going to broadcast / Will they broadcast** the music awards live tomorrow night?
8 **Do they broadcast / Are they broadcasting** the music awards live tomorrow night?
9 According to the timetable, the train for Oxford **leaves / is leaving** at 10.15.
10 **Does the restaurant open / Is the restaurant opening** next Sunday?

## C Write a word or short phrase in each gap.

At the end of this month, I'll (**1**) .................................................. working on my physics project for about six weeks, but I've still got a lot to do before I hand it in. I'll (**2**) .................................................. spending the whole day in the physics lab next Saturday doing experiments, and in fact, I (**3**) .................................................. playing football the weekend after either because I've got to go back to the lab then, too. I guess I'll (**4**) .................................................. doing lots of similar projects when I'm at university, so it's good practice. Thinking about it, when I leave university in about four years, I will (**5**).................................................. studying physics for over thirteen years, so I should be quite good at it by then!

## D Complete using the future perfect simple or future perfect continuous of the verbs in brackets.

1 I .................................................. (**cook**) dinner by the time you get home.
2 In a few minutes, I .................................................. (**wait**) here for Craig for over two hours. Where can he be?
3 We'll be halfway through the sponsored swim in one hour so we .................................................. (**swim**) for forty-eight hours non-stop by then.
4 They .................................................. (**not / finish**) painting the house by the time we get back from holiday.
5 If she's still on the phone at eight o'clock, .................................................. (**Jan / talk**) to Melissa for over two hours.
6 At six o'clock this evening, we .................................................. (**not / climb**) for five hours but for seven hours!
7 This time next month, you .................................................. (**probably / pass**) your driving test!
8 .................................................. (**you / do**) all your homework by bedtime?
9 Tomorrow .................................................. (**Elaine / work**) on the project for ten days.
10 We .................................................. (**probably / not / leave**) by the time you get home.

## E Complete each second sentence using the word given, so that it has a similar meaning to the first sentence. Write between two and five words in each gap.

1 We'll get home and then we'll have something to eat. **got**
We'll have something to eat .................................................................................. home.
2 I'll finish marking the exams and then I'll tell you your results. **soon**
I'll tell you your results .................................................................................. marking the exams.
3 You'll be travelling across the Sahara next week so remember to wear lots of sunscreen! **while**
Remember to wear lots of sunscreen .................................................................................. across the Sahara next week!
4 They'll show *Titan* at the cinema and then they'll release the DVD. **before**
They won't release the DVD .................................................................................. at the cinema.
5 My science exam starts at ten tomorrow morning. **taking**
At ten past ten tomorrow .................................................................................. my science exam.
6 Let's watch the space documentary before we have supper. **watched**
Let's have supper .................................................................................. the space documentary.
7 I'll send out all the invitations before lunchtime. **have**
By lunchtime, .................................................................................. all the invitations.
8 Do some revision and then I 'll give you a test. **until**
I won't give you a test .................................................................................. some revision.
9 When you visit us, we'll have moved into our new house. **by**
We'll have moved into our new house .................................................................................. you visit us.
10 We'll get some more information and then we'll make a decision. **once**
Let's make a decision .................................................................................. got some more information.

**F** Read the information and write a question for each answer given.

## Watkins Tours

**Isles of Scilly Day Trip - 22nd July**

| | |
|---|---|
| 5.30 am | coach departs from Plymouth Bretonside Bus Station |
| 8.15 am | arrive Penzance |
| 9.15 am | ferry (Scillonian III) departs |
| 12.00 noon | arrive St Mary's |
| 12-1.30 pm | walk round the town |
| 1.30-2.30 pm | picnic lunch (on Garrison overlooking harbour) |
| 2.30-4 pm | swimming or boat trip round island |
| 4.30 pm | ferry (Scillonian III) departs |
| 7.15 pm | arrive Penzance |
| 7.30 pm | coach departs |
| 10.15 pm | arrive Plymouth Bretonside Bus Station |

*Example:*
*What time does the coach leave Plymouth?*
It leaves at 5.30 am.

1 ..............................
He'll be driving the coach to Penzance.

2 ..............................
It'll arrive at 8.15 am.

3 ..............................
It's going to set sail at 9.15 am.

4 ..............................
It will have been sailing for two hours.

5 ..............................
They will just have arrived in St Mary's.

6 ..............................
They'll be walking round the town.

7 ..............................
They'll be having a picnic lunch.

8 ..............................
They'll be leaving the beach at 4 pm.

9 ..............................
They'll have just finished a boat trip round the island.

10 ..............................
It's leaving at 4.30 pm.

11 ..............................
They get back at 10.15 pm.

## G Write *on*, *in* or *at* in each gap.

1 I'll be 100 years old ........................ the year 2095!
2 Sasha's not going to have a party ........................ her birthday this year.
3 See you ........................ August!
4 See you ........................ Tuesday!
5 See you ........................ eight o'clock!
6 See you ........................ the morning!
7 See you ........................ a couple of hours!
8 It's difficult to sleep ........................ night ........................ the summer because of the heat.
9 My grandfather left home ........................ the age of fourteen!
10 We got there just ........................ time for the movie.
11 He's never late, and he's never early; he always arrives right ........................ time.
12 My birthday's ........................ April 1st.

## H Each of the words in bold is incorrect. Rewrite them correctly.

1 My Australian cousins are coming **in** Greece next month! ........................
2 Turn left **on** the post office, then go straight on. ........................
3 There weren't any chairs, so we had to sit **at** the floor. ........................
4 The TV's **on** the corner of the room. ........................
5 There's a photo of the author **at** the back cover of the book. ........................
6 We should arrive **at** Paris at six in the morning. ........................
7 Could you go out **from** the room for a moment, please? ........................
8 Walk **in** the station, but turn left a couple of blocks before you get there. ........................
9 I'll meet you **in** the corner of your street. ........................
10 There should be a broom **on** the back of the cupboard, somewhere. ........................
11 They should arrive **in** the airport in about an hour. ........................
12 The CD should be next **from** the CD player. ........................

## I Write one word in each gap.

### Defining the Age

Ages, eras and wars will always be defined (**1**) ........................ they are over, or at least well after they (**2**) ........................ started. (**3**) ........................ the year 1914, for example, no one said: 'Tomorrow I'm going (**4**) ........................ go and fight in the First World War.' Why not? Because it wasn't generally called the First World War until the Second World War had started. Similarly, no one ever said: 'Next year (**5**) ........................ be the start of the Industrial Revolution.' The era now known as the Industrial Revolution only started being called that once it was well under way.

(**6**) ........................ the time we are old, we will all (**7**) ........................ experienced enormous technological advances. We might even (**8**) ........................ walking round with computer chips implanted in our bodies, or perhaps computer chip technology will have (**9**) ........................ replaced by even more advanced technology. There's talk (**10**) ........................ the moment that human skin itself might make an excellent electronic circuit board. We can all make predictions, but nobody knows for sure. And nobody knows what the era we will live in (**11**) ........................ the near future will be called by future historians. If we already live in the Computer Age or the Information Age as some people suggest, the present-day era (**12**) ........................ be referred to by future historians, then who knows what era we're just (**13**) ........................ the beginning of right now?

## Science and technology

### Topic vocabulary in contrast

see page 187 for definitions

| | | |
|---|---|---|
| artificial / false | aim / cause / reason | progress / development |
| natural / physical | estimate / calculate | modern / new |
| true / accurate | electric / electronic | industry / factory |
| method / way | invent / discover | award / reward |
| engine / machine / motor | research / experiment | take place / occur |

### Phrasal verbs

| | |
|---|---|
| **break down** stop working (for a machine, etc) | **give off** produce sth such as heat or a smell |
| **carry out** perform an experiment, etc | **narrow down** reduce the number of possibilities |
| **come off** succeed | **plug in** connect to the electricity supply |
| **come on** develop or make progress | **put through** connect by phone |
| **come up with** think of (an idea, a plan, etc) | **turn into** change into sth different |
| **cut off** stop the supply of sth | **turn off** stop a machine working |
| **find out** discover information, etc | **work out** find the solution to a problem, etc |

### Phrases and collocations

| | |
|---|---|
| **attempt** | make an attempt (at sth/doing / to do); attempt to do; in an attempt to do |
| **average** | on average |
| **beginning** | in the beginning; at the beginning (of sth); beginning with |
| **bottom** | at/on the bottom (of sth) |
| **cause** | (be/find/look for/etc) the cause of sth |
| **conclusion** | come to/reach the conclusion (that); in conclusion |
| **experiment** | do/perform/carry out an experiment (on sth); experiment with sth/doing |
| **fact** | in fact; as a matter of fact; the fact (of the matter) is (that); face the facts |
| **introduction** | with the introduction of sth; an introduction to sth/sb |
| **phone call** | make/receive/get a phone call |
| **photo(graph)** | take a photo (of sth/sb) |
| **research** | carry out / do research (on/into sth) |

### Word patterns

| | |
|---|---|
| **cause** sth (to do) | **look** at/for sth/sb; look forward to sth/doing |
| **consider** sth/doing; consider if/whether; consider sb for sth; consider it strange, etc (for sb to do) | **manage** to do |
| **discuss** sth/doing (with sb) | **plan** sth; plan to do |
| **explain** that; explain sth (to sb) | **possible** (for sb) to do; find sth possible; find it impossible to do |
| **intend** to do/doing | **result** of sth/doing; result in sth; result in (your) doing; result from sth/doing; as a result of sth |
| **know** (about) sth/doing; know of sb; be known as sth | **wonder** about sth/doing; wonder if/whether/why |

### Word formation

| | | |
|---|---|---|
| **appear** appearance, apparently | **introduce** introduction, introductory | **research** researcher |
| **build** builder, building | **invent** inventor, invention | **revolution** revolutionary |
| **discover** discovery | **observe** observer, observation | **science** scientist, (un)scientific(ally) |
| **explain** explanation | **possible** impossible, (im)possibility, (im)possibly | **technology** technological(ly), technical(ly); technician, technique |
| **important** unimportant, importance, importantly | **psychology** psychologist, psychological(ly) | **wood** wooden |

### Topic vocabulary in contrast

## A Choose the correct answer.

### Modern science

It seems entirely (**1**) ........... to us that there are teams of scientists in universities and other institutions around the world, attempting to (**2**) ........... the way the world works. However, it hasn't always been that (**3**) ........... . Although the scientific method is now four or five hundred years old, the ancient Greeks, for example, believed that they could work out the (**4**) ........... of natural events just by the power of thought.

During the 17th century, more and more people began to realise that they could (**5**) ........... their scientific ideas by designing a relevant (**6**) ........... and seeing what happened. A lot of (**7**) ........... was made in this way by individual scientists. These men and women often worked alone, carrying out (**8**) ........... into many different areas of science, and they often received very little (**9**) ........... for their hard work. At the start of the 20th century, though, it became (**10**) ........... that science was becoming more complicated and more expensive. The individual scientist disappeared, to be replaced by highly qualified teams of experts. Modern science was born.

| | | | | |
|---|---|---|---|---|
| **1** | A physical | B natural | C typical | D real |
| **2** | A create | B invent | C construct | D discover |
| **3** | A route | B method | C way | D technique |
| **4** | A aims | B reasons | C causes | D impulses |
| **5** | A calculate | B estimate | C measure | D test |
| **6** | A experiment | B research | C attempt | D analysis |
| **7** | A development | B movement | C progress | D evolution |
| **8** | A research | B experiment | C discovery | D education |
| **9** | A award | B prize | C gift | D reward |
| **10** | A clear | B true | C accurate | D actual |

## B Circle the correct word.

1. Many materials have been used for **artificial / false** teeth, including wood.
2. Be careful! You might give yourself an **electric / electronic** shock!
3. I'm afraid the problem with your washing machine is the **engine / motor**.
4. Many employers in the chemicals **industry / factory** object to the new law.
5. My computing exam is **taking place / occurring** next week.
6. Technology is a fundamental part of **new / modern** life.
7. We had our car serviced and it seems there's a problem with the **engine / machine**.

### Phrasal verbs

## C Complete using the correct form of the words in the box.

**plug • turn • carry • narrow • put • work • come • break**

1. A lorry had .................................. down on the motorway and we had to wait for over an hour.
2. I have .................................. it down to two computer games, but I still can't make up my mind.
3. I wish you would .................................. the TV off and go outside and get some exercise.
4. Scientists are trying to .................................. out ways to reduce pollution from aircraft.
5. Tomorrow, we will be .................................. out an experiment to test this theory.
6. Who .................................. up with the idea of the ball-point pen?
7. I'll just .................................. you through to our research department. Please hold on.
8. No wonder the vacuum cleaner isn't working. You haven't .................................. it in!

## D Match to make sentences.

1 Alex's electricity was cut ...........
2 Wear a mask because these chemicals give ...........
3 I'm writing an essay and I need to find ...........
4 I was pleased that our gamble came ...........
5 Alchemists spent years trying to turn ...........
6 Your teacher says you've really come ...........

A off because she forgot to pay the bill.
B metals such as lead into gold.
C out who discovered penicillin.
D on in physics over the last year.
E off fumes that can be harmful.
F off and the experiment was a success.

### Phrases and collocations

## E Choose the correct answer.

1 I don't think people should be allowed to perform experiments ........... animals.
A for B over C on D to

2 There was an explosion in technology ........... the beginning of the 20th century.
A in B at C through D on

3 Let's face ........... – we are destroying the environment and we need to do something now.
A truth B facts C things D information

4 The distance from the Earth to the Sun is, ........... average, about 149 million kilometres.
A by B on C from D in

5 It's amazing that creatures survive ........... the bottom of the ocean.
A in B by C at D to

6 Fox Talbot ........... the first photograph in 1835.
A gave B did C drew D took

7 Researchers have ........... to the conclusion that your personality is affected by your genes.
A come B got C reached D arrived

8 Do you mind if I just ........... a quick phone call from here?
A do B take C have D make

9 Many lives were saved ........... the introduction of antibiotics.
A into B at C with D in

10 The ........... of the nuclear accident is still unknown.
A reason B cause C base D motive

11 My father works at the university, doing research ........... weather control.
A on B to C of D from

12 The telescope will photograph distant galaxies, ........... an attempt to understand their past.
A on B for C with D in

### Word patterns

## F Find the extra word in each line.

**The future**

1 ........................ We were discussing about the future in class today. Some people were
2 ........................ wondering it whether we would have to live in space when we destroy
3 ........................ our own planet. I explained them that the answer lies in technology because
4 ........................ scientists are intend to develop forms of energy that will not damage the
5 ........................ environment. The problems caused as being a result of technology will be
6 ........................ solved by technology. I am look forward to our next discussion.

## G Complete each second sentence using the word given, so that it has a similar meaning to the first sentence. Write between two and five words in each gap.

1 The mistake by scientists caused a massive explosion. **in**
The mistake by scientists ............................................................................ a massive explosion.
2 Dr Atherton finally succeeded in discovering the secret formula. **managed**
Dr Atherton finally ............................................................................ the secret formula.
3 Another name for iron oxide is 'fool's gold'. **as**
Iron oxide ............................................................................ 'fool's gold'.
4 Many local residents intend to protest about the nuclear power plant. **plan**
Many local residents ............................................................................ about the nuclear power plant.
5 We are thinking of appointing Dr Knight to the position of Professor. **considering**
We ............................................................................ the position of Professor.
6 We cannot live in outer space without special equipment. **us**
It ............................................................................ to live in outer space without special equipment.

**Word formation**

## H Use the word given in capitals at the end of each line to form a word that fits in the gap in the same line.

### Qualcomp Powertop

| | |
|---|---|
| Qualcomp have just brought out their (**1**) .............................. new handheld | **REVOLUTION** |
| computer, the Powertop. It's (**2**) .............................. not to love it, with its | **POSSIBLE** |
| smooth, shiny (**3**) .............................. and its bright screen. It might not be the | **APPEAR** |
| best (**4**) .............................. to handheld computing because it is quite advanced, | **INTRODUCE** |
| but you'll find an (**5**) .............................. of all the features in the detailed manual. | **EXPLAIN** |
| The Powertop has been (**6**) .............................. designed to fit a lot of computing | **SCIENCE** |
| power in your palm. The (**7**) .............................. of a unique wireless Internet | **INVENT** |
| connection means there's a world of (**8**) .............................. just waiting for you. | **DISCOVER** |
| We give the Powertop nine out of ten. | |

## I Complete the sentences by changing the form of the word in capitals when this is necessary.

1 Did you know that George Washington had .............................. (**WOOD**) teeth?
2 The old astronomer patiently made his .............................. (**OBSERVE**) and wrote down what he saw.
3 .............................. (**RESEARCH**) have announced that a major breakthrough has been made.
4 I'm planning to train as a .............................. (**PSYCHOLOGY**) when I grow up.
5 That red .............................. (**BUILD**) over there is the Science Department.
6 The scientist said she had an announcement of international .............................. (**IMPORTANT**).
7 *Science Weekly* has a special .............................. (**INTRODUCE**) offer – the first issue is free!
8 If there are aliens out there, do you think they are much more .............................. (**TECHNOLOGY**) advanced than we are?

## A Use the word given in capitals at the end of each line to form a word that fits in the gap in the same line.

### Egypt and South America

| | |
|---|---|
| There is still no adequate (**1**) .............................. why, several thousand years | **EXPLAIN** |
| ago, cultures in both Egypt and South America saw the (**2**) .............................. | **INTRODUCE** |
| of pyramids. Was it coincidence? Many (**3**) .............................. believe that it | **SCIENCE** |
| was, and state that there is no (**4**) .............................. at all that people from | **POSSIBLE** |
| two distant continents traded information on (**5**) .............................. techniques. | **BUILD** |
| However, some (**6**) .............................. theories in recent years, based on the | **REVOLUTION** |
| (**7**) .............................. that the two cultures also share key myths, legends | **DISCOVER** |
| and beliefs, suggest that the (**8**) .............................. of pyramids on opposite | **APPEAR** |
| sides of the world was no coincidence at all. One (**9**) .............................. | **RESEARCH** |
| working on this, Crystal Davis, said: 'The (**10**) .............................. of finding | **IMPORTANT** |
| out the truth here cannot be exaggerated. It could change our whole | |
| understanding of the history of the world.' | |

(1 mark per answer)

## B Match to make sentences.

**11** The fax machine has broken ...........
**12** A number of experiments have been carried ...........
**13** Whoever came ...........
**14** The electricity was cut ...........
**15** I'd like to find ...........
**16** This chemical gives ...........
**17** Cancer treatments have come ...........
**18** I wonder if you could put me ...........

**A** out by physicists which prove that time can speed up and slow down.
**B** on enormously in recent years.
**C** off for over three hours yesterday.
**D** down, so I'm afraid you'll have to wait until tomorrow.
**E** off a very nasty smell when it's heated.
**F** up with that idea should have won the Nobel Prize.
**G** through to the Radiology Department, please.
**H** out much more about technology in the Bronze Age.

(1 mark per answer)

## C Complete the second sentence using the word given, so that it has a similar meaning to the first sentence. Write between two and five words in each gap.

**19** I can't wait until we do some experiments in the science lab. **forward**
I'm really .............................................................................. some experiments in the science lab.

**20** Communication changed completely when the telephone was introduced. **with**
Communication changed completely .............................................................................. the telephone.

**21** Dr Frankenstein was finally successful in bringing the monster to life. **managed**
Dr Frankenstein .............................................................................. the monster to life.

**22** I can't understand how they built the Pyramids. **impossible**
I .............................................................................. how they built the Pyramids.

**23** Fleming discovered penicillin as a result of a little luck. **resulted**
A little luck .............................................................................. penicillin.

**24** People sometimes call nurses 'angels'. **known**
Nurses .............................................................................. 'angels'.

**25** Einstein eventually realised that he was wrong. **conclusion**
Einstein eventually ............................................................................... that he was wrong.

**26** Our physics teacher tried to explain the Theory of Relativity. **attempt**
Our physics teacher ............................................................................... explaining the Theory of Relativity.

**27** We'll save enough money and then we'll buy a computer. **soon**
We'll buy a computer ............................................................................... saved enough money.

(2 marks per answer)

## D Choose the correct answer.

**28** This time next week, we ............ the chemistry exam.
A have finished
B have been finishing
C will have finished
D will have been finishing

**29** When I grow up, ............ an inventor.
A I'm being
B I'm going to be
C I will have been
D I will be being

**30** Shirley will ............ her research for the next few weeks.
A have done
B be doing
C have been doing
D have been done

**31** Next year, Sam will ............ patients at this hospital for twenty-five years.
A have been treating
B treat
C be treating
D be going to treat

**32** 'What is it?'
'We won't know until ............ at it under a microscope.'
A we're going to look
B we'll have looked
C we'll be looking
D we've looked

**33** You won't get any radio reception while ............ through the tunnel.
A you've driven
B you'll drive
C you're driving
D you'll be driving

**34** 'I'm going to set up the equipment in a minute.'
'............ give you a hand?'
A Shall I
B Will I
C Would I
D Do I

(1 mark per answer)

## E Choose the correct answer.

**35** Do you know who ............ the fact that sound travels in waves?
A invented C discovered
B developed D found

**36** I'm thinking of getting a fax ............ .
A machine C motor
B engine D instrument

**37** The ............ of the outbreak of the disease is still unknown.
A aim C cause
B reason D motive

**38** Ten million text messages are sent on ............ every minute.
A normal C general
B common D average

**39** Once they've finished the extension to the ............ , there'll be room for them to take on a lot more workers.
A manufacturing C industry
B trade D factory

**40** Shannen doesn't dye her hair; it's ............ blonde.
A physically C logically
B naturally D organically

**41** I've ............ it in at the mains but it still doesn't seem to work.
A worked C narrowed
B turned D plugged

(1 mark per answer)

**Total mark: ...... / 50**

## Articles / countable and uncountable nouns / quantifiers

### Indefinite article

There are two indefinite articles in English: 'a' and 'an'. 'An' is used before vowel sounds.

| Use | Example |
|---|---|
| Singular countable nouns (when we are not being specific or when we mention something for the first time) | *There's **a** good film on TV tonight.* |

**Watch out!**

- Whether we use 'an' or 'a' depends on the sound, **not** the spelling.
  ✓ *The news is on TV in **an** hour.*
  ✗ ~~*The news is on TV in **a** hour.*~~
  ✓ *Being in a film was **a** unique experience for me.*
  ✗ ~~*Being in a film was **an** unique experience for me.*~~

### Definite article

There is one definite article in English: 'the'.

| Use | Example |
|---|---|
| Singular countable nouns (when we are being specific) | *Where's **the** DVD you were talking about?* |
| Singular countable nouns (when we are talking generally) | ***The** radio seemed amazing to people at first.* |
| Plural countable nouns (when we are being specific) | *I didn't believe **the** rumours about the prime minister.* |
| Uncountable nouns (when we are being specific) | *I followed **the** advice my lawyer gave me.* |

**Watch out!**

- The way we say 'the' changes depending on the sound at the start of the next word.
  Before a consonant sound (*the media, the USA, the programme*), we pronounce it /ðə/.
  Before a vowel sound (*the announcer, the actor, the editor*), we pronounce it /ðɪ/.
- We often use 'the' when we are talking about something there is only one of.
  ✓ ***the** sky, **the** sun, **the** moon, **the** Prince of Wales, **the** North Pole, **the** World Cup*

### Zero article

We often don't use an article at all. This is sometimes called the zero article.

| Use | Example |
|---|---|
| Plural countable nouns (when we are talking generally) | *Journalists often face dangerous situations.* |
| Uncountable nouns (when we are talking generally) | *News travels fast these days.* |

### Articles in phrases and expressions

Notice how we use articles in the following phrases and expressions. Many of these are examples of general categories. For example, '***the** River Thames*' means that we use 'the' for all rivers.

| Use | Example |
|---|---|
| Time | definite article: *in **the** 1990s, in (**the**) summer, in **the** morning*<br>zero article: *in 2008, in June, on Friday, at night* |
| People and work | indefinite article: *have **a** job, work as **a** ...*<br>definite article: ***the** queen, **the** principal, **the** president, **the** French*<br>zero article: *become president, go to work, be at work, have work to do, he's French.* |
| Places | definite article: ***the** Alps, **the** Atlantic Ocean, **the** River Thames, **the** Earth, **the** Arctic, **the** USA, **the** UK, **the** Cyclades*<br>zero article: *Mount Everest, Paris, America, Mars/Venus/Jupiter etc, Oxford Street, Lake Superior, Crete* |
| Entertainment and sport | definite article: ***the** media, on **the** radio, play **the** guitar, go to **the** cinema, watch (**the**) TV*<br>zero article: *listen to music, on television, play tennis/football etc* |

| Use | Example |
|---|---|
| Organisations | definite article: ***the*** *army,* ***the*** *police,* ***the*** *fire brigade* |
| Education | definite article: *go to* ***the*** *school (as a visitor), be in* ***the*** *first year*<br>zero article: *go to school (as a student), be in Class 3B, maths* |
| Travel | indefinite article: *take* ***a*** *taxi, catch* ***a/the*** *bus*<br>definite article: *on* ***the*** *bus*<br>zero article: *on foot, go home, go by bus* |
| Health | indefinite article: *have* ***a*** *cold/headache/cough*<br>definite article: *have (****the****) flu/measles*<br>zero article: *have toothache* |
| Public buildings | definite article: ***the*** *bank,* ***the*** *tax office, go to* ***the*** *hospital/prison (as a visitor)*<br>zero article: *go to hospital/prison/church (as a patient/prisoner/worshipper)* |

**US vs UK Grammar**

- Speakers of American English do not usually use *hospital* without an article.
  **US**: *The ambulance took Simon to* ***the*** *hospital.*
  **UK**: *The ambulance took Simon to hospital.*

## Countable and uncountable nouns

| Type | Example |
|---|---|
| Countable nouns<br>● Use *a, the, some, many*<br>● Use a singular or plural verb | *I want to be* ***a journalist****.*<br>*Where is* ***the newspaper****?*<br>*There are* ***some*** *good* ***articles*** *in the paper.*<br>*How* ***many channels*** *do you get?* |
| Uncountable nouns<br>● Use *the, some, much*<br>● Use a singular verb | *Did you hear* ***the news****?*<br>***Some*** *important* ***news*** *has just come in.*<br>*How* ***much information*** *do we have about it?*<br>*Your* ***advice was*** *very useful.* |
| Common uncountable nouns:<br>*advice, coffee, furniture, glass, hair, homework, information, knowledge, luggage, money, news, paper, work* | |

**Watch out!**

- Most uncountable nouns are singular, but a few are plural. These include *clothes, scissors, jeans, spectacles, trousers, groceries*, etc. With these words, we use a plural verb.
  ✓ *Oh, no! My new clothes* ***are*** *dirty!*
- Some nouns are countable with one meaning and uncountable with another meaning.
  ✓ *Do you think you could bring me* ***a*** *clean* ***glass****?* (countable)
  ✓ *We should make computer monitors out of recycled* ***glass****.* (uncountable)

## Quantifiers

| Quantifier | Use | Example |
|---|---|---|
| *many* | ● countable nouns, usually in negative statements and questions | *There aren't* ***many*** *programmes on TV that I find interesting.* |
| *much* | ● uncountable nouns, usually in negative statements and questions | *My dad never shows* ***much*** *interest in the news.* |
| *a lot of / lots of* | ● countable and uncountable nouns in positive statements | *That film has won* ***a lot of / lots of*** *awards.*<br>*What* ***a lot of*** *luggage you've got!* |
| *a few* | ● countable nouns, means 'some' | *There have been* ***a few*** *scandals in the papers recently.* |
| *a little* | ● uncountable nouns, means 'some' | *They say that* ***a little*** *knowledge is a dangerous thing.* |
| *few* | ● countable nouns, means 'not many' | *Richard has* ***few*** *interests outside work.* |
| *little* | ● uncountable nouns, means 'not much' | *The police have* ***little*** *information about the robbery.* |

**Watch out!**

- The phrase 'only a few' means 'not many'. The phrase 'only a little' means 'not much'.
  ✓ *There are* ***only a few*** *programmes on TV that I like watching.*
  ✓ *There's* ***only a little*** *sugar left, so get some when you go out.*

## A Circle the correct word or phrase.

1 I love this time in **evening / the evening** when the sun is going down.
2 People play **cricket / the cricket** in South Africa, Australia and Sri Lanka.
3 It's too far to walk so I think I'll catch **bus / the bus**.
4 Jane had to go home from school because she had **a headache / the headache**.
5 The robber was sent to **prison / the prison** for a total of three years.
6 My cousin works as **waiter / a waiter** in a cafe near where we live.
7 The underground doesn't run this late so we'll have to take **a taxi / the taxi**.
8 I like to listen to **music / the music** in my free time.
9 My favourite subject at school is **chemistry / the chemistry**.
10 Jazz music appeared in America **in 1920s / in the 1920s**.

## B Choose the correct answer. If no word is needed, choose 'D'.

1 Oh, I didn't tell you! We've got ............ new English teacher.
A a B an C the D *no word*

2 Here's ............ DVD you asked to borrow.
A a B an C the D *no word*

3 We're out of ............ coffee, so could you get some from the supermarket?
A a B an C the D *no word*

4 The prize is ............ unique opportunity to travel the world!
A a B an C the D *no word*

5 It looks like ............ glass in your bedroom window is cracked.
A a B an C the D *no word*

6 It's ............ honour to be here this evening to speak to you.
A a B an C the D *no word*

7 There's ............ good chance we'll be late for the meeting.
A a B an C the D *no word*

8 Reports are coming in of a major oil spill in ............ Mediterranean.
A a B an C the D *no word*

9 I went to see the doctor because I'm finding it difficult to sleep at ............ night.
A a B an C the D *no word*

10 Do you think that they'll ever send a manned mission to ............ Venus?
A a B an C the D *no word*

## C Circle the extra word in each line.

### Being in the news

1 The many people who appear in the news for the first time
2 find that a sudden fame has a negative effect on their lives.
3 The national press can be an unforgiving and the loss of
4 the privacy that comes with fame is an extra problem at a
5 difficult time. This is especially the case when a someone is
6 in the news because of a tragedy or the serious crime. Just
7 at the moment when you are under a most stress, you find
8 microphones and the cameras in your face. The media have
9 a responsibility to inform the public, but an innocent people
10 are often hurt by the demand for the scandal.

## D Complete using the correct form of the verb in brackets.

1 The clothes you bought me for my birthday .................................................. (**be**) wonderful!
2 It turned out that the information we had received .................................................. (**be**) wrong.
3 My new jeans .................................................. (**be**) in the wash and I wanted to wear them tonight.
4 The luggage on a plane .................................................. (**take**) up a lot of room.
5 Your hair .................................................. (**look**) really nice and shiny.
6 I could tell by the look on her face that the news .................................................. (**not / be**) good.
7 Oh, no! My money .................................................. (**be**) in my other jacket!

## E Find ten mistakes in this passage and correct them.

**Newflash!**

1 'We interrupt your usual schedule to bring you an important news. We are receiving
2 informations about a spaceship that has landed outside the White House. The large
3 ship seems to be made of glasses. Reports say that a short time ago aliens came out
4 of the craft. Eye-witnesses described them as short and said their clothes was made
5 of metal and their hairs was bright green. Strangely, one of them appeared to be
6 wearing a jean. Much people said that they seemed to be friendly. The President of the
7 United States is currently holding a meeting with the visitors in the hope that we can
8 exchange knowledges. Police advice are to stay indoors and under no circumstances
9 approach the spaceship. We will be back with another news as soon as we can. And
10 now, back to your usual programme, *Gardening for Beginners*.'

## F Complete each second sentence using the word given, so that it has a similar meaning to the first sentence. Write between two and five words in each gap.

1 Not many people came to the party. **only**
There .................................................................................. people at the party.

2 The witness described the mugger to the police. **a**
The witness .................................................................................. of the mugger.

3 There isn't much sugar left. **a**
There .................................................................................. sugar left.

4 I am thinking of becoming a firefighter when I leave school. **brigade**
I am thinking of .................................................................................. when I leave school.

5 We were shocked by the news and didn't know what to do. **shocking**
The news .................................................................................. didn't know what to do.

6 There aren't many good films out at the moment. **only**
There .................................................................................. good films out at the moment.

7 I didn't eat much dessert because I'm on a diet. **only**
I .................................................................................. dessert because I'm on a diet.

8 You have lots of hats! **lot**
What .................................................................................. you have!

## G Match to make sentences.

1 I'm quite busy so I've got ...........
2 Happily, we have had ...........
3 My dad just got a good job so we have ...........
4 Pollution is improving now that ...........
5 My mum has lost her job so we have ...........
6 My lesson's been cancelled so I've got ...........
7 It's a shame that ...........
8 Unfortunately, we have had ...........

A a little time to talk to you now.
B a few people recycle their rubbish.
C a few complaints from hotel guests recently.
D little money for luxuries.
E few people recycle their rubbish.
F very few complaints from hotel guests recently.
G a little money for luxuries.
H very little time to talk to you now.

## H Choose the correct answer.

1 If you have ........... time at the end of the exam, check your answers.
A few B a few C little D a little

2 Give me ........... minutes and I'll be ready.
A few B a few C little D a little

3 We've only got ........... milk left so get some when you go shopping.
A few B a few C little D a little

4 Just ........... practice every day and you'll soon be able to play the piano.
A few B a few C little D a little

5 We were disappointed that ........... of the members came to the youth club party.
A few B a few C little D a little

6 Sprinkle ........... sugar on the strawberries.
A few B a few C little D a little

7 I suppose now I'm 43, I have ........... hope of playing football for England.
A few B a few C little D a little

8 Could you help me with ........... exercises I don't understand?
A few B a few C little D a little

9 There's ........... coffee left, if anyone wants some.
A few B a few C little D a little

10 Becoming an astronaut is so demanding that ........... people manage it.
A few B a few C little D a little

11 I'll meet you in half an hour - I've got ........... e-mails to write first.
A few B a few C little D a little

12 Many people feel there's ........... point in voting, even in a general election.
A few B a few C little D a little

## I Write an article in each gap where necessary. If an article is not necessary, write a dash (–).

**Ray:** Hello?
**Sandy:** Hi. Is that Ray? It's (**1**) ........................ Sandy.
**Ray:** Oh, hi! How was (**2**) ........................ film?
**Sandy:** Great! We took (**3**) ........................ taxi to (**4**) ........................ cinema and (**5**) ........................ taxi driver got lost, so we almost missed (**6**) ........................ start. What about you? What did you do (**7**) ........................ last night?
**Ray:** Oh, I just stayed at (**8**) ........................ home. I listened to (**9**) ........................ music for a while and then watched (**10**) ........................ news.
**Sandy:** Oh, yes? So what's happening in (**11**) ........................ world? Anything I should know about?
**Ray:** Well, I know you don't like (**12**) ........................ politics, but there was (**13**) ........................ interesting report on (**14**) ........................ Asia. It gave me (**15**) ........................ few ideas for (**16**) ........................ geography essay we were talking about (**17**) ........................ other day.
**Sandy:** Ah, right. Anything else?
**Ray:** Nothing important. Just that (**18**) ........................ lead singer of your favourite band is getting married – to (**19**) ........................ actress, (**20**) ........................ one who was in that film ...
**Sandy:** What?! Why didn't you tell me? I have to check this out on (**21**) ........................ Internet! See you at (**22**) ........................ school tomorrow. Bye!
**Ray:** Okay. Bye.

## J Rewrite the sentences correctly, adding articles where necessary.

**1** We went to theatre last night and saw great play, although some of acting was bit poor.
..........................................................................................

**2** Give me ring tomorrow before I go to work and we'll arrange to meet at office.
..........................................................................................

**3** Prime minister told reporter that government wanted to pass law banning hunting.
..........................................................................................

**4** I asked hotel manager where pool was and she directed me to seventh floor.
..........................................................................................

**5** They said on news on radio that Mount Vesuvius, volcano that destroyed Pompeii, could erupt again.
..........................................................................................

**6** Car has revolutionised transport and is absolutely vital to economy of most countries.
..........................................................................................

**7** Judge read jury's verdict aloud and then sentenced accused to five years in prison.
..........................................................................................

**8** Job in media can be quite stressful because of pressure you are under to do things on time.
..........................................................................................

**9** Very few people in 19th century went to school or university and most started work at very young age.
..........................................................................................

**10** I have little free time since I gave up karate, so I'm thinking of trying new hobby, like learning musical instrument.
..........................................................................................

# The media

## Topic vocabulary in contrast

see page 188 for definitions

| | | |
|---|---|---|
| deny / refuse | talk show / quiz show / game show | press / media |
| agree / accept | announcer / commentator | programme / program |
| headline / heading | tabloid / broadsheet | channel / broadcast |
| feature / article | journalist / columnist | bulletin / newsflash |

## Phrasal verbs

| | |
|---|---|
| **bring up** start discussing a subject | **look up** try to find information in a book or list, etc |
| **come on** start to be broadcast | **make out** pretend that something is true; see, hear or understand sb or sth with difficulty |
| **come out** be published | **make up** invent an explanation, excuse, etc; create a story, poem, etc |
| **fill in** add information in the spaces on a document | **put forward** suggest |
| **flick through** turn and look at the pages of a magazine, etc quickly | **see through** recognise that sth is not true and not be tricked by it |
| **go into** deal with sth in detail | **stand out** be easy to see because of being different |
| **hand out** give things to people in a group | **turn over** turn a page so that the other side is towards you |

## Phrases and collocations

| | |
|---|---|
| **control** | in control (of sth); take control (of sth); under control; under the control of sb; out of control |
| **description** | give a description of sth/sb |
| **difference** | make a difference (to sth/sb); tell the difference (between); there's no/some/little/etc difference between |
| **granted** | take sth/sb for granted |
| **influence** | influence sth/sb; have/be an influence on sth/sb |
| **Internet** | on the Internet; over the Internet; surf the Internet |
| **news** | in the news; on the news; hear the news; newsflash; newspaper |
| **place** | take place; in place of; at a place |
| **question** | ask/answer a question; question sth/sb; in question; question mark |
| **view** | have/hold/take a view; be sb's view that; in my view; in view of; look at/see the view; view of sth; view from sth/swh |
| **watch** | watch sth/sb; watch (out) for sth/sb; keep watch |

## Word patterns

| | |
|---|---|
| **according** to sb | **inform** sb that; inform sb about/of sth |
| **announce** sth (to sb); announce that | **likely** to do; likely that |
| **believe** sth; believe in sth; believe that; believe to be | **persuade** sb to do; persuade sb that; persuade sb of sth |
| **comment** on sth; make a comment (to sb) about sth | **point** (in) doing |
| **confuse** sth/sb with sth/sb; confused about/by sth | **send** sb sth; send sth (to sb) |
| **correspond** with sth/sb | **surprise** by surprise; surprised at/by sth |
| **describe** sth/sb as; describe sth/sb to sb | **tell** sb sth; tell sb that; tell sb about sth/doing; tell sb (not) to do |
| **hear** sth/sb; hear about sth/sb; hear from sb | |

## Word formation

| | | |
|---|---|---|
| **announce** announcement, (un)announced | **edit** editor, editorial, edited | **power** powerful(ly), powerless(ly), empower |
| **belief** disbelief, believe, (un)believable, (un)believably | **humour** humorous, humourless | **ridicule** ridiculous(ly), ridiculousness |
| **communicate** communication, (un)communicative, communicator | **inform** information, (un)informed, (un)informative | **second** secondly, secondary |
| **convince** convinced, (un)convincing | **journal** journalist, journalism, journalistic | **write** writer, writing, wrote, (un)written |
| **discuss** discussion | **politics** political(ly), politician | |

## Topic vocabulary in contrast

### A Complete using the correct form of the words in the box.

| deny |
| --- |
| refuse |

1 John Sanders, MP, ........................ any involvement in the scandal when asked about it yesterday.
2 The politician ........................ to say more when questioned by reporters this morning.

| agree |
| --- |
| accept |

3 Johnny Depp rarely ........................ invitations to do interviews.
4 Johnny Depp ........................ to appear at a press conference to promote his latest film.

| heading |
| --- |
| headline |

5 Did you see the newspaper ........................ this morning?
6 If you give every paragraph of your report a ........................ , it'll be easier to read.

| feature |
| --- |
| article |

7 *Living Today* has got a special ........................ this month on healthy diets. There are interviews with nutritionists, menus, recipes, and loads of other things too.
8 There's an interesting ........................ in the paper about the Constitution of the European Union.

| press |
| --- |
| media |

9 I generally trust what I hear on the news, but rarely believe anything I read in the ........................ .
10 The ........................ involve print journalism, TV, radio and even electronic forms of communication such as the Internet.

| bulletin |
| --- |
| newflash |

11 We interrupt this programme to bring you an urgent ........................ .
12 And we'll be back with our regular ........................ at seven o'clock.

### B Circle the correct word or phrase.

1 It's a great computer **programme / program** once you get the hang of it.
2 I hate **tabloid / broadsheet** newspapers; they're just full of gossip, scandal and lies!
3 As a **journalist / columnist** for a local paper, you don't have to interview people or attend events. You just have to express your opinions about the issues of the day.
4 There's a great **talk / quiz / game** show on BBC1 tonight. Contestants have to race through a supermarket as quickly as they can, filling up their trolleys as they go.
5 On some TV channels, **an announcer / a commentator** tells you what the next programme is going to be.
6 Join us at half past nine for a live **broadcast / channel** of the State Opening of Parliament.

## Phrasal verbs

### C Write one word in each gap.

1 Please do not ........................ over your examination papers until you are instructed to do so.
2 I had to ........................ in so many forms. It took me hours!
3 I'd like everyone here to ........................ forward as many suggestions as possible.
4 There was a guy in the street ........................ out free tickets to that new quiz show.
5 He ........................ out that he'd worked in children's TV, but in fact he's never been near a TV studio!
6 Could you ........................ up her number in the phone book?
7 She ........................ out as one of the finest contemporary British novelists around at the moment.

**D** Complete each second sentence using the word given, so that it has a similar meaning to the first sentence. Write between two and five words in each gap.

1 Her latest bestseller was published last month. **out**
Her latest bestseller ............................................................................ last month.
2 That story's not true, is it? **up**
You ............................................................................ , didn't you?
3 The programme starts at half past six. **on**
The programme ............................................................................ at half past six.
4 The documentary didn't really explore why the rainforests are being cut down. **into**
The documentary didn't really ............................................................................ why the rainforests are being cut down.
5 I had a quick look at the magazine in the dentist's waiting room. **through**
I ............................................................................ in the dentist's waiting room.
6 I don't think we need to mention that now. **up**
I don't think we need to ............................................................................ now.
7 Your lies don't fool me! **through**
I can ............................................................................ your lies!

### Phrases and collocations

**E** Choose the correct answer.

1 It's not always easy to ............ the difference between fact and opinion.
A make C say
B do D tell

2 The debate will ............ place tonight.
A be C take
B have D make

3 In my ............ , freedom of the press must be maintained.
A mind C sight
B view D thought

4 Media mogul Ronald Morduck has ............ control of another tabloid.
A made C given
B found D taken

5 They ............ a description of the robber on *CrimeTime* and it sounded like you!
A made C said
B told D gave

6 J. K. Rowling has ............ an enormous influence on children's literature.
A had C done
B given D set

7 I could spend hours ............ the Internet!
A surfing C sailing
B diving D swimming

8 They said ............ the news that the price of petrol is going up again.
A from C on
B in D at

9 The issue ............ question is more complex than you think.
A from C on
B in D at

10 Watch ............ for words like 'so-called' in articles as they express the writer's bias.
A about C over
B around D out

### Word patterns

**F** Each of the words in bold is incorrect. Rewrite them correctly.

1 He's been described by several critics **for** our greatest living poet. ........................
2 I think you've confused tabloids **by** broadsheets. ........................
3 Do you believe **about** telepathy? ........................
4 There's no point **of** trying to get an interview with him. He never does interviews! ........................
5 According **from** this report, scientists have discovered a new planet. ........................
6 The facts in this article don't correspond **about** my own experience at all. ........................

## G Water has damaged part of this text about an anouncement. Read it and decide what you think each of the original words was. Write the words in the blank spaces.

### The announcement

The editor sent an e-mail ........ every journalist on the news desk 1 ........................
announcing ........ there would be an emergency editorial meeting 2 ........................
at one o'clock. I had heard ........ the problems the paper was facing 3 ........................
and I heard ........ one of my colleagues that the paper might be 4 ........................
going to close. Whatever it was, it was likely ........ be bad news. 5 ........................
At the meeting, the editor told us ........ to tell anyone else yet, but 6 ........................
the paper had been taken over by Ronald Morduck. He said he had
only been informed ........ the decision that morning. We were all 7 ........................
so surprised ........ the news that nobody knew what to say. I made 8 ........................
a comment ........ a colleague that it was time to start looking for a 9 ........................
new job. The editor heard this, and finally managed to persuade us not
........ quit until we had seen what changes would be made. 10 ........................

**Word formation**

## H Complete the sentences by changing the form of the word in capitals when this is necessary.

1 Why do press photographers think they can turn up at a celebrity's house completely .............................. (**ANNOUNCE**)?
2 How many means of .............................. (**COMMUNICATE**) do you use on a regular basis?
3 Could you write an .............................. (**EDIT**) for the next issue of the school magazine?
4 You have to have a sense of .............................. (**HUMOUR**) to work on children's TV!
5 There's an .............................. (**WRITE**) rule on tabloid newspapers that the truth always takes second place to a good story.
6 When Jill was at .............................. (**SECOND**) school she used to dream of being a DJ on local radio.
7 Are you thinking of a career in .............................. (**JOURNAL**)?
8 You don't actually get a lot of .............................. (**INFORM**) from a news report on radio or TV.

## I Complete the text by changing the form of the word in capitals.

**Politics on TV**

I love watching (**1**) .............................. (**DISCUSS**) programmes, and I love politics, so you'd think I'd enjoy watching (**2**) .............................. (**POLITICS**) being interviewed on TV. But I don't. All too often, (**3**) .............................. (**JOURNAL**) ask them the most (**4**) .............................. (**RIDICULE**) questions, and, when they do get an interesting question, I sit there watching in (**5**) .............................. (**BELIEVE**) as some of the most (**6**) .............................. (**POWER**) people in the country give totally (**7**) .............................. (**CONVINCE**) responses. It's as if they don't care whether their reply is (**8**) .............................. (**BELIEVE**) or not. Often, they're very poor (**9**) .............................. (**COMMUNICATE**), and they're frequently even more (**10**) .............................. (**INFORM**) about key issues than I am. I don't expect them to be particularly (**11**) .............................. (**HUMOUR**) – they are serious people, after all – but at least they could say something interesting occasionally. It makes me want to stand for election myself!

## A If a line is correct, put a tick (✓) next to the number. If there is an extra word in a line, write it next to the number.

### Quiz Show

1 ........................ Last month, I wrote to a few local television station asking if
2 ........................ they gave away the free tickets to any shows. A week later,
3 ........................ they sent to me two tickets for a quiz show. I went with my
4 ........................ best friend Angie last night. It was an excellent! The show
5 ........................ is called *Know Them Or Not?* and contestants have to
6 ........................ answer questions about a lots of different people in their lives,
7 ........................ like friends, relatives and colleagues. There are ten contestants
8 ........................ to start with but one of them gets knocked out at the end of
9 ........................ each round. I'd like to go into on a show like that one day
10 ........................ but, for now, I'm much happy just to have been in the audience.

(1 mark per answer)

## B Complete the sentences by changing the form of the word in capitals when this is necessary.

11 Why can't .............................. (**POLITICS**) ever just say 'yes' or 'no' when they're asked if they agree with something?
12 I was hoping this book would help me with my history project but in fact it wasn't very .............................. (**INFORM**).
13 My cousin Dan has kept a .............................. (**JOURNAL**) since he was twelve years old.
14 Did you hear that .............................. (**ANNOUNCE**) on the radio about the water shortage?
15 There's an .............................. (**WRITE**) rule in our house about how late we can stay up to watch TV.
16 I just stood there in .............................. (**BELIEVE**) when I heard I'd been selected to go on the quiz show.
17 The Internet is an incredibly powerful means of .............................. (**COMMUNICATE**).
18 I wouldn't describe the film as a comedy, but one or two scenes are mildly .............................. (**HUMOUR**).

(1 mark per answer)

## C Complete the second sentence using the word given, so that it has a similar meaning to the first sentence. Write between two and five words in each gap.

19 These two dictionaries are similar. **little**
There .............................................................................. these two dictionaries.
20 My first editor greatly influenced me. **influence**
My first editor .............................................................................. me.
21 They described the robber on the evening news. **gave**
They .............................................................................. the robber on the evening news.
22 Robert Maxdoch has just bought the newspaper. **control**
The newspaper is now .............................................................................. Robert Maxdoch.
23 You'll be wasting your time if you try to get tickets for that show. **point**
There .............................................................................. to get tickets for that show.
24 I believe that adverts do influence people's buying habits. **view**
It .............................................................................. that adverts do influence people's buying habits.

**25** The prime minister will probably make a statement this afternoon. **likely**
The prime minister .................................................................................. a statement this afternoon.

**26** A programme about the royal family will be shown instead of *Friends* this evening. **place**
This evening, .................................................................................. *Friends*, a programme about the royal family will be shown.

**27** The Hollywood star wouldn't say anything about the allegations. **comment**
The Hollywood star refused .................................................................................. the allegations.

(2 marks per answer)

## D Use the words in the box only once to complete the sentences in Table A. The meaning of the sentences in Table B will help you. There is one word you won't need.

**few • little • lot • lots • many • most • much • some**

| Table A | Table B |
|---|---|
| **28** How ........................ information do we have at the moment? | *asking about an amount* |
| **29** Only a ........................ print journalists manage to move into television. | *describing a small amount* |
| **30** This magazine's got ........................ of adverts in it. | *describing a large amount* |
| **31** I won ........................ money on a quiz show once. | *describing an imprecise amount* |
| **32** There's ........................ chance of getting rich from starting a website. | *describing a small amount* |
| **33** I think that ........................ children's TV programmes these days are educational. | *describing a majority* |
| **34** There aren't ........................ opportunities for poets to get published. | *describing a small amount* |

(1 mark per answer)

## E Choose the correct answer.

**35** The programme usually ............ on at half past eight.
A looks C turns
B does D comes

**36** I saw the interview while I was ............ through a magazine at the hairdresser's.
A clicking C picking
B flicking D ticking

**37** Why did you have to bring that subject ............ at dinner?
A up C over
B out D off

**38** They mentioned it in the article but they didn't ............ into detail.
A make C come
B take D go

**39** The tabloids completely ............ that story about Bruce Willis. It's not true at all!
A stood out C made up
B filled in D turned over

**40** They were ............ out free tickets to the concert to everyone in the shopping centre.
A handing C carrying
B holding D bringing

**41** We had the volume turned down, so I couldn't make ............ what they were talking about.
A up C in
B out D off

(1 mark per answer)

**Total mark: ...... / 50**

## Conditionals: zero, first, second, third, mixed, inverted / unless, in case, as/so long as, provided (that)

### Zero conditional

**Form** *if* + present simple, present simple

| Use | Example |
|---|---|
| General or scientific facts and definitions | *If you **have** faith in something, you **believe** in something you cannot prove.* |

### First conditional

**Form** *if* + a present tense, *will* + bare infinitive

| Use | Example |
|---|---|
| Real or likely conditions in the present or future and their results in the present and future | *If you **have** a birthday party, you**'ll get** loads of cool presents!* |
| | *If you**'re working** till half past six, we**'ll have** dinner at about eight.* |
| | *If you **have revised** properly, you **won't have** any problems in the test next week.* |

**Watch out!**

- We can also use *may, might, can, could, shall, should, ought to, have to* instead of *will*, depending on the meaning.
  ✓ *If you **have** a birthday party, you **might get** loads of cool presents!*
- We can also use *should* + bare infinitive instead of present simple. This suggests the situation is possible, but unlikely to happen.
  ✓ *If you **should bump** into Alex at the concert, you'll be able to get a lift home.*
- We can also use a form of the first conditional to give instructions about real or likely situations in the present or future. This is: *if* + a present tense, imperative.
  ✓ *If you **decide** to have a birthday party, **tell** me!*

### unless, in case, as/so long as, provided (that)

| Word or Phrase | Meaning | Example |
|---|---|---|
| *unless* | 'except if' or 'if…not' | *I'll be there at six **unless** I get delayed.* ( = except if I get delayed / if I don't get delayed) |
| *in case* | 'because he/she/it/etc might' | *Let's take our wellies **in case** it's muddy.* ( = because it might be muddy) |
| *as/so long as* | 'if' or 'only if' | ***As long as** I'm happy, my parents don't care what job I do.*<br>***So long as** I'm happy, my parents don't care what job I do.* |
| *provided (that)* | 'if' or 'only if' | ***Provided (that)** I'm happy, my parents don't care what job I do.* |

### Second conditional

**Form** *if* + past simple or past continuous, *would* + bare infinitive

| Use | Example |
|---|---|
| Impossible, unlikely or hypothetical conditions in the present or future and their results in the present or future | *If you **had** a beard, you **would look** just like Charles Dickens!*<br>*If you **were flying** to Rio, **would** you **get** there much quicker?* |
| Advice | *If I **were** you, I would think very carefully about my future.* (more formal)<br>*If I **was** you, I'd have a party at the weekend!* (more informal) |

**Watch out!**

- We can also use *might* or *could* instead of *would*, depending on the meaning. (Note: *could* here often means *would be able to*.)
  ✓ *If we **were** older, we **could go** on holiday on our own.*
- We can also use *could* in the *if* clause. Here, it means *was/were able to*.
  ✓ *If I **could** drive, I'd buy a car.*

## Third conditional

**Form** *if* + past perfect (simple or continuous), *would* + *have* + past participle

| Use | Example |
|---|---|
| Hypothetical conditions in the past and their results in the past | *If you **had worn** a fake beard, no one **would have known** who you were!* ( = You didn't wear a fake beard so people knew who you were.)<br>*If she**'d been wearing** her new glasses, I **would have noticed** them.* ( = She wasn't wearing her new glasses so I didn't notice them.) |

**Watch out!**

- We can also use *might*, *could* or *should* instead of *would*, depending on the meaning.
  ✓ *If I **had done** some revision, I **might / could / should** have passed the exam.*

## Mixed conditionals

**Form** *if* + past perfect (simple or continuous), *would* + bare infinitive

| Use | Example |
|---|---|
| Hypothetical past condition and a present result | *If I **had listened** to my parents, I **wouldn't be** in so much trouble now.* ( = I didn't listen to my parents so I'm in lots of trouble now.) |

**Form** *if* + past simple or past continuous, *would* + *have* + past participle

| Use | Example |
|---|---|
| Hypothetical present condition and a past result | *If I **had** a mobile, I **would have called** you last night.* ( = I don't have a mobile so I didn't call you last night.) |

## Inverted conditionals

**Form**
*Should I/you/he/etc* ... instead of *If I/you/he/etc should* ...
*Were I/you/he/etc* ... instead of *If I/you/he/etc were* ...
*Had I/you/he/etc* ... instead of *If I/you/he/etc had* ...

| Use | Example |
|---|---|
| More formal form of the first conditional (with *should*) | ***Should** the situation worsen, the United Nations is prepared to send in a peacekeeping force.* ( = If the situation should worsen...) |
| More formal form of the second conditional | ***Were** the situation to worsen, the United Nations would be prepared to send in a peacekeeping force.* ( = If the situation were to worsen...) |
| More formal form of the third conditional | ***Had** the situation worsened, the United Nations would have been prepared to send in a peacekeeping force.* ( = If the situation had worsened...) |

**Watch out!**

- For all conditional sentences (first, second, third, mixed, inverted), when the condition comes before the result it is usually followed by a comma. When the result comes first, no comma is necessary.
  ✓ *If I had a mobile, I would have called you last night.*
  ✓ *I would have called you last night if I had a mobile.*
- In conditional sentences, modals (*will*, *would*, *could*, etc) are sometimes followed by a continuous infinitive.
  ✓ *We**'d** still **be waiting** if you hadn't turned up.*

**US vs UK Grammar**

- With second and third conditionals in informal conversation, speakers of American English sometimes use *would* or *would have* in the *if* clause. This is very unusual in British English.
  **US**: *How would you feel if this **happened / would happen** to you?*
  **UK**: *How would you feel if this **happened** to you?*
  **US**: *I would have felt awful if that **had happened / would have happened** to me.*
  **UK**: *I would have felt awful if that **had happened** to me.*

## A Write *Yes* or *No* to answer the questions about each sentence.

1 If Carl doesn't come to the party, I'll be really upset.
Is it possible that Carl won't come to the party? ........................

2 If my neighbour became prime minister, he'd give everyone a million euros.
Is it likely that the neighbour will become prime minister? ........................
Is it possible that the neighbour will become prime minister? ........................

3 If Helen weren't here, I don't know what we'd do.
Is Helen here now? ........................

4 If Tarek had had enough money, he'd have bought a car.
Did Tarek have enough money? ........................
Did he buy a car? ........................

5 If Debbie hadn't gone to the UK, she wouldn't have met Will.
Did Debbie go to the UK? ........................
Did she meet Will? ........................

6 If the police had investigated the case thoroughly, they wouldn't have arrested Keren.
Did the police investigate the case thoroughly? ........................
Did they arrest Keren? ........................

7 Had she not gone to university, she might not have started her own business.
Did she go to university? ........................
Did she start her own business? ........................

## B Complete the definitions using your own ideas.

*Example:*
If you trust someone, you believe that they won't let you down.

1 If you bully someone, ........................
2 If you accuse someone, ........................
3 If you are a liar, ........................
4 If you are rich, ........................
5 If you are lucky, ........................
6 If you are lazy, ........................
7 If you look up to someone, ........................
8 If you look down on someone, ........................

## C Complete using the correct form of the verbs in the box.

| **be** • **call** • **find** • **forget** • **get** • **leave** • **see** • **take** • **want** • **work** |
|---|

1 If she ........................ at five o'clock, she'll be there by half past seven.
2 We ........................ you if we have any problems.
3 It might not be a good idea to go out tonight if you ........................ an important test in the morning.
4 If you ........................ ill all day, you shouldn't come to the club tonight.
5 If you should ........................ my wallet, call me on my mobile immediately!
6 Let's get a different DVD if you ........................ that one already.
7 If Sean ........................ so hard lately, he'll welcome the chance to have a few days off.
8 If you're going into town, ........................ a video for tonight while you're there!
9 If you see Carol tonight, ........................ to say hello from me!
10 Don't feel you have to come if you ........................ to.

## D Circle the correct word or phrase.

1 This time in six months I'll be at university **unless / if** I decide to take a year off first.
2 We'd better leave early tomorrow **unless / in case** there's a lot of traffic when we get to Doncaster.
3 You can watch the film **as long as / in case** you promise to go straight to bed when it finishes.
4 Let's go to *Mirabella's* tonight **unless / if** you haven't been there before.
5 **Unless / So long as** I've still got my health, I don't mind how poor I am!
6 You'd better take a sweater with you now **if / in case** it gets cold tonight.
7 Do what you like **provided / unless** you don't make any noise.
8 I'm not going to worry **unless / as long as** she hasn't called by midnight.

## E Write sentences using the second conditional.

*Example:* I don't want to buy that CD so I'm not going to.
If I wanted to buy that CD, I would.

1 I don't live alone so I don't get lonely.

........................................

2 Don's got such a lot of homework that he's not going to play football tonight.

........................................

3 I can't swim so I'm not going scuba diving with Terry.

........................................

4 We're not going to order a pizza because we don't have enough money.

........................................

5 We're not staying in the same hotel, so we can't share a room.

........................................

6 I'm not you, but I think you should call Antony right now!

........................................

7 I can't come because I have to help my dad with something.

........................................

8 I don't go to bed as late as you so I'm able to get up early in the morning.

........................................

## F Read the text and complete the sentences using the third conditional.

Some scientists, such as Stephen Hawking, believe it's possible that there are billions and billions of universes. Each universe has a different possible consequence for every action. In the universe we live in, for example, George Bush became President of the USA in January 2001, and Greece won the European Cup in July 2004. But in other universes different things happened. Imagine if that's true! In some universes, your parents didn't meet, so you weren't born. In another universe, a meteor didn't strike the Earth, so the dinosaurs didn't become extinct. In a different universe, your best friend won the lottery last summer and moved to a bigger house. In another parallel universe, you started learning English a year earlier, so you did this book last year! Somewhere else, Madonna wasn't discovered, and so didn't make any records. In another universe, Van Gogh was recognised as a great painter during his lifetime, and so didn't die in poverty. And perhaps in several universes, there were enough lifeboats on the *Titanic* and so everyone on board survived. It makes you think, doesn't it?

1 If I'd started learning English a year earlier, ..............................
2 If a meteor hadn't struck the Earth, ..............................
3 If my best friend had won the lottery last summer, ..............................
4 If my parents ..............................
5 Everyone on board the *Titanic* ..............................
6 Van Gogh ..............................
7 Madonna ..............................
8 If George Bush ..............................
9 If Greece ..............................

## G Choose the correct answer.

If this theory about parallel universes (**1**) ........... correct, it (**2**) ........... that we're living in more than one universe at the same time. But if that (**3**) ........... true – if I was doing different things in different universes – (**4**) ........... about it. And if I (**5**) ........... about it, how could it be me doing these things? If I (**6**) ........... the lottery last year in a parallel universe, and decided to sail round the world, how is that 'me'? It doesn't make sense!
And another thing. If I do something, it (**7**) ........... consequences. For example, if I (**8**) ........... study, I might not pass my exams. I can't start thinking about different universes where the consequences are different. If I just (**9**) ........... about the universe I actually live in, then I'm sure (**10**) ........... okay!

| | | | | |
|---|---|---|---|---|
| **1** | A will be | B is | C would have been | D has been |
| **2** | A has meant | B meant | C had meant | D means |
| **3** | A will be | B was being | C were | D has been |
| **4** | A I'd know | B I'll know | C I have known | D I know |
| **5** | A wouldn't know | B don't know | C won't know | D didn't know |
| **6** | A had won | B was winning | C have won | D win |
| **7** | A would have | B would have had | C will have | D had had |
| **8** | A won't | B haven't | C don't | D hadn't |
| **9** | A think | B to think | C am thinking | D have thought |
| **10** | A I'd be | B I've been | C I'd have been | D I'll be |

## H Complete using the correct form of the verbs in brackets.

1 If .............................. (**you / do**) your homework last night, you'd know the answer to this question!

2 We .............................. (**not / stand**) by the side of the road at the moment trying to get a lift if .............................. (**we / bring**) a spare tyre with us.

3 If I .............................. (**not / stay up**) so late last night, I .............................. (**not / feel**) so tired this morning!

4 .............................. (**I / be**) in terrible trouble right now if you .............................. (**not / help**) me.

5 If I had a video recorder, .............................. (**I / record**) the match last night.

6 .............................. (**I / ask**) for Andy's phone number when I met him if I .............................. (**not / already / have**) a boyfriend!

7 If Cody .................................................. (**not / live**) so far away, he ..................................................
(**not / be**) so late to the barbecue yesterday.

8 Tracy .................................................. (**not / need**) extra lessons last month if she
.................................................. (**be**) as good at maths as you are.

9 .................................................. (**you / got**) a job when you left school if the university
.................................................. (**not / offer**) you a place?

10 If you .................................................. (**have**) as much money as she does,
.................................................. (**you / retire**) by now?

## I Complete the sentences so that the meaning remains the same.

1 If her condition should improve, we'll inform you immediately.
Should ..................................................................................................................................

2 Jade will ask lots of difficult questions if she gets to interview a famous politician.
Should ..................................................................................................................................

3 If you were able to go abroad for the summer, where would you go?
Were ..................................................................................................................................

4 If I was to become a vet, I'd find putting animals down very difficult.
Were ..................................................................................................................................

5 The world would be much better off if all environmental pollution stopped today.
Were ..................................................................................................................................

6 If the hole in the ozone layer had been discovered sooner, fewer people would have got skin cancer.
Had ..................................................................................................................................

7 I wouldn't have become a teacher if I hadn't had such a good English teacher at school.
Had ..................................................................................................................................

## J If a line is correct, put a tick (✓) next to the number. If there is an extra word in a line, write it next to the number.

### Being an only child

1 ................ I'm an only child. People often say to me: 'Wouldn't you be a lot
2 ................ happier if you have had brothers and sisters?' but I don't see it like that.
3 ................ It's true that if I had had a brother or sister, I would have someone closer
4 ................ to my own age to talk to and play with at home, but I don't think that's
5 ................ very important provided for you have close friends, which I do. If my
6 ................ parents would had more children, they wouldn't be able to spend so much
7 ................ time with me. And we have great fun together! Also, except if I had a
8 ................ brother or sister, I'd have it to share a bedroom with them. That might be
9 ................ fun, but what would happen if I wanted to play my CDs and he or she had
10 ................ to study? No – I don't want a brother or sister, unless it will happens, of
course. In that case, I'll think it's the best thing in the world!

## People and society

### Topic vocabulary in contrast

see page 189 for definitions

| | | |
|---|---|---|
| relationship / connection | support / assist | company / group |
| blame / fault | kind / polite | popular / famous |
| old / ancient | sympathetic / likeable | typical / usual / ordinary |
| crowd / audience | nervous / bad-tempered | close / near |
| enjoy / please | sensitive / sensible | unknown / infamous |

### Phrasal verbs

| | |
|---|---|
| **ask after** ask for news about | **make up** become friends again after an argument |
| **bring up** look after a child until he or she becomes an adult | **pass away** die |
| **fall for** fall in love with; believe (a lie/trick/etc) | **pick on** keep treating someone badly or unfairly |
| **fall out (with)** have an argument with and stop being friends | **put down** criticise, make someone feel stupid |
| **get on (with)** have a good relationship (with) | **settle down** become calm after being upset, etc; stay in one place or get married and live quietly |
| **grow up** become older | **stand up for** support in an argument or fight |
| **look down on** think that you are better than | **take aback** surprise (usually in passive voice) |
| **look up to** admire and respect | |

### Phrases and collocations

| | |
|---|---|
| **approval** | show/give (your) approval of/for sth; meet with sb's approval |
| **argument** | have an argument (with sb) (about sth/doing); win/lose an argument |
| **care** | take care (of sth/sb); care for/about sth/sb |
| **courage** | have the courage to do; it takes courage to do |
| **disguise** | in disguise; wear a disguise; disguise yourself; disguised as sth/sb |
| **dream** | have a dream (about sth/sb/doing); daydream; dream of/about doing |
| **family** | have/start a family; nuclear family; extended family |
| **favour** | do/owe sb a favour; be in favour of |
| **friend** | make/become/be/stay friends (with sb); best friend |
| **love** | be/fall in love with sb |
| **mood** | in a good/bad mood; in the right/wrong mood; in the mood for sth |
| **pity** | pity sb; take pity on sb; feel pity for sb; it's a pity (that) |
| **promise** | promise to do; give/make sb a promise; break a/your promise |

### Word patterns

| | |
|---|---|
| **agree** with/on/to sth; agree with sb; agree to do; agree that | **force** sb to do sth; force sb into sth/doing |
| **allow** sb to do; allow sth | **independent** of/from sth |
| **approve** of sth/doing; approve sth | **let** sb do sth |
| **ask** sb sth; ask sb to do sth (for you); ask about/for sth; ask if/whether | **object** to sth/doing |
| **attack** sth; attack sb for sth/doing; an attack on sth/sb | **pretend** to be; pretend to do; pretend that |
| **ban** sb from sth/doing; ban sth | **rely** on sth/sb |
| **convince** sb (of sth); convince sb to do; convince sb that | |

### Word formation

| | | |
|---|---|---|
| **able** unable, (in)ability, disabled, disability | **happy** unhappy, (un)happiness, (un)happily | **obey** disobey, (dis)obedient(ly), (dis)obedience |
| **achieve** achievement | **jealous** jealousy, jealously | **person** (im)personal(ly), personality |
| **argue** argument, argumentative | **kind** unkind, (un)kindness, kindly | **polite** impolite, (im)politely, (im)politeness |
| **care** careful(ly), careless(ly), (un)caring | **marry** marriage, (un)married | **relate** relative(ly), relation, relationship |
| **correspond** correspondence | **nerve** nervous(ly), nervousness | **willing** unwilling, (un)willingness, (un)willingly |
| **friend** friendship, (un)friendly | | |

### Topic vocabulary in contrast

## A Choose the correct answer.

1 Everyone said they had ………… themselves at the wedding.
A enjoyed C pleased
B impressed D excited

2 Mary seems to go out with a different ………… of friends almost every night.
A group C company
B band D collection

3 People can become very ………… when they are stuck in traffic for a long time.
A nervous C stressful
B bad-tempered D pressed

4 More and more people are living into ………… age and it's a serious social problem.
A high C far
B ancient D old

5 Stephanie seems to be very ………… with her classmates.
A likeable C known
B famous D popular

6 Most ………… people have no idea what it's like to be famous.
A usual C typical
B ordinary D medium

7 When my parents got divorced, my best friend was very ………… and listened to all my problems.
A likeable C sympathetic
B amusing D enjoyable

8 Rita's very ………… and easily gets upset when people criticise her.
A level-headed C sensible
B sensitive D open-minded

9 Police were called in when the ………… of people began to get violent.
A crowd C audience
B company D herd

10 My dad says he once met Robbie Williams when he was still ………… .
A unknown C infamous
B hidden D unrelated

## B Circle the correct word.

1 These days, many parents find it difficult to **assist / support** a large family.
2 Forgetting to thank us for dinner is **usual / typical** of George.
3 My grandma doesn't have any **close / near** family her own age left.
4 In **ancient / old** times, people had a very different view of the world.
5 Who was to **blame / fault** for the argument?
6 Don't you know it's **kind / polite** to close your mouth when you are eating?
7 Nathan's parents were very **enjoyed / pleased** when they saw him in the school play.
8 I have a very good **connection / relationship** with my mother.

### Phrasal verbs

## C Complete using the words from the box. You need to use one word twice.

**get • make • put • look • bring • fall • grow**

### Personality

Some of us seem to be infinitely kind, while others seem to (**1**) …………………… down on everyone around them. Some of us never forget an argument, while others (**2**) …………………… up and forgive easily. As we (**3**) …………………… up, our personality develops and we find that we (**4**) …………………… on with certain people more than others. Who we are seems to have a large genetic element, but is also influenced by those who (**5**) …………………… us up. If we (**6**) …………………… up to our parents or other family members, we may want to be like them. On the other hand, if our parents seem to (**7**) …………………… us down all the time and we (**8**) …………………… out with them a lot, then perhaps we will develop quite different personalities.

## D Write a phrasal verb in the correct form to replace the words in italics. Add any other words you need.

1 The doctor said that the old woman had *died* .............................................. peacefully in her sleep.
2 I always *support* .............................................. my brother when he gets into trouble.
3 Tony seems to have really *fallen in love with* .............................................. Vanessa.
4 Mark is such a bully and *treats badly* .............................................. the younger boys at school.
5 I was *surprised* .............................................. when Michaela said I'd hurt her feelings.
6 Richard finally met the woman of his dreams and *got married and started to live quietly* .............................................. in Australia.
7 I saw Mrs Khan in the centre of town and she *asked for news about* .............................................. you.

### Phrases and collocations

## E Write one word in each gap.

1 Could you ........................ me a favour and ask Oliver to see me in my office?
2 I don't have many ambitions, but I'd like to graduate and then ........................ a family.
3 As we walked down the street, Helen ........................ pity on the beggar and gave him some money.
4 Nadia's hair looked awful, but I didn't ........................ the courage to tell her.
5 My dad can't stand ........................ an argument and always has to have the last word.
6 The new law seemed to ........................ with everyone's approval.
7 Can you ........................ care of your little sister for a minute while I go to the shop?
8 When you first ........................ in love, the whole world seems a beautiful place.
9 I don't really ........................ friends very easily because I'm quite shy.
10 I didn't recognise Ed when I saw him because he was ........................ disguise.
11 You're in a very good ........................ . Why are you so happy?
12 If you keep ........................ your promises, people won't trust you any more.
13 I ........................ a really strange dream last night about my best friend.

### Word patterns

## F Choose the correct answer.

1 The government is trying to convince people ............ the need for higher taxes.
A with C that
B of D for

2 I believe that judges should be independent ............ the government.
A to C with
B from D on

3 Local residents object ............ the new power station in their area.
A to have C of having
B having D to having

4 Do you think they should ban people ............ smoking in public places?
A from C in
B that D of

5 The MP asked ............ the prime minister was aware of the growing social problem.
A that C if
B him D what

6 Most people seem to agree ............ the newspapers' criticism of the government.
A on C with
B to D that

7 I don't think people should rely ............ the state, even if they are unemployed.
A to C on
B with D by

8 The mayor was attacked ............ public money.
A for wasting C he waste
B to waste D of wasting

## G Find the extra word in each line.

### Living together in society

1 ........................ Hell, said Jean-Paul Sartre, is other people, and whether you agree with
2 ........................ or not, we are all have to learn to live together. We may not always
3 ........................ approve of that other people's behaviour, but we do have to live with it.
4 ........................ It is impossible to force other people in to behave exactly how we think
5 ........................ they should behave. Of course, the law bans from all kinds of behaviour
6 ........................ and if you can convince to enough people, you might be able to get the
7 ........................ government to pass a new law. Mostly, though, you have to let off people
8 ........................ live their own lives, in the same way you expect them to allow you for to
9 ........................ live your life. You don't have to pretend it that you like how some other
10 ........................ people live, but letting them to be themselves is often the only choice.

**Word formation**

## H Use the word given in capitals at the end of each line to form a word that fits in the gap in the same line.

I had a really stupid (**1**) .............................. with my best friend the other day. It all **ARGUE**
started because we were talking about (**2**) .............................. and having a family. **MARRY**
I said that (**3**) .............................. is important when you are married and she said **POLITE**
that she thought that was rubbish and that (**4**) .............................. is much more **KIND**
important. Well, we were (**5**) .............................. to agree and, in the end, she left **ABLE**
without saying goodbye. I do hope it doesn't spoil our (**6**) .............................. . **FRIEND**

## I Complete the sentences by changing the form of the word in capitals when this is necessary.

1 My best friend has a great .............................. (**PERSON**) and everyone likes her.
2 I have a good .............................. (**RELATE**) with my mum and I can talk to her about anything.
3 They've just published a book of George Bush's .............................. (**CORRESPOND**) and it looks really interesting.
4 Jenny seemed .............................. (**WILLING**) to talk about her argument with Nancy but I eventually got the facts.
5 As I waited for Kelly to arrive at the cinema, I bit my nails .............................. (**NERVE**).
6 Ignore what Sharon says about you. It's just .............................. (**JEALOUS**).
7 In the past, children were expected to be very .............................. (**OBEY**).
8 Brenda blames her .............................. (**HAPPY**) on being single, but I'm not so sure.
9 Tom knew that being chosen as class president was a real .............................. (**ACHIEVE**).
10 Kevin's so sensitive that you have to be very .............................. (**CARE**) what you say to him.

## A Write one word in each gap.

### CULTURE SHOCK

Many people dream (**1**) ........................ living in a foreign country. It can be an amazing experience for those who (**2**) ........................ the courage to leave their family and friends and settle (**3**) ........................ in a new place. However, there's one potential problem you should be aware of: culture shock. Culture shock is the feeling we get from living in a place that is so different to where we (**4**) ........................ up that we are not sure how to deal with it. Societies are organised in many different ways, and we can often be (**5**) ........................ aback by some of the things we find in foreign countries. Customs and traditions can be very different and that can sometimes make it difficult to (**6**) ........................ on with local people and to (**7**) ........................ friends. They might not approve (**8**) ........................ things you do or might object (**9**) ........................ things you say. You might even be banned (**10**) ........................ doing things in another country that are perfectly legal in your own. (**11**) ........................ you were to move to a country such as Singapore, say, you might find some of the laws very strict. There, people can be forced (**12**) ........................ pay a large fine just for dropping litter. Eventually, though, most people who live abroad (**13**) ........................ in love with their adopted country and learn to accept its differences. It does (**14**) ........................ real courage to make such a big change to your life, but many people agree (**15**) ........................ it is worth it in the end.

(1 mark per answer)

## B Complete the sentences by changing the form of the word in capitals when this is necessary.

**16** My .............................. (**FRIEND**) with Harriet is one of the most important things in my life.
**17** Many parents complain of their children's .............................. (**OBEY**), but I think they were probably exactly the same.
**18** Don't listen to Mary – she's just .............................. (**JEALOUS**) of you.
**19** We all watched .............................. (**NERVE**) as Mark made his speech of thanks.
**20** Don't you think that we should make sure that .............................. (**ABLE**) people have the same rights as everyone else?
**21** Terry is really .............................. (**ARGUE**) and is always looking for fights with other people.
**22** Hasn't anyone ever told you that it's very .............................. (**POLITE**) to interrupt when other people are talking?

(1 mark per answer)

## C Complete the second sentence using the word given, so that it has a similar meaning to the first sentence. Write between two and five words in each gap.

**23** I promised my mum that I would work hard this year. **made**
I ........................................................................ that I would work hard this year.

**24** My parents allowed me to go out even though it was very late. **let**
My parents ........................................................................ even though it was very late.

**25** Margaret and I have had an argument, so we're not talking to each other. **out**
Margaret and I ........................................................................ , so we're not talking to each other.

**26** Nobody approved of the new law when it was introduced. **approval**
The new law didn't ........................................................................ when it was introduced.

**27** I didn't want to have an argument, so I changed the subject. **mood**
I wasn't ........................................................................ an argument, so I changed the subject.

**28** Tina was depressed because she couldn't make friends at summer camp. **inability**
Tina was depressed because .................................................................................. friends at summer camp.

**29** 'Could you open the door for me, please?' said Simon. **me**
Simon .................................................................................. the door for him.

**30** Make sure you look after your little brother while I'm out. **care**
Make sure you .................................................................................. your little brother while I'm out.

(2 marks per answer)

## D Choose the correct answer.

**31** If I ............ the lottery, I'd give some of the money to each member of my family.
A win
B have won
C will win
D won

**32** 'Did you have an argument with Francis?'
'If you had been there, you ............ the same.'
A did
B would have done
C had done
D will do

**33** If you see Nina on Friday, ............ her to give me a ring.
A you will tell
B tell to
C you would have told
D tell

**34** If I'd known you were coming, I ............ a cake.
A would have baked
B would bake
C will bake
D baked

**35** Remind Tony about the party ............ he's forgotten.
A in case
B unless
C provided that
D except

**36** 'Did you have a message for Dan?'
'Tell him I'll call him on Friday if you ............ him.'
A had seen
B see
C will see
D saw

(1 mark per answer)

## E Choose the correct answer.

**37** This fascinating book covers some of the most ............ crimes of the twentieth century.
A unknown C covered
B hidden D infamous

**38** The government should do more for ............ people.
A usual C everyday
B ordinary D typical

**39** Ivan tells me he really ............ himself at your barbecue last week.
A pleased C enjoyed
B played D interested

**40** I know we had an argument, but now I'd quite like to ............ .
A look down C fall out
B make up D bring up

**41** Harry and Sam both denied that the fight was their ............ .
A blame C criticism
B cause D fault

**42** The curtain went up, the ............ grew silent and the actors on stage began to speak.
A crowd C jury
B congregation D audience

(1 mark per answer)

**Total mark: ...... / 50**

## Comparatives and superlatives / so, such, enough, too

### Comparative and superlative adjectives

| | adjective | comparative | superlative |
|---|---|---|---|
| regular adjectives with one syllable | *black* | + *-er*<br>*blacker* | + *-est*<br>*blackest* |
| regular adjectives with one syllable (ending in vowel + consonant) | *thin* | double final letter + *-er*<br>*thinner* | double final letter + *-est*<br>*thinnest* |
| regular adjectives with two syllables (ending in *-y*) | *funny* | replace *-y* with *-ier*<br>*funnier* | replace *-y* with *-iest*<br>*funniest* |
| regular adjectives with two or more syllables | *intelligent* | *more / less* + adj<br>*more intelligent* | *most / least* + adj<br>*most intelligent* |
| irregular adjectives / quantifiers | *good*<br>*bad*<br>*far*<br>*little*<br>*much*<br>*many* | *better*<br>*worse*<br>*farther / further*<br>*less*<br>*more*<br>*more* | *best*<br>*worst*<br>*farthest / furthest*<br>*least*<br>*most*<br>*most* |

| Use | Example |
|---|---|
| Comparative<br>To compare things or people that are different | *The crime rate in this area is **higher** than in other parts of the country.* |
| Superlative<br>To compare one member of a group of people or things with the whole group | *The robbery was **the biggest** in the bank's history.* |

**Watch out!**

- Regular adjectives with two syllables can often also form the comparative and superlative like adjectives with one syllable.
  ✓ ***clever, cleverer, cleverest***
- Adjectives with one syllable that end in *-e* add *-r* and *-st*.
  ✓ ***white, whiter, whitest***
- Remember that comparative forms are often followed by *than*.
  ✓ *Crime is a much **bigger** problem in this country **than** in many other countries.*
- Remember that superlative forms are often preceded by *the*.
  ✓ *Our local police force is **the best** in the country.*

### Comparative and superlative adverbs

| | adverb | comparative | superlative |
|---|---|---|---|
| regular adverbs | *easily* | *more / less* + adv *more easily* | *most / least* + adv *most easily* |
| irregular adverbs | *badly*<br>*early*<br>*far*<br>*fast*<br>*hard*<br>*late*<br>*often*<br>*near*<br>*soon*<br>*well* | *worse*<br>*earlier*<br>*farther / further*<br>*faster*<br>*harder*<br>*later*<br>*more often*<br>*nearer*<br>*sooner*<br>*better* | *worst*<br>*earliest*<br>*farthest / furthest*<br>*fastest*<br>*hardest*<br>*latest*<br>*most often*<br>*nearest*<br>*soonest*<br>*best* |

| Use | Example |
|---|---|
| Comparative<br>To compare actions that are different | *Lock your door **more carefully** next time and maybe you won't get burgled!* |
| Superlative<br>To compare actions of one member of a group of people or things with the whole group | *Only the criminal who ran **fastest** managed to escape from the police.* |

## So

| Form | |
|---|---|
| | *so* + adjective + *that*<br>*so* + adverb + *that*<br>*so* + *many/much* + noun + *that* |

| Use | Example |
|---|---|
| To show the results of a situation or action | *The burglar was **so** clever **that** no one could catch him.*<br>*Jane took the money **so** quickly **that** no one saw her.*<br>*There was **so** much money **that** the robber couldn't carry it all.* |

**Watch out!**

- The word *that* is not usually necessary to introduce the second clause.
  ✓ *The crime rate is **so** high people are very frightened.*
- The word *so* has a number of other uses. Try not to get confused between them.
  ✓ *The crime rate is **so** high **that** people are very frightened.*
  ✓ *I saw that burglar leaving the house, **so** I called the police.*

## Such

| Form | |
|---|---|
| | *such* + *a/an* + adjective + singular noun + *that*<br>*such* + adjective + plural noun + *that*<br>*such* + *a lot of* + noun + *that* |

| Use | Example |
|---|---|
| To show the results of a situation or action | *It was **such** a terrible crime **that** the man was sent to prison for life.*<br>*The security guard had **such** good hearing **that** he heard the door open immediately.*<br>*There is **such** a lot of crime here **that** the police can't cope.* |

## Enough

| Form | |
|---|---|
| | *enough* + noun (+ *for* and/or + full infinitive)<br>adjective + *enough* (+ *for* and/or + full infinitive)<br>adverb + *enough* (+ *for* and/or + full infinitive) |

| Use | Example |
|---|---|
| To show the results of a situation or action where there is/isn't the right amount/number of something | *There aren't **enough** police officers on the streets to keep us safe.*<br>*It wasn't dark **enough** for the burglar to start working.*<br>*Did the police respond quickly **enough** to help?* |

**Watch out!**

- A common mistake is to put *enough* before an adjective when the correct word is *quite* or *fairly*.
  ✓ *It's **quite** / **fairly** dangerous around here so don't go out alone.*
  ✗ ~~*It's **enough** dangerous around here so don't go out alone.*~~

## Too

| Form | |
|---|---|
| | *too* + adjective (+ *for* and/or + full infinitive)<br>*too* + adverb (+ *for* and/or + full infinitive)<br>*too* + *many/much* + noun (+ *for* and/or + full infinitive) |

| Use | Example |
|---|---|
| To describe something that is more than necessary and which has a negative effect | *The young man was **too** young to go to prison.*<br>*We arrived **too** late for the start of the trial.*<br>*We send **too** many innocent people to prison.* |

**Watch out!**

- We do not use *too* when we want to describe something we consider to be positive. Instead, we use *very*, *really* or *extremely*.
  ✓ *You were **very** / **really** / **extremely** lucky not to get caught.*
  ✗ ~~*You were **too** lucky not to get caught.*~~

## A Complete using the comparative forms of the words in capitals.

1 Your brother is much .................................................. (**TALL**) than mine.
2 This island used to be much .................................................. (**GREEN**) before the forest fires.
3 Slow down! You're .................................................. (**FIT**) than me and I can't keep up!
4 Veronica seems .................................................. (**HAPPY**) since she moved schools.
5 It's actually .................................................. (**TRENDY**) to wear your hair up this year.
6 As the time for the performance got nearer, I got .................................................. (**NERVOUS**).
7 Old people are often .................................................. (**WISE**) than young people.
8 Why don't you try and find a .................................................. (**CHEAP**) computer game and save some money?
9 Matt seems to have got even .................................................. (**LAZY**) than he used to be and almost never studies.
10 If the problem gets any .................................................. (**SERIOUS**), we may need to inform the manager about it.
11 If you work .................................................. (**QUICKLY**), you'll finish sooner and then you can go home earlier.
12 Ben says he's feeling much .................................................. (**WELL**) after his illness.
13 I have even .................................................. (**LITTLE**) free time this year than I did last year.
14 The news was much .................................................. (**BAD**) than anyone had feared.
15 You'll need to be able to run .................................................. (**FAR**) than this if you're going to do the marathon.

## B Complete using the superlative forms of the words in capitals.

1 I think Mohammed Ali was the .................................................. (**GREAT**) boxer that ever lived.
2 It was the .................................................. (**BORING**) film I had ever seen.
3 Our teacher told us that the student with the .................................................. (**HIGH**) mark would get a prize.
4 Ginger is one of the .................................................. (**LUCKY**) cats alive – he's been hit by a car three times and has never been hurt!
5 Out of all the students in my music school, I practise .................................................. (**OFTEN**).
6 The Pacific is the .................................................. (**DEEP**) ocean in the world.
7 That's the .................................................. (**UGLY**) fish I've ever seen!
8 I was ill before the exam and I did .................................................. (**BADLY**) out of the whole class.
9 The .................................................. (**FAR**) I've run in one day is about ten kilometres.
10 Don't you think this would be the .................................................. (**LOVELY**) spot for a picnic?
11 But that's the .................................................. (**CRAZY**) idea I've ever heard!
12 I asked the assistant to show me the .................................................. (**MODERN**) phone they had.
13 I told the manager that it was the .................................................. (**BAD**) hotel I had ever stayed in.
14 Who do you think is the .................................................. (**LITTLE**) talented actor to win an Oscar?
15 Out of all the members of the choir, Jason sang .................................................. (**WELL**).

## C Circle the correct word.

### FILM REVIEW

*Crime Does Pay*, the (**1**) **later / latest** comedy from director Sam Martin, has to be one of the (**2**) **little / least** interesting films I have ever seen. The acting is terrible and the story is much (**3**) **worse / worst** than Martin's other flop, *Escape*. *Crime Does Pay* was apparently (**4**) **more / most** expensive than any other film this year, but it's hard to see where the money went. The plot concerns a gang of burglars who decide to steal the (**5**) **more / most** valuable painting in the world. Fine, except these criminals are far (**6**) **less / least** amusing than they should be. There isn't a single real laugh in the whole movie. When I saw it, even (**7**) **younger / youngest** members of the audience thought it was stupidly childish. Dean Richards, playing Scarnose, does a slightly (**8**) **better / best** job than the others, but there isn't much in it. When will Hollywood realise that as ticket prices get (**9**) **higher / highest**, more people are finding that the (**10**) **well / best** form of entertainment is to spend an evening at home with a DVD?

## D Complete each second sentence using the word given, so that it has a similar meaning to the first sentence. Write between two and five words in each gap.

1 I have never read a better book than this one. **ever**
This is the ............................................................................ read.

2 Nobody has ever been this far into the jungle. **the**
This is ............................................................................ has ever been into the jungle.

3 I have never worked so hard in my whole life. **ever**
It was the ............................................................................ in my whole life.

4 Liam is the tallest boy in the class. **than**
Every other boy in the class ............................................................................ Liam.

5 This is the nicest beach along this part of the coast. **than**
This ............................................................................ the others along this part of the coast.

6 I read that Mount Everest is the highest mountain. **no**
I read that ............................................................................ Mount Everest.

7 Has anyone ever been this far north before? **the**
Is ............................................................................ has ever been?

8 The painting Ed did is the ugliest one you can imagine. **than**
You can't imagine ............................................................................ the one Ed did.

9 This stamp is rarer than any other in my collection. **more**
The other stamps in my collection ............................................................................ this one.

10 Nobody in the class runs as fast as Pedro. **runner**
Pedro ............................................................................ in the class.

## E Rewrite each sentence using *so ... that*.

1 John can see over the wall because he is tall.

............................................................................................................................

2 I'm sure my sister will go to university because she is clever.

............................................................................................................................

3 I can't stop playing this computer game because it's good.

............................................................................................................................

4 Tim can't come out because he has a lot of work to do.

..................................................................................................................................

5 It's hot, which means I can't sleep.

..................................................................................................................................

6 Tina arrived late, which meant she missed the train.

..................................................................................................................................

7 We don't have any money for luxuries because we have a lot of bills to pay.

..................................................................................................................................

8 It takes a day to get to Australia because it's very far away.

..................................................................................................................................

## F Match to make sentences.

1 Last year, winter started so ............
2 Last winter, there were so ............
3 Last year, we had such ............
4 Last winter, there was so ............
5 Last winter, there was such a lot of ............
6 Last winter was so ............

A many storms that we had floods.
B cold that the water in the pipes froze.
C a cold winter that I had to sleep with a hat on!
D suddenly that many people were taken by surprise.
E much snow that I skied nearly every day.
F snow that many wild animals died.

## G Circle the correct word or phrase.

1 I don't think there's **enough pizza / pizza enough** for everyone.
2 I'm afraid you're not **enough old / old enough** to see this film.
3 Luckily, we got to the box office **enough early / early enough** and got the tickets.
4 Anne's **enough sensible / sensible enough** to realise she needs to work hard this year.
5 If you don't train **enough hard / hard enough**, you'll never win the race.
6 Have you got **enough credits / credits enough** to call Yiota on your mobile?
7 It should be **enough warm / warm enough** for a picnic this weekend.
8 I don't think I'm good enough **for getting / to get** into the swimming team.
9 Are you sure you've got enough chairs for **us all to sit down / we all sit down**?
10 In mountaineering, you have to be strong enough **for pull / to pull** yourself up with your fingers.

## H Tick (✓) the correct sentences. If a sentence is incorrect, write another word to replace the word in bold.

1 I wanted to get some new trainers but they were **too** expensive. ...............................
2 Japanese is a **too** difficult language for Westerners to learn. ...............................
3 Daniel's **too** good at art and he's starting art school next year. ...............................
4 Don't invite **too** many people to the party or we won't have enough room. ...............................
5 If you try to write your essay **too** quickly, you'll make mistakes. ...............................
6 My new computer is **too** fast and can run all the latest programs. ...............................
7 Joanne was fined for driving **too** fast. ...............................
8 Carol couldn't climb over the wall because it was **too** high. ...............................
9 Cornwall is **too** beautiful and we go there every year on holiday. ...............................

10 My grandparents are **too** old to work now and have retired. ..............................
11 It was **too** dark for me to see the map and I got lost. ..............................
12 My best friend is **too** funny and always makes me laugh. ..............................

## I Choose the correct answer.

1 It was ........... windy that I couldn't stand up!
A so C enough
B such D too

2 Everyone had ........... a good time when we went bowling that we agreed to go again.
A so C enough
B such D too

3 Emma and Karen used to be ........... good friends that I'm surprised they don't get on now.
A so C enough
B such D too

4 I hope I've got ........... money to pay for this meal!
A so C enough
B such D too

5 I'm sorry, but I've got ........... much work to do to come to the beach today.
A so C enough
B such D too

6 My mum was ........... angry that I knew I'd better disappear for a while.
A so C enough
B such D too

7 They were ........... beautiful shoes that I decided I had to get them.
A so C enough
B such D too

8 The earthquake was ........... powerful that the town was destroyed.
A so C enough
B such D too

9 The shot was ........... quick for the goalkeeper and the ball hit the back of the net.
A so C enough
B such D too

10 I had ........... a bad headache that I went to lie down for a while.
A so C enough
B such D too

## J Write one word in each gap.

**CRIMESTOPPERS**

'Hello, and welcome to *Crimestoppers*, the show that lets you, the viewer, help the police. We've had (**1**) ........................ a lot of letters this week that it's difficult to know where to begin. We'll start with the story of Mrs Pat Williams, of Cambridge. Last Friday, Pat decided to go into town with her baby daughter. It's (**2**) ........................ far to walk so they went to the bus stop. They waited (**3**) ........................ a long time that baby Caroline started to cry. Pat picked the baby up out of the pram and she was (**4**) ........................ busy she didn't notice the man beside her until it was (**5**) ........................ late. He grabbed her handbag and ran off (**6**) ........................ quickly for her to catch him. It all happened (**7**) ........................ fast that there was nothing anyone could do. Police are appealing for witnesses. Maybe you were in the area. Maybe you think that what you saw is (**8**) ........................ unimportant that the police won't be interested. Remember that no detail is (**9**) ........................ small to be useful to the police. Call us here at *Crimestoppers* now.'

## The law and crime

### Topic vocabulary in contrast

see page 190 for definitions

| | | |
|---|---|---|
| proof / evidence | rule / law / justice / right | vandal / hooligan |
| suspect / arrest / charge | judge / jury | sentence / imprison |
| suspect / accused | prosecute / persecute | innocent / guilty |
| decision / verdict | capital punishment / corporal punishment | witness / bystander |
| commit / break | robber / burglar / thief | lawyer / solicitor |

### Phrasal verbs

| | |
|---|---|
| **back down** stop demanding sth, stop saying that you will do sth | **hand in** give to a person in authority |
| **break out** escape (from prison) | **hold up** rob while threatening violence; delay |
| **bring in** introduce a new law or system | **let off** give little or no punishment; make a bomb, etc explode |
| **chase after** follow sb/sth quickly in order to catch them | **look into** investigate |
| **come forward** offer help or information | **make off** escape |
| **get away with** escape punishment for | **take down** write down what someone says |
| **go off** explode; be fired (for a gun, usually accidentally) | **take in** trick sb into believing sth that is not true |

### Phrases and collocations

| | |
|---|---|
| **account** | on account of; take into account; account for sth |
| **advantage** | take advantage of sth/sb; have an advantage over sth/sb; at an advantage; an/one/etc advantage (of sth) |
| **blame** | be to blame (for sth/doing); get/take the blame (for sth/doing); put the blame on sth/sb; blame sth (on sb); blame sb for sth/doing |
| **damage** | do/cause damage (to sth) |
| **fault** | at fault; find fault with sth/sb |
| **intention** | have the/no intention of doing |
| **mistake** | make a mistake; a mistake (to do); mistake sb for sb; do sth by mistake |
| **necessary** | necessary (for sb) to do |
| **order** | in order; put sth in order; in order to do; give an order (to sb) (to do) |
| **permission** | give sb permission to do; ask (sb) for permission to do; have/ask for/get permission (from sb) to do |
| **purpose** | do sth on purpose; purpose of sth |
| **reason** | reason why; reason for sth; reason with sb |
| **solution** | have/find/think of/work out/come up with/figure out a solution (to sth) |
| **wrong** | do wrong; do the wrong thing; the wrong thing to do; go wrong; the wrong way up |

### Word patterns

| | | |
|---|---|---|
| **accuse** sb of sth/doing | **doubt** sth; doubt that; doubt if/whether | **make** sb do; be made to do |
| **arrest** sb for sth/doing | **forgive** sb for sth/doing | **refuse** to do sth; refuse sth |
| **charge** sb with sth | **glimpse** sth; catch a glimpse of sth | **respect** sth; respect sb for sth/doing; have respect for sth/sb |
| **claim** to be/do; claim that | **guilty** of sth/doing | **threaten** to do, threaten sb with sth |
| **deny** sth/doing | **legal** (for sb) to do | |

### Word formation

| | | |
|---|---|---|
| **accuse** accused, accusation | **honest** dishonest, (dis)honesty, (dis)honestly | **prison** prisoner, imprison(ed), imprisonment |
| **addict** addicted, addictive, addiction | **investigate** investigative, investigation, investigator | **prove** proof, (un)proven, disprove |
| **convict** convicted, conviction | **law** lawyer, (un)lawful | **rob** robbery, robber |
| **crime** criminal | **murder** murderer | **secure** insecure, (in)security |
| **evident** evidence, evidently | **offence** offensive, offend, offender | **theft** thief |
| **forge** forgery, forger | | |

### Topic vocabulary in contrast

## A Each of the words in bold is in the wrong sentence. Write the correct word on the line.

1 All twelve members of the **witness** were convinced of Davidson's guilt. ....................
2 I don't think I'd ever **break** a serious crime. ....................
3 If the school **laws** aren't written down anywhere, how are we supposed to know what they are? ....................
4 A psychiatrist was called as an expert **judge** during the trial. ....................
5 If a parent smacks a child, that's an example of **commit** punishment. ....................
6 Everyone should have the **jury** to a fair trial. ....................
7 If you **sentenced** the law, you deserve to be punished! ....................
8 Governments must be allowed to introduce, change and scrap **bystanders**. ....................
9 Can you imagine what it's like being **justice** for years in a cell? ....................
10 It's very important that **capital** is seen to be done. ....................
11 Another phrase for '**right** punishment' is 'the death sentence'. ....................
12 The spy was **imprisoned** to life imprisonment. ....................
13 A number of **rules** watched the robbers speed off in a getaway car. ....................
14 'Silence in court!' shouted the **corporal** angrily. ....................

## B Complete the crossword.

**Across**

2 A football … is someone who causes trouble at a football match. (8)
4 the decision of a judge or jury (7)
8 a burglar, robber or any other person who steals (5)
10 It might not be absolute proof of someone's guilt, but it is used to show that someone could be guilty. (8)
11 a person the police think might have committed a crime (7)
12 The jury found her not … of all charges. (6)
13 take someone to court (9)

**Down**

1 A solicitor is a specific type of … . (6)
3 put someone in handcuffs and take them to the police station, for example (6)
4 a person who puts graffiti on walls, smashes windows, etc (6)
5 not guilty (8)
6 If the police feel sure a person is guilty, they … that person with the crime. (6)
7 frequently attack or annoy; treat someone badly and deny them their rights (9)
9 the person in court who is on trial (also known as the defendant) (7)

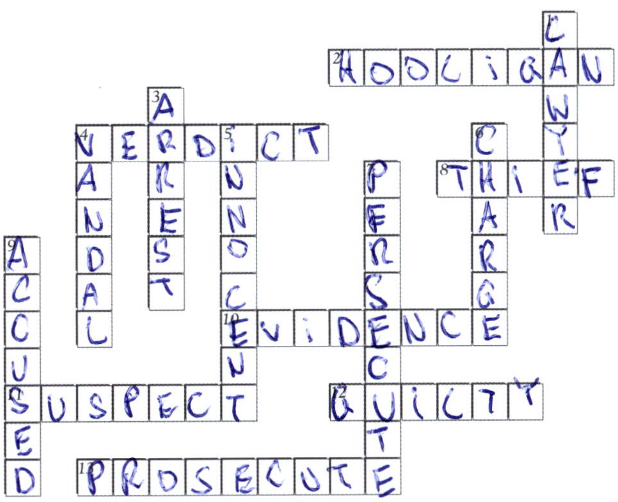

### Phrasal verbs

## C Complete using the correct form of the phrasal verbs in the box.

| |
|---|
| **break out • bring in • chase after • come forward • go off** |
| **hold up • look into • make off** |

1 So many witnesses have ............................................ that it will take days to interview them all.
2 The two robbers ............................................ on a motorbike.
3 Police are ............................................ allegations of corruption in the mayor's office.
4 The government is thinking of ............................................ a law to allow on-the-spot fines for hooligans.
5 A robber has ............................................ three banks in town in the last week.
6 They spent two years planning their escape before they finally ............................................ of prison.
7 The policewoman ............................................ the pickpocket, brought him to the ground and finally arrested him.
8 Luckily, the bomb disposal squad defused the bomb before it ............................................ .

## D Write one word in each gap.

### You've been framed!

The most incredible thing happened to me yesterday. I was walking home from school when I saw a wallet on the ground full of money. I picked it up, and was just about to take it to the police station to (**1**) ...................... it in, when a police officer jumped out and told me I was under arrest for stealing. I tried to explain the situation but he wouldn't (**2**) ...................... down. 'I won't let you get (**3**) ...................... with this,' he said. 'You're a thief, and thieves have to be punished.' He handcuffed me and drove me to the police station, where he took (**4**) ...................... my name and address. I started crying, and begged him to (**5**) ...................... me off, again trying to explain that I wasn't going to keep the money. Suddenly, my best friend Adrian and a TV presenter came in and the police officer started laughing. It was a practical joke for a TV show, and I'd been completely (**6**) ...................... in!

### Phrases and collocations

## E Circle the correct word.

1 I don't know why you're **putting** / **taking** the blame on me.
2 Shelley has no **intention** / **purpose** of admitting she lied.
3 It **doesn't** / **isn't** necessary to set the burglar alarm.
4 The judge **made** / **gave** us permission to call a suprise witness.
5 We don't know who was at **fault** / **damage** yet, but we'll find out.
6 Sorry, I mistook you **for** / **with** someone else.
7 Should judges take children into **reason** / **account** when sentencing their parents?
8 The plan **went** / **had** wrong, didn't it?
9 We need prisons in **solution** / **order** to keep society safe from dangerous criminals.
10 Many people are **making** / **taking** advantage of the change in the tax law.

### Word patterns

## F Match to make sentences.

1 They accused me ............
2 Our next-door neighbour was arrested ............
3 Three people have been charged ............
4 She denied ............
5 I doubt whether ............
6 I caught a glimpse ............
7 My friends made me ............
8 She says she was made ............
9 It is illegal for ............

A for shoplifting.
B she's guilty.
C someone to steal something from a shop.
D of someone shoplifting.
E stealing the clothes.
F to steal something from the shop.
G steal something from the shop.
H with theft.
I of shoplifting.

## G Write one word in each gap.

**Newton Archer** ***The Voice of Sanity***

# You've let us down, Owen!

Owen Davis used to be my hero. One of the greatest athletes of his generation, Owen made us think that everything was possible. I had so much respect (**1**) ........................ him, particularly in terms of his 'no drugs in sport' campaign. And now there's no doubt that all the time Davis was claiming (**2**) ........................ drugs were damaging sport, he himself was taking them. Last week, the International Athletics Association found Davis guilty (**3**) ........................ taking banned body-enhancing substances. Davis has been banned from taking part in national and international events for the next five years, and the IAA are threatening (**4**) ........................ ban future drug-takers for life. I hope they do. I refuse (**5**) ........................ accept that we should show sympathy towards Davis at a time like this. We should never forgive people like Owen Davis (**6**) ........................ bringing sport into disrepute.

### Word formation

## H Each of the words in bold is in the wrong form. Write the correct form on the line.

1 I'm not sure that sending young **offence** to prison is such a good idea. ..............................
2 There's absolutely no solid **prove** that he was anywhere near the scene of the crime. ..............................
3 I'm not saying another word until I've spoken to my **law**. ..............................
4 You shouldn't make **accuse** like that without evidence. ..............................
5 When she left the police force, she worked as a private **investigate** for a while. ..............................
6 'I hope that your **prison** has shown you the error of your ways,' said the prison governor. ..............................
7 He was initially sent to a maximum **secure** prison. ..............................
8 Lying and stealing are both forms of **honest**. ..............................
9 Police are looking carefully at the forensic **evident**. ..............................
10 There's no doubt this painting is a **forge**. ..............................
11 Drug **addict** is no excuse – no one should hold up a petrol station! ..............................
12 The **rob** took place at half past ten in the morning. ..............................
13 No one is born a **theft**, and no one has to remain one their whole life. ..............................
14 The **convict** of a number of senior executives has left the whole business community in shock. ..............................
15 The problem with prisons is that they're full of **crime** who can teach new inmates all their tricks and skills! ..............................
16 Should a **murder** be given the death penalty? ..............................

# Units 11 and 12 — Review 6

## A Use the word given in capitals at the end of each line to form a word that fits in the gap in the same line.

**STOP PRESS**

| | |
|---|---|
| Frank Turner, the (**1**) ....accused.... in a trial that has attracted national | **ACCUSE** |
| attention, was today convicted of murder. The police (**2**) ....investigations.... | **INVESTIGATE** |
| lasted for a year and during the trial over 100 hours of (**3**) ....evidence.... | **EVIDENT** |
| were heard. Turner's (**4**) ....lawyers.... had all argued that he was not in the | **LAW** |
| area at the time, but could not provide the necessary (**5**) ....proof.... . | **PROVE** |
| Police described Turner as a well-known (**6**) ....thief.... who was | **THEFT** |
| responsible for many (**7**) ....robberies.... in the local region. This is not | **ROB** |
| Turner's first (**8**) ....conviction.... . Seven years ago, he was found guilty of | **CONVICT** |
| (**9**) ....forgery.... and served three years in prison. The judge is expected | **FORGE** |
| to sentence Turner to a period of (**10**) ....imprisonment.... later this week. | **PRISON** |

(1 mark per answer)

## B Match to make sentences.

**11** I heard that they're going to bring ............
**12** Police are appealing for members of the public to come ............
**13** Nobody was convinced when the man claimed the gun had gone ............
**14** The policewoman started to take ............
**15** Lots of old people have been taken ............
**16** Peterson was found guilty of holding ............
**17** Many people get ............
**18** The policeman decided to let Shaun ............

**A** off accidentally in his hand.
**B** away with serious crimes every day.
**C** in by this trick and have lost a lot of money.
**D** forward with any information they feel might be useful.
**E** up the bank and was sentenced to five years in prison.
**F** off this time, but told him that he wouldn't be so lucky next time.
**G** in a law banning smoking in public places.
**H** down everything I was saying and I knew I was in serious trouble.

(1 mark per answer)

## C Complete the second sentence using the word given, so that it has a similar meaning to the first sentence. Write between two and five words in each gap.

**19** Police said there hadn't been a crime as bad as this in over ten years. **the**
Police described it ........................................ over ten years.

**20** Some people don't respect the law. **have**
Some people ........................................ the law.

**21** The laws in some countries are so strict that people have very little freedom. **such**
Some countries ........................................ people have very little freedom.

**22** The girl was too young to go to prison. **old**
The girl ........................................ to go to prison.

**23** The witness thought I was the thief, but realised that she was wrong. **for**
The witness ........................................ , but realised that she was wrong.

**24** Nobody in the country knows the law as well as Mr Parkhurst. **than**
Mr Parkhurst knows the law ........................................ in the country.

**25** There have been so many robberies lately that people are afraid. **such**
There have been ........................................ robberies lately that people are afraid.

**26** Even though we weren't old enough, we managed to get into the night club. **too**
Even though we .................................................................................. , we managed to get into the night club.

**27** The judge told the jury to consider the man's past life. **account**
The judge told the jury to .................................................................................. the man's past life.

(2 marks per answer)

## D Choose the correct answer.

**28** I had ........... a bad time in prison that I never want to go there again.
A too
B so
C such
D quite

**29** One problem is that we don't have ........... officers on the streets.
A so a lot of
B too many
C enough
D such many

**30** I can't get a car yet because I'm not ........... to drive.
A enough old
B quite old
C so old
D old enough

**31** Some crimes seem to be ........... in this country than in others.
A much less common
B the least common
C too little common
D little common enough

**32** Police blamed the robberies ........... a local gang.
A with
B on
C for
D to

**33** My grandma says there was ........... a lot of crime when she was young that nobody trusted anybody else.
A too
B so
C such
D quite

**34** It became ........... as I walked home and I began to get slightly nervous.
A enough dark
B such dark
C quite dark
D so dark enough

(1 mark per answer)

## E Choose the correct answer.

**35** The prisoner knew he had ........... a mistake and would regret it forever.
A got C done
B taken D made

**36** The boy ........... that he had had anything to do with the break-in.
A refused C objected
B denied D rejected

**37** Suddenly, someone shouted, 'Thief!' and the man quickly ........... on a motorbike.
A took in C came forward
B made off D handed in

**38** Do you have ........... to take that bicycle?
A allowance C willingness
B exception D permission

**39** He said it was an accident, but I know he did it on ........... .
A purpose C goal
B aim D reason

**40** Things started to ........... wrong for the robbers when the alarm went off.
A take C go
B have D come

**41** The sign says that all shoplifters will be ........... .
A persecuted C prosecuted
B disproved D prohibited

(1 mark per answer)

**Total mark: ...... / 50**

# Unit 13 Grammar

## Modals: ability, permission, advice, criticism, obligation and necessity, degrees of certainty

**Form**

- All modals (*will, would, shall, should, can, could, may, might, must*) and the semi-modal *ought to* have only one form.
- Modals are followed by the bare infinitive (simple or continuous) or the bare perfect infinitive eg *Toby **should be** very fit by now.*
  *Toby **should have recovered** by now.*
- The semi-modals *have to* and *need to* change their form depending on person and tense eg *The doctor said I **had/needed to** give up red meat.*

### Modals: ability

| Use | Modal | Example |
|---|---|---|
| Expressing ability now or generally | *can* | *I **can** run a kilometre in four minutes.* |
| Expressing decisions made now about future ability | *can* | *We **can** meet at the gym tomorrow, if you like.* |
| Expressing ability in the past | *could* | *I **could** do fifty press-ups with one hand when I was younger.* |
| Expressing ability in present, future or general hypothetical situations | *could* | *If only I **could** quit smoking!* |
| Expressing ability in past hypothetical situations | *could* + perfect infinitive | *I **could have roasted** the potatoes, but I decided that boiling them was healthier.* |

**Watch out!**

- We use *be able to* for the infinitive and other tenses.
  ✓ *I'd love **to be able to** fit into these jeans again!* (infinitive)
  ✓ *I'**ll be able to** leave hospital in a few weeks, apparently.* (future)
  ✓ *I'**ve been able to** swim since I was five.* (present perfect)

### Modals: permission

| Use | Modal | Example |
|---|---|---|
| Asking for and giving permission now, for the future or generally | *may*<br>*could*<br>*can* | ***May / Could / Can** I see the doctor, please?* |

**Watch out!**

- *May* is more polite than *could*, and *could* is more polite than *can*.
- We don't usually use a modal to talk about past permission.
  ✓ *I **was allowed to** wear a knee support during the match.*
  ✗ ~~*I **could** wear a knee support during the match.*~~
- However, we do use *could* to talk about past permission in reported speech.
  ✓ *The coach said I **could** wear a knee support during the match.*

### Modals: advice

| Use | Modal | Example |
|---|---|---|
| Asking for and giving advice now, for the future or generally | *should*<br>*ought to* | *You **ought to / should** cut down on the amount of red meat you eat.* |

### Modals: criticism

| Use | Modal | Example |
|---|---|---|
| Criticising past behaviour | *should*<br>*ought to*<br>(+ perfect infinitive) | *He **ought to / should have made** more of an effort with his diet.* |

## Modals: obligation and necessity

| Use | Modal | Example |
|---|---|---|
| Expressing obligation or necessity | *must / have to / need to* | *I* ***must / have to / need to*** *pick up that prescription from the chemist on the way home.* |
| Expressing lack of obligation or necessity | *needn't / don't have to / don't need to* | *You* ***needn't / don't have to / don't need to*** *pick up that prescription from the chemist as I'll get it while I'm in town.* |
| Expressing past obligation | *had to* | *I* ***had to*** *take the pills three times a day for two weeks.* |
| Expressing lack of past obligation | *needn't* ( + perfect infinitive) / *didn't have to / didn't need to* | *I* ***needn't have gone / didn't have to go / didn't need to go*** *to the doctor.* |

**Watch out!**

- There is usually no difference in meaning between *must* and *have to.* However, we are sometimes more likely to use *must* for personal obligation (making our own decision about what we must do) and *have to* for external obligation (someone else making a decision about what we must do).
- We can also use *will have/need to* to express future obligation.
  ✓ *You'****ll have/need to*** *be more careful about what you eat in future.*
- It is unusual to use *must* for questions. We usually use *have/need to.*
  ✓ ***Do*** *I* ***have/need to*** *take this medicine before every meal?*
- *Must* cannot be used as an infinitive. Use *to have to.*
  ✓ *I'd hate* ***to have to*** *have injections every day.*
  ✗ ~~*I'd hate* ***to must*** *have injections every day.*~~
- *Mustn't* and *don't/doesn't have/need to* have different meanings.
  ✓ *You* ***mustn't*** *do that!* (Don't do that!)
  ✓ *You* ***don't have/need to*** *do that.* (You can do that if you want to but it's not necessary.)
- *Needn't* ( + perfect infinitive) always refers to an action that happened.
  *Didn't have to* and *didn't need to* can refer to actions that did or didn't happen.
  ✓ *I* ***needn't have gone*** *to the doctor.* (I went but it wasn't necessary.)
  ✓ *I* ***didn't have/need to*** *go to the doctor because I suddenly felt better.* (I didn't go.)
  ✓ *I* ***didn't have/need to*** *go to the doctor but I went just to be on the safe side.* (I did go.)
- Be careful with the verb *need.* It can also take the *-ing* form.
  ✓ *I need to sterilise this syringe.*
  ✓ *This syringe needs sterilis****ing****.*

## Modals: degrees of certainty

| Use | Modal | Example |
|---|---|---|
| Expressing certainty (or near certainty) about now or generally | *must*<br>*can't*<br>*couldn't* | *That* ***must*** *be the district nurse at the door.*<br>*These* ***can't / couldn't*** *be the pills; they're the wrong colour.* |
| Expressing certainty (or near certainty) about the past | *must*<br>*can't*<br>*couldn't*<br>(+ perfect infinitive) | *She* ***must have been*** *in a lot of pain.*<br>*His leg* ***can't / couldn't have been*** *in plaster for two years!* |
| Expressing probability about now, the future or generally | *should*<br>*ought to* | *You* ***ought to / should*** *feel better in a few days, as long as you get lots of rest.* |
| Expressing probability about the past | *should*<br>*ought to*<br>(+ perfect infinitive) | *The bruise* ***ought to / should have disappeared*** *days ago. I wonder why it didn't.* |
| Expressing possibility about now, the future or generally | *could*<br>*may*<br>*might* | *You should talk to your doctor first because that diet* ***could / may / might*** *be dangerous.* |
| Expressing possibility about the real past | *could*<br>*may*<br>*might*<br>(+ perfect infinitive) | *That* ***could / may / might have been*** *the doctor who rang earlier while we were out.* |
| Expressing possibility about a hypothetical past | *could*<br>*might*<br>(+ perfect infinitive) | *It's a good thing you went to the doctor or you* ***could / might have become*** *quite ill.* |

## A If a word or phrase in bold is correct, put a tick (✓). If it is incorrect, rewrite it correctly on the line.

1 Can you **to speak** French? ..................................................
2 I **can** give you a hand tomorrow morning, if you like. ..................................................
3 I'll **can** take my driving test after a few more lessons. ..................................................
4 Jack **can** play the guitar before he learnt to talk! ..................................................
5 If only I **can** afford to buy that top! ..................................................
6 We **can** have gone up the Eiffel Tower while we were in Paris, but we decided to go to the Louvre instead. ..................................................
7 I could **get** a more expensive computer, but it didn't seem worth it. ..................................................
8 I wish I **could** get out of the maths test tomorrow! ..................................................
9 I bet you'd love to be **can** to get satellite TV. ..................................................
10 You'd better tell the coach if you can't **playing** on Saturday. ..................................................

## B Circle the correct word or phrase. If both options are correct, circle both.

1 Hello. **Could / Can** I speak to Mrs Johnson, please?
2 We **could / were allowed to** go home early yesterday because our teacher was ill.
3 The head teacher said we **could / were allowed to** go home.
4 Do you think I **should / could** be worried about these spots on my forehead?
5 You **ought to / should** enter that talent contest!
6 You **couldn't / shouldn't** talk to people like that! It's rude!
7 Alan should **write / have written** two essays in the exam yesterday, not one!
8 No, you **may / should** not go out tonight. You know you're grounded!
9 Diana should have **waited / been waiting** for me at the corner. I wonder where she went.
10 What were you doing in the park? You ought to have **done / been doing** your homework then!
11 Yes, of course you **can / are able to** open the window if you're too hot!

## C Write a form of *must, have to, need* or *need to* in each gap to complete the sentences. If more than one possibility is correct, write all possibilities.

1 Oh, I .................................................. remember to get some potatoes on the way home tonight.
2 Jason .................................................. see the headmaster during the next break. I wonder what it's about?
3 We .................................................. light lots of candles during the power cut two nights ago.
4 I'll .................................................. start doing my Christmas cards soon. It's nearly December.
5 Carl, you .................................................. run into the street like that without looking first. It's dangerous!
6 People with solar-powered cars .................................................. worry about the price of petrol.
7 I wouldn't like to .................................................. get up at five o'clock every morning.
8 We .................................................. do any washing-up after the picnic because we'd used disposable plates and cutlery.
9 Do professional musicians .................................................. practise every day?
10 I .................................................. have bothered cooking all that food; they'd eaten before they arrived.

## D Complete each second sentence using the word given, so that it has a similar meaning to the first sentence. Write between two and five words in each gap.

**1** His lights are on so I'm pretty sure Dan is at home. **as**
Dan ............................................................................ his lights are on.

**2** Susie's car's not here so she's almost certainly taking Dobber to the vet. **be**
Susie ............................................................................ Dobber to the vet since her car's not here.

**3** There's no way that boy's Simon. He's much taller! **boy**
That ............................................................................ Simon. He's much taller!

**4** I'm certain the Winners don't think we're coming tonight; we arranged it for next Tuesday. **expecting**
The Winners ............................................................................ tonight; we arranged it for next Tuesday.

**5** I bet you were exhausted after such a long journey! **have**
You ............................................................................ exhausted after such a long journey!

**6** The only explanation is that Evan was on the phone to someone in Australia! **talking**
Evan ............................................................................ on the phone to someone in Australia!

**7** There's no way Casey won the disco dancing competition – he's got two left feet! **have**
Casey ............................................................................ the disco dancing competition – he's got two left feet!

**8** I don't believe Helen's been trying to call us all day. The phone hasn't rung once. **been**
Helen ............................................................................ to call us all day. The phone hasn't rung once.

## E Use the words in the box only once to complete the sentences in Table A. The meaning of the sentences in Table B will help you.

**able • cannot • could • had • have • might • must**
**needn't • mustn't • ought • should • will**

| Table A | Table B |
|---|---|
| **1** I ........................ have left my bag on the bus. | *expressing certainty* |
| **2** In a few months, I'll be ........................ to buy a car. | *expressing future ability* |
| **3** I ........................ drive when I was thirteen years old! | *expressing past ability* |
| **4** No, you ........................ have any more pocket money! | *refusing a request* |
| **5** I think you ........................ consider a career in the armed forces. | *giving advice* |
| **6** I ........................ forget to phone Julie tonight! | *expressing personal obligation* |
| **7** I ........................ to have a filling at the dentist's. | *expressing external obligation in the past* |
| **8** You don't ........................ to do Exercise D for homework. | *expressing a lack of obligation* |
| **9** You ........................ have to work a lot harder if you want to get a good report. | *expressing future obligation* |
| **10** They ........................ to arrive at about 8. | *expressing probability* |
| **11** Sean ........................ have got stuck in traffic. | *expressing possibility* |
| **12** I ........................ have worried so much about Jan's present. She loved it! | *expressing a lack of past obligation* |

## F Circle the correct answer.

1 ............ I have a look at those shoes in the window, please?
A Must
B Would
C Should
D Could

2 We ............ pay for the tickets as Josie won them in a competition.
A mustn't
B didn't have to
C couldn't
D hadn't to

3 You really ............ make such a mountain out of a molehill!
A can't
B won't
C mightn't
D shouldn't

4 You won't ............ to connect to the Internet once you've got broadband as you're online twenty-four hours a day.
A need
B must
C ought
D able

5 I hope we ............ find the cinema easily.
A could
B may
C might
D can

6 We couldn't find a hotel room so we ............ sleep in the car. It was awful!
A must
B should
C had to
D could

7 We'd love to ............ afford to go on a round-the-world cruise.
A can
B be able to
C will have to
D have to

8 Fiona can't ............ about the meeting. I reminded her this morning!
A forget
B be forgetting
C have forgotten
D have been forgetting

9 She could ............ in the garage when we came round, which would explain why she didn't hear the bell.
A work
B be working
C have worked
D have been working

10 You'll ............ tell the police that your house was broken into.
A have to
B must
C had to
D should

## G Write a modal or semi-modal in each gap to replace the phrase in brackets. Add any other words you need.

1 Bruce ................................................ (*is able to*) finish most crosswords in under ten minutes.
2 Charlotte didn't get to the Craig David concert because she ................................................ (*wasn't able to*) get tickets.
3 I ................................................ (*had the opportunity to go*) to Oxford but I decided to go to a more modern university.
4 You ................................................ (*were wrong to tell*) Angus. You know he can't keep a secret!
5 If you have a cashpoint card, you ................................................ (*are not forced to*) go into the bank to get money from your account.
6 We ................................................ (*were made to*) apologise to the police for wasting their time.
7 That ................................................ (*almost definitely wasn't*) the last can of soda in the fridge. I bought loads this morning!
8 ................................................ (*Were you obliged to*) talk about two photographs during the interview?
9 Children ................................................ (*are not allowed to*) be left unattended.
10 The weather ................................................ (*will probably*) be good tomorrow.

## H Choose the correct answer.

### Choosing a gym

Choosing to go to a gym regularly (**1**) ........... change your life for the better. Don't let it be a decision you regret!
Good gyms have a lot to offer. They (**2**) ........... provide exercise equipment that is just too expensive to buy and their trained staff are (**3**) ........... to provide quality health and fitness advice. But if you're planning to join a gym, you (**4**) ........... definitely ask to look round before you become a member. There are a number of things to bear in mind before choosing which gym to join.
Before the law changed a few years ago, anyone (**5**) ........... set up a gym and even today gyms (**6**) ........... employ trained fitness instructors. Find out what qualifications the staff have. If they're untrained, it's best to go elsewhere.
You (**7**) ........... be put off by the gym's hard sell. Just because they want you to sign up – they want your money, after all – that doesn't mean you (**8**) ........... decide there and then. See a few gyms before you make your final decision.
Ask yourself: What kind of equipment and facilities do they have? There's little point joining a gym and then thinking a few months later, 'I (**9**) ........... have chosen a gym with a pool.' Do you (**10**) ........... book equipment in advance, or can you just turn up and use it? How busy does the gym get? It (**11**) ........... be very pleasant turning up to find there's no room in the changing room and there's a huge queue for each piece of equipment. It (**12**) ........... also be a good idea to talk to people who already go to that gym to find out their opinion.

| | | | | |
|---|---|---|---|---|
| **1** | A must | B would | C should | D will have to |
| **2** | A can | B could | C would | D must |
| **3** | A made | B forced | C allowed | D able |
| **4** | A should | B would | C might | D will |
| **5** | A can | B could | C might | D may |
| **6** | A mustn't | B don't have to | C can't | D shouldn't |
| **7** | A mustn't | B couldn't | C won't | D mightn't |
| **8** | A can't | B can | C would | D have to |
| **9** | A ought to | B must | C have to | D can't |
| **10** | A able | B must | C have to | D allowed |
| **11** | A won't have to | B doesn't have to | C mustn't | D won't |
| **12** | A must | B might | C has to | D ought to |

## I Write one word in each gap.

When I broke my arm a week ago, I guess it (**1**) ......................... to have hurt. But it didn't! We were doing PE at school, and we were making a pyramid. We (**2**) ......................... to stand on each other's shoulders. I was right at the top. We (**3**) ......................... have been doing it properly because suddenly the pyramid collapsed and we all fell. I landed on my arm.
Mr Jenkins (**4**) ......................... have known immediately that I'd broken my arm because he sent someone to call an ambulance. 'Sit still, and don't move your arm at all until the ambulance comes,' he said. I (**5**) ......................... still remember the feeling – my arm was numb, and looked very strange, but there was no pain at all. I remember thinking: 'It (**6**) ......................... be broken. If it was broken, I'd be in agony.' I suppose not feeling any pain (**7**) ......................... have been because I was in shock.
The plaster (**8**) ......................... come off in about three weeks but it (**9**) ......................... have to stay on longer. It depends on whether the break has healed properly or not. The next three weeks may (**10**) ......................... be the best three weeks of my life – no basketball, no playing in the playground, no swimming – but I'm counting my blessings. It (**11**) ......................... have been a lot worse!

## Health and fitness

### Topic vocabulary in contrast

see page 191 for definitions

| | | |
|---|---|---|
| prescription / recipe | thin / slim | infection / pollution |
| operation / surgery | remedy / cure / therapy | plaster / bandage |
| sore / hurt / pain | effect / result | ward / clinic |
| illness / disease | healthy / fit | dose / fix |
| injured / damaged | examine / investigate | fever / rash |

### Phrasal verbs

| | |
|---|---|
| **break out** start suddenly (for a war, fire, etc) | **give up** stop doing sth you do regularly |
| **bring on** cause (an illness, etc) | **look after** take care of |
| **come down with** start to suffer from a minor illness | **pass out** suddenly become unconscious |
| **come round/to** become conscious | **pull through** survive (a serious illness, etc) |
| **cut down (on)** do less of (smoking, etc); reduce an amount of | **put down** kill (a sick/old animal) |
| **feel up to** feel well enough to do | **put on** gain (weight) |
| **get over** recover from (an illness, etc) | **wear off** stop being effective (for a drug, etc) |

### Phrases and collocations

| | |
|---|---|
| **alternative** | alternative medicine/therapy; find an alternative (to sth) |
| **appointment** | make/have/break an appointment |
| **bath** | have/take a bath; run a bath (for sb) |
| **danger** | in danger; out of danger |
| **exercise** | do an exercise; do exercise; take/get (some) exercise |
| **fit** | get/stay/keep/be fit; fit and healthy |
| **good** | do sb good; sth does you good; good for sb (to do) |
| **health** | in good/bad/poor/etc health; health centre; health care |
| **injection** | have an injection (for/against sth); give sb an injection |
| **medicine** | take/prescribe medicine; practise/study medicine; the best medicine; alternative medicine |
| **shape** | get in/into shape; stay/keep in shape; the shape of sth; in the shape of |
| **spread** | spread sth; spread sth over/on sth; spread to a place |

### Word patterns

| | |
|---|---|
| **addicted** to sth | **need** to do; need doing; in need of; no need for |
| **attempt** to do | **operate** on sb/sth |
| **benefit** from sth; a benefit of sth | **suffer** from sth; suffer sth |
| **complain** (to sb) (about sth/sb doing); complain of sth | **tired** of sth/doing |
| **cope** with sth/doing | **try** to do; try sth/sb/doing; try and do |
| **inject** sth into sth/sb | **worry** about sth/sb doing; worried that; worried about/by |
| **lead** to sth/(your) doing | **worth** sth/doing |
| **likely** to do; it is (un)likely that | |

### Word formation

| | | |
|---|---|---|
| **allergy** allergic | **fit** unfit, fitness | **poison** poisonous, poisoning |
| **aware** unaware, awareness | **ill** illness | **recover** recovery |
| **benefit** beneficial | **inject** injection | **strong** strength, strengthen, strongly |
| **comfort** discomfort, (un)comfortable, (un)comfortably | **injure** injury, injuries | **surgery** surgeon, surgical(ly) |
| **emphasis** emphasise, emphatic | **operate** operation, operator, operating, cooperate, cooperation, (un)cooperative | **treat** treatment |

### Topic vocabulary in contrast

## A Complete using the correct form of the words in the box.

**prescription**
**recipe**

1 My doctor said I have to stay in bed and gave me a .................................................. for some medicine.
2 You must give me the .................................................. for that wonderful chocolate cake you made!

**remedy**
**cure**
**therapy**

3 Many rock stars seem to end up in drug .................................................. .
4 Do you think a .................................................. for cancer will ever be found?
5 My grandma uses an old-fashioned .................................................. for her arthritis.

**examine**
**investigate**

6 I lifted my shirt so the doctor could .................................................. my chest.
7 Police have begun to .................................................. the break-in at the hospital.

**operation**
**surgery**

8 My mum's thinking of having an .................................................. to have her nose straightened.
9 Dr Key told the old man that he needed .................................................. on his leg.

**pain**
**sore**
**hurt**

10 My arm is really .................................................. and I can't move it.
11 Mind you don't .................................................. yourself! Oh, too late. Sorry.
12 I had a really bad .................................................. in my foot so I decided to see a doctor.

## B Circle the correct word.

1 Tim looks really pale and **thin / slim**. I'm worried he might be ill.
2 It's important to eat a **fit / healthy** diet with lots of vegetables.
3 After picking the flowers, I noticed I had a **fever / rash** all over my hands.
4 When I broke a rib, I had to wear a **bandage / plaster** around my chest.
5 Make sure you wash your cut properly so that you don't get a/an **infection / pollution**.
6 Half an hour after taking the pill, I began to feel the **results / effects**.
7 The doctor walked along the **ward / clinic**, chatting to all the patients she passed.
8 Two people have been slightly **injured / damaged** in an accident on the M1.
9 It's good for children to get minor **diseases / illnesses**, such as colds.
10 The medicine bottle said the recommended **dose** / **fix** was two teaspoons twice a day.

### Phrasal verbs

## C Complete each second sentence using the word given, so that it has a similar meaning to the first sentence. Write between two and five words in each gap.

1 Dan couldn't work because he caught the flu. **down**
Dan .................................................................................. , which meant he couldn't work.
2 If you smoke, then stopping can really improve your health. **up**
If you .................................................................................. , you'll really improve your health.
3 We asked the vet to kill the dog to stop her suffering any longer. **put**
We asked the vet .................................................................................. to stop her suffering any longer.
4 I don't really have enough energy to play tennis. **up**
I don't really .................................................................................. tennis.
5 Is it true that getting wet can cause a cold? **on**
Is it true that getting wet can .................................................................................. a cold?
6 The flu epidemic started suddenly in June and lots of people got ill. **out**
Lots of people got ill when the flu epidemic .................................................................................. in June.

## D Write a phrasal verb in the correct form to replace the words in bold.

1 Gill slowly ............................................ after the operation. (**became conscious**)
2 My dad is trying to ............................................ on smoking. (**do less**)
3 I think the medicine is beginning to ............................................ . (**stop being effective**)
4 Bill decided that he needed to go on a diet after ............................................ weight. (**gaining**)
5 It was so hot in the stadium that a number of people ............................................ . (**became unconscious**)
6 I finally ............................................ the cold that I had had all week. (**recover from**)
7 We thought we were going to lose our horse when he got ill, but he managed to ............................................ . (**survive**)
8 My dentist told me to ............................................ my teeth. (**take care of**)

### Phrases and collocations

## E Choose the correct answer.

1 Let me ............ you a nice warm bath and you'll feel a lot better.
A make B run C get D build
2 When the snake bit Mike in the forest, he knew he was ....... serious danger.
A to B with C on D in
3 Being ............ an injection wasn't as painful as I thought it was going to be.
A given B done C made D taken
4 Hello? Yes, I'd like to ............ an appointment for tomorrow with Dr Fletcher, please.
A form B do C break D make
5 My grandfather's over 95 and is ............ pretty poor health these days.
A on B to C with D in
6 I was told to ............ the medicine three times a day, before meals.
A take B eat C get D do
7 I like to ............ fit by going to the gym at least twice a week.
A continue B make C keep D set
8 Eat your vegetables. They'll ............ you good.
A make B get C have D do
9 The key to losing weight is to ............ more exercise.
A get B make C go D create
10 You should try to ............ an alternative to all those sugary snacks you eat.
A make B find C take D do
11 I'm going to make a real effort to get ............ shape for the summer.
A on B to C in D from
12 Try spreading something low fat ............ your bread instead of butter.
A in B through C around D on

### Word patterns

## F Match to make sentences.

1 It is said that people who eat poorly are likely ............
2 Did you know that you can have your eyes operated ............
3 I'm getting really tired of ............
4 Why don't you try ............
5 It really is worth ............

**A** on with lasers these days?
**B** going to the gym more often?
**C** losing a bit of weight.
**D** telling my dad to give up smoking.
**E** to have health problems later in life.

**G** Water has damaged part of this text about the drug problem. Read it and decide what you think each of the original words was. Write the words in the blank spaces.

### THE DRUG PROBLEM

Many people today are worried ~~~ drugs. It seems that more and more people are becoming addicted ~~~ substances, such as heroine and cocaine, that damage their health. But what leads ~~~ people becoming addicts? What makes someone inject a drug ~~~ their veins? Is it because of their inability to cope ~~~ problems in their everyday lives? One thing is for sure. When we complain ~~~ the problems caused by hard drugs, we need ~~~ remember that people suffer ~~~ all kinds of health problems caused by legal drugs, such as alcohol and tobacco. We would all benefit ~~~ more education and the government should attempt ~~~ make sure we all know the risks involved.

1 ........................
2 ........................
3 ........................
4 ........................
5 ........................
6 ........................
7 ........................
8 ........................
9 ........................
10 ........................

**Word formation**

**H** Complete the sentences by changing the form of the word in capitals when this is necessary.

1 Most people seem to be .............................. of the harmful effects of their diet. (**AWARE**)
2 I'm .............................. to peanuts so I have to be very careful what I eat. (**ALLERGY**)
3 Jade's .............................. turned out to be much more serious than anyone imagined. (**ILL**)
4 Did you know Australia has the highest number of .............................. species of snake? (**POISON**)
5 After a couple of weeks, the plaster cast on my leg became really .............................. and I couldn't wait to take it off. (**COMFORT**)
6 I was really impressed by the .............................. levels of all the athletes. (**FIT**)
7 Luckily, Ted's .............................. weren't serious. (**INJURE**)
8 Working out can really .............................. your muscles. (**STRONG**)

**I** Use the word given in capitals at the end of each line to form a word that fits in the gap in the same line.

### The no-surgery solution!

| | |
|---|---|
| These days, it seems there's an (**1**) .............................. for everything. Whether you | **OPERATE** |
| want something made smaller or you want to (**2**) .............................. your best | **EMPHASIS** |
| features, you can bet that plastic (**3**) .............................. claim to have the solution. | **SURGERY** |
| We at *BodySculpt* know, though, that you don't want the (**4**) .............................. | **COMFORT** |
| associated with surgery. But you can't enjoy the (**5**) .............................. effects | **BENEFIT** |
| without going under the knife, can you? Yes! No need for (**6**) .............................. | **SURGERY** |
| procedures with a long (**7**) .............................. period! Our unique service consists | **RECOVER** |
| of a series of (**8**) .............................. that will give you the results you've always | **INJECT** |
| wanted! Call now and speak to one of our (**9**) .............................. . | **OPERATE** |

## A Use the word given in capitals at the end of each line to form a word that fits in the gap in the same line.

### Scorpion Fish

Have you ever heard of scorpion fish? I was completely (**1**) .............................. **AWARE**
they existed until I trod on one in the sea. I can't (**2**) .............................. enough **EMPHASIS**
how painful it was! The fish has a spike which gives you an (**3**) .............................. **INJECT**
of a (**4**) .............................. substance. It's not dangerous, but you begin to feel **POISON**
extremely (**5**) .............................. , and the pain just gets worse and worse. Luckily, **COMFORT**
there was a doctor on the beach – she was a (**6**) .............................. at the local **SURGERY**
hospital – and she told me what the best (**7**) .............................. was. I had to bathe **TREAT**
my foot in warm, salty water and then apply an ammonia-based solution.
After my holiday, my foot still seemed to be a little infected, so my local
GP gave me a (**8**) .............................. for antibiotics. Unfortunately, it turned out **PRESCRIBE**
I was (**9**) .............................. to them, so I came out in a red rash all over my body. **ALLERGY**
It was over a week before I had made a complete (**10**) .............................. . **RECOVER**

(1 mark per answer)

## B Complete the second sentence using the word given, so that it has a similar meaning to the first sentence. Write between two and five words in each gap.

**11** Thankfully, Adrian doesn't need to have an operation. **no**
Thankfully, there .............................................................................. to have an operation.

**12** The minister had to resign because of ill health. **led**
Ill health .............................................................................. resignation.

**13** You won't benefit from seeing the doctor if you've just got a cold. **worth**
It .............................................................................. the doctor if you've just got a cold.

**14** I'm seeing the nutritionist at three tomorrow. **appointment**
I've .............................................................................. the nutritionist at three tomorrow.

**15** I don't want to be a vegan any more! **tired**
I .............................................................................. a vegan!

**16** Your arm probably won't heal before the match on Saturday. **unlikely**
You arm .............................................................................. heal before the match on Saturday.

**17** I wish I could do a hundred press-ups in one go. **able**
I'd love .............................................................................. a hundred press-ups in one go.

**18** Do you think I should reduce the amount of chocolate I eat? **on**
Do you think I should .............................................................................. chocolate?

(1 mark per answer)

## C Write a phrasal verb in the correct form to replace the words in bold.

**19** Dan's .......................................... flu, so he can't come to work today. **(started to suffer from)**

**20** It took Shirley a long time to .......................................... the death of her hamster. **(recover from)**

**21** Many people feel sick when they .......................................... after a general anaesthetic. **(regain consciousness)**

**22** It was so hot and stuffy, I nearly .......................................... . **(suddenly lost consciousness)**

**23** Fern's .......................................... a lot of weight recently. **(gained)**

**24** Disease is more likely to .......................................... in areas of extreme poverty. **(suddenly start)**

25 I don't know what's been ........................................ my terrible headaches. **(causing)**
26 My grandfather's decided to ........................................ red meat completely. **(stop eating)**

(2 marks per answer)

## D Choose the correct answer.

**27** I ........... have joined a gym but in the end I decided to exercise at home.
A must
B could
C will
D may

**28** 'I've been feeling under the weather recently.'
'You ........... more exercise.'
A should get
B should have got
C would get
D would have got

**29** 'It was hard work getting back from the hospital with my leg in plaster.'
'You should ........... me. I'd have picked you up.'
A call
B be calling
C have called
D have been calling

**30** ........... write with your left hand when you broke your arm?
A Did you had to
B Did you have to
C Needed you to
D Must you

**31** You ........... have huge muscles to look good, you know!
A don't have to
B mustn't
C can't
D shouldn't

**32** That ........... be Ted at the door. He's in bed with chicken pox.
A hasn't to
B oughtn't to
C mustn't
D can't

**33** You must ........... thrilled when the doctor said it wasn't serious.
A be
B have been
C be being
D have been being

**34** 'Colin's got to stay in bed for eight weeks.'
'I'd hate to ........... do that.'
A will have to
B must
C have to
D will

(1 mark per answer)

## E Choose the correct answer.

**35** The doctor ........... the cut on my knee and said it had completely healed up.
A investigated
B researched
C examined
D looked into

**36** Dr Parker gave my mum a lovely ........... for spaghetti carbonara.
A recipe
B prescription
C receipt
D paper

**37** My feet are ........... . I guess my new shoes are a bit tight.
A hurt
B pain
C ache
D sore

**38** I was shocked when I crashed the car, but at least I wasn't ........... .
A injured
B damaged
C broken
D spoilt

**39** Diana looks terribly ........... . You don't think she's ill, do you?
A slim
B thin
C slender
D slight

**40** Some drugs produce bad side ........... .
A consequences
B products
C results
D effects

**41** I was very sad when the vet said he'd have to ........... Gertie, our labrador.
A put down
B pull through
C feel up to
D wear off

**42** Going on this diet has really ........... me good. I've lost weight and I feel fantastic!
A made
B taken
C done
D had

(1 mark per answer)

**Total mark: ...... /**

# Progress Test 1

## A Choose the correct answer.

### THE HISTORY OF WRITING

The development of writing (**1**) ........... a huge difference to the world and we might see it as the beginning of the (**2**) ........... . Pieces of pottery with marks on that are probably numbers have been (**3**) ........... in China that date from around 4000 BC. Hieroglyphics and other forms of 'picture writing' developed in the (**4**) ........... around Mesopotamia (modern-day Iraq), where the (**5**) ........... Sumerian civilization was based, from around 3300 BC onwards. However, the first (**6**) ........... alphabet was used by the Phoenicians around 1050 BC. Their alphabet had 22 letters and it is (**7**) ........... that it lasted for 1000 years. The first two signs were called 'aleph' and 'beth', which in Greek became 'alpha' and 'beta', which gave us the (**8**) ........... word 'alphabet'.

The modern European alphabet is based on the Greek and (**9**) ........... to other European countries under the Romans. A number of changes took (**10**) ........... as time (**11**) ........... . The Romans added the letter G, and the letters J and V were (**12**) ........... to people in Shakespeare's time.

If we (**13**) ........... the history of punctuation, we also find some interesting facts. The Romans used to write *quaesto* at the end of a sentence in (**14**) ........... to show that it was a question. They started to write *Qo* in (**15**) ........... of the whole word, and then put the *Q* above the *o*. In the end, that became the question mark '?'.

| | | | | |
|---|---|---|---|---|
| **1** | A did | B had | C made | D took |
| **2** | A media | B bulletin | C programme | D journalism |
| **3** | A invented | B displayed | C discovered | D appeared |
| **4** | A distance | B area | C length | D earth |
| **5** | A antique | B old-fashioned | C ancient | D dated |
| **6** | A true | B accurate | C exact | D precise |
| **7** | A observed | B measured | C counted | D estimated |
| **8** | A new | B trendy | C modern | D fashionable |
| **9** | A spread | B appeared | C was | D occurred |
| **10** | A place | B part | C control | D account |
| **11** | A spent | B passed | C went | D developed |
| **12** | A infamous | B unpopular | C unknown | D hidden |
| **13** | A look into | B bring on | C make off | D hold up |
| **14** | A turn | B fact | C order | D intention |
| **15** | A position | B space | C spot | D place |

(1 mark per answer)

## B Choose the correct answer.

**16** I was disappointed that the restaurant had ........... flowers on the table.
A false C artificial
B untrue D forged

**17** Sarah and Michael's ........... seems to make both of them unhappy.
A connection C relationship
B bond D link

**18** Anybody found stealing from this shop will be ........... .
A prosecuted C provoked
B persuaded D persecuted

**19** Grace thinks she's very ........... , but I don't think many people like her, really.
A famous C recognisable
B known D popular

**20** I glanced at the newspaper and saw that the ........... said 'President Resigns'.
A headline C heading
B subtitle D chapter

**21** If our flight is delayed, will we ........... our connection in Los Angeles?
A drop C lose
B miss D lack

**22** The doctor told Bill that he needed ............ on his arm.
A operation C remedy
B surgery D cure

**23** The judge looked at the ............ and reminded him that he had to tell the whole truth.
A bystander C witness
B onlooker D viewer

**24** I think my favourite ............ is probably table tennis.
A athletics C sport
B exercise D gym

**25** The actor, Michael Read, was today ............ with robbery.
A charged C arrested
B accused D suspected

(1 mark per answer)

## C Write one word in each gap.

### Your first telescope

Many people look up at (**26**) ........................ night sky and become fascinated by the wonders of the universe. (**27**) ........................ that sounds like you, then perhaps it's time you got your own telescope. Astronomy (**28**) ........................ be a great hobby and we've provided this simple guide for those of you thinking of (**29**) ........................ it up.

*What if I don't have much money?*

Try a pair of binoculars. You can still see a lot, as (**30**) ........................ as you don't expect to see so (**31**) ........................ detail. Explore the Moon and the stars – and who knows? You might (**32**) ........................ discover a comet! Remember, though, that you (**33**) ........................ never look at the Sun directly through binoculars or a telescope.

*What kind of telescope do I need?*

Depending on what you want to do, you need to choose (**34**) ........................ a refracting and a reflecting telescope. A refracting telescope (with two glass lenses) is (**35**) ........................ great way of quickly (**36**)) ........................ your way around the heavens. As well as more stars (**37**) ........................ you can imagine, there are the planets to explore! You should have no difficulty (**38**) ........................ finding Mars and even Saturn, with its fantastic rings. If you want to really explore the universe, then you (**39**) ........................ need a reflecting telescope (with a mirror). These telescopes are much (**40**) ........................ at collecting light and allow you to see things in amazing detail!

Whatever you decide, welcome to the wonderful world of astronomy!

(1 mark per answer)

## D Choose the correct answer.

**41** I think the discussion has gone on ............ and we should make a decision.
A enough long B such long C long enough D so long

**42** 'Did you call John?'
'No, because I ............ go out. I'll try him later today.'
A had to B must C might D need

**43** There ............ be a lot more open space around here before they built the new underground station.
A would B used to C used D got used to

**44** If you hadn't lost the pieces, we ............ a game of chess.
A couldn't have had B can't have C may have D could have

**45** 'Why are you taking your PlayStation games?'
'Oh, just ........... Tommy wants to borrow them.'
A as long as B in case C provided that D unless

**46** I suppose we really ........... to book our ferry tickets in advance.
A should B can C must D ought

**47** I'm afraid we've run out of ........... this week, so we'll see you at the same time tomorrow for *It's Worth a Million*!
A the time B some time C time D a time

**48** The man might have got away with the crime if the policeman ........... him.
A wasn't seeing B hadn't seen C didn't see D wouldn't have seen

**49** 'I've been reading a great book.'
'I seem to be ........... busy to find the time for reading these days.'
A so B too C such D enough

**50** The hotel has a poor reputation and ........... people want to stay there.
A little B a few C a little D few

(1 mark per answer)

## E Match to make sentences. There is one extra letter you will not use.

**51** The Pattersons have decided to pull ...........
**52** Mr Greene seems to find it difficult to get ...........
**53** We haven't made a final decision, but we've narrowed it ...........
**54** Dad thought it might be a good idea to look ...........
**55** It seems that Matt has fallen ...........
**56** I think it was Bob who came ...........
**57** The holiday started okay and then turned ...........

**A** down to France or Spain for this summer's holiday.
**B** up the train times on the Internet.
**C** up with the idea of going to Poland.
**D** out with Dave over their holiday plans.
**E** on with our holiday as if nothing had happened.
**F** out of our trip together because Angie's got a fever.
**G** into a bit of a nightmare when our luggage got lost.
**H** on with people from other countries.

(1 mark per answer)

## F Complete the second sentence using the word given, so that it has a similar meaning to the first sentence. Write between two and five words in each gap.

**58** I lost my keys once before this month. **second**
This is the .................................................................. my keys this month.

**59** I started playing squash six years ago. **for**
I .................................................................. six years.

**60** I can't wait until I'm old enough to go to a match on my own. **forward**
I'm really .................................................................. old enough to go to a match on my own.

**61** Accidents are often caused by careless driving. **results**
Careless driving .................................................................. accidents.

**62** It's a waste of time denying that you did it when we've got proof. **point**
There .................................................................. that you did it when we've got proof.

**63** Don't you wish you could travel into space? **able**
Wouldn't you love ........................................................................................ into space?

**64** I called the travel agent to check that I had the right timetable. **make**
I called the travel agent to ........................................................................................ I had the right timetable.

**65** I'm afraid you're too young to go down the water slide. **old**
I'm afraid you ........................................................................................ to go down the water slide.

**66** My mum says doctors weren't so expensive in the past. **used**
My mum says doctors ........................................................................................ so expensive.

(2 marks per answer)

## G If a line is correct, put a tick (✓) next to the number. If there is an extra word in a line, write it next to the number.

### Our media project

**67** ........................ I had a great week at school! We were been having a media
**68** ........................ studies lesson when our teacher told to us that we were going
**69** ........................ to make a radio advert for the school! I was really keen on
**70** ........................ to be involved because I've always had been interested in a
**71** ........................ career in the television. She asked us to plan our advert in
**72** ........................ detail and to write a script. Most people found it out difficult
**73** ........................ to come up with ideas, but I didn't. I decided that I would have
**74** ........................ interviews with people who were used to go to the school,
**75** ........................ commenting on how they had benefited them from going to that
**76** ........................ school. My teacher thought it was a great idea and said I should
**77** ........................ to see if I could find some ex-students. I asked the head and
**78** ........................ she gave me a few phone numbers. When I called them and
**79** ........................ explained them what I wanted to do, they were all happy to
**80** ........................ help. I am going to visit them with a tape recorder and record
**81** ........................ that what they say. Media studies is definitely turning out to be
my favourite subject!

(1 mark per answer)

## H Use the word given in capitals at the end of each line to form a word that fits in the gap in the same line.

### DISHONEST AND DUMB

Some (**82**) ............................ become known for their intelligence and avoid being **CRIME**
caught for years. Others are just so stupid that it seems (**83**) ............................ . **RIDICULE**
Take, for instance, one (**84**) ............................ , who decided that he was feeling a **ROB**
little tired half-way through burgling a house. Seeing the (**85**) ............................ **COMFORT**
bed, he decided to take a nap. It may seem (**86**) ............................ , but he was still **BELIEF**
asleep when the owners got home! They (**87**) ............................ called the police, **NERVOUS**
who came to arrest Sleeping Beauty right away! Another (**88**) ............................ **HUMOUR**
story is that of the man who stole a (**89**) ............................ camera. He managed to **SECURE**
steal the camera (**90**) ............................ , but left the tape behind. It was used as **EQUIP**
(**91**) ............................ in court because, of course, it showed him taking the camera! **EVIDENT**

(1 mark per answer)

**Total mark: ...... / 100**

## ● The passive / the causative / direct and indirect objects

### The passive

| Form | noun + *be* in the correct form + past participle (+ *by/with* + noun) | |
|---|---|---|
| | **Active** | **Passive** |
| present simple | *They grow bananas in tropical areas.* | *am/is/are* + past participle<br>*Bananas* ***are grown*** *in tropical areas.* |
| present continuous | *They are redecorating the café.* | *am/is/are* + *-ing* + past participle<br>*The café* ***is being redecorated****.* |
| present perfect simple | *Has anyone peeled the carrots?* | *has/have* + *been* + past participle<br>***Have*** *the carrots* ***been peeled****?* |
| past simple | *They served the meal in an elegant dining room.* | *was/were* + past participle<br>*The meal* ***was served*** *in an elegant dining room.* |
| past continuous | *We asked for coffee while they were preparing the bill.* | *was/were* + *-ing* + past participle<br>*We asked for coffee while the bill* ***was being prepared****.* |
| past perfect simple | *Someone had eaten all the food by the time I got there.* | *has* + *been* + past participle<br>*All the food* ***had been eaten*** *by the time I got there.* |
| *will* future | *We will deliver your pizza in forty minutes.* | *will* + *be* + past participle<br>*Your pizza* ***will be delivered*** *in forty minutes.* |
| *be going to* future | *Overweight customers are going to sue Burgerland.* | *is/are going to* + *be* + past participle<br>*Burgerland* ***is going to be sued*** *by overweight customers.* |
| future perfect simple | *They will have harvested all the grapes by the end of September.* | *will* + *have* + *been* + past participle<br>*All the grapes* ***will have been harvested*** *by the end of September.* |
| modal | *You should brush the chicken breast with oil and then fry it.* | modal + *be* + past participle<br>*The chicken breast* ***should be brushed*** *with oil and then fried.* |
| modal + perfect infinitive | *They should have delivered the groceries by now.* | modal + *have* + *been* + past participle<br>*The groceries* ***should have been delivered*** *by now.* |
| - *ing* (gerund) | *I don't like people telling me what to do in the kitchen.* | *being* + past participle<br>*I don't like* ***being told*** *what to do in the kitchen.* |

| Use | Example |
|---|---|
| When we don't know who does/did something | *My groceries* ***have been stolen****!* |
| When it's obvious who does/did something | *A boy* ***was arrested*** *in town yesterday for stealing an apple.* |
| When it's not important who does/did something | *The French bistro* ***is being knocked down****.* |
| When we want to emphasise new information or use a formal style | *The potato* ***was brought*** *to Europe by Sir Walter Raleigh.* |

**Watch out!**

- We do not normally use verbs in the passive in the present perfect continuous, past perfect continuous, future continuous or future perfect continuous tenses. Instead, we use a different phrase.
  ✓ *The restaurant has been* ***under construction*** *for four yours.*
  ✗ ~~*The restaurant* ***has been being built*** *for four years.*~~
  ✓ *Dave has been* ***in training*** *as a chef for three years.*
  ✗ ~~*Dave* ***has been being trained*** *as a chef for three years.*~~
- We only normally use '*by*' to say who did something when it is important information.
  ✓ *Margarine was invented* ***by*** *a French chef.*
  ✓ *The best pizzas are made* ***by*** *the Italians.*
  ✗ ~~*Waiter! This steak has been overcooked* ***by*** *someone.*~~
- We usually use '*with*' when we talk about the thing used to do something.
  ✓ *The soup should then be stirred* ***with*** *a spoon.*
  ✗ ~~*The soup should then be stirred* ***by*** *a spoon.*~~
- Some verbs are not normally used in the passive. They include intransitive verbs (without objects), such as *appear* and *die*, and some common transitive verbs, such as *have*, *let*, *lack*, etc.

## The impersonal passive

To express other people's opinions in a formal style, we can use two special forms of the passive.
They can be used with a number of verbs, including: *say, believe, think, claim, estimate,* etc.
Some other verbs (*argue, suggest, calculate,* etc) are usually used with only the second structure.

**Form** noun + *is/are said to* + bare infinitive/perfect infinitive
*It is said that* + clause

| Active | Passive |
|---|---|
| *People **think** he **is** a great chef.* | *He **is thought to be** a great chef.*<br>***It is thought that he is** a great chef.* |
| *People **believe** he **was** a great chef.* | *He **is believed to have been** a great chef.*<br>***It is believed that he was** a great chef.* |
| *People **claim** he **has had** an influence on many other chefs.* | *He **is claimed to have had** an influence on many other chefs.*<br>***It is claimed that he has had** an influence on many other chefs.* |
| *People **say** he **has been making** the best cheese in the area for over thirty years.* | *He **is said to have been making** the best cheese in the area for over thirty years.*<br>***It is said that he has been making** the best cheese in the area for over thirty years.* |
| *People **estimated** that his restaurant **was** worth over $10 million.* | *His restaurant **was estimated to be / to have been** worth over $10 million.*<br>***It was estimated that his restaurant was** worth over $10 million.* |
| *People **have suggested** that he **is** a great chef.* | ***It has been suggested that he is** a great chef.* |

## The causative

**Form** noun + *have/get* in the correct form + noun + past participle (+ *by/with* + noun)

| Use | Example |
|---|---|
| To show that someone arranges for someone else to do something for them | *I **have** my groceries **delivered** by the supermarket once a week.*<br>*We **are having** a new cooker **put in** tomorrow.*<br>*We **had** a large wedding cake **made**.*<br>***Have** you **had** your kitchen **decorated**?*<br>*We **are going to have** the food for the party **made** by a catering company.* |
| To refer to an unpleasant situation which hasn't been arranged | *We **had** our herb garden **vandalised** while we were away.*<br>*The Smiths **have had** their new microwave **stolen**.* |

**Watch out!**

- Using the verb *get* is usually more informal than using *have*.
  ✓ *Can you go and **get** this recipe **photocopied** for me?*
- We can also use *get somebody to do* and *have somebody do* when we want to refer to the person we arrange to do something for us.
  ✓ *Why don't you **get the chef to prepare** you a vegetarian meal?*
  ✓ *Why don't you **have the chef prepare** you a vegetarian meal?*

## Direct and indirect objects

Some verbs can be followed by both a direct and an indirect object (usually a person).
These verbs include:
*bring, buy, get, give, lend, make, offer, owe, pass, promise, send, show, take, teach, tell, write,* etc.

| Active | Passive |
|---|---|
| We can put the indirect object either immediately after the verb, or at the end of the sentence with a preposition (*for/to*, etc).<br>*A friend gave **my sister** this cookery book.*<br>*A friend gave this cookery book **to my sister**.* | The subject of the sentence can be either the indirect object or the direct object of the active sentence.<br>***My sister** was given this cookery book by a friend.*<br>***This cookery book** was given to my sister by a friend.* |

## A Choose the correct word or phrase.

1 The prime minister **was / has** criticised for his recent actions.
2 When I walked past the Wilsons' house, their new sofa **was / has** being delivered.
3 Our teacher **was / has** told us to take our favourite book to school tomorrow.
4 I think my mobile **was / has** been stolen!
5 Jonathan **was / has** chosen to play the lead role in the school play.
6 I'm sleeping downstairs because my bedroom **is being painted / has been painting**.
7 This picture **was / has** probably taken during the winter.
8 Your essays must **be / have** handed in on Friday morning.
9 Someone **was / has** left their wallet on the floor.
10 Did you hear about the bank **being / having** robbed?
11 *Treasure Island* **was / has** written by Robert Louis Stevenson.
12 It was a real shock when my dad **was / has** fired from his job.
13 The Vikings had visited America before it **was / has** discovered by Columbus.
14 When we got to the airport, we learned that our flight **was / had** been delayed.
15 **Was / Has** your ticket for the concert tomorrow paid for by you or your parents?

## B Complete using the correct passive form of the verbs in brackets.

1 The Earth ............................................ (**hold**) by the gravity of the Sun and orbits around it.
2 The first feature-length comedy film ............................................ (**create**) by Charlie Chaplin.
3 The award for best video ............................................ (**present**) later this evening.
4 By the time you read this, I ............................................ (**arrest**) for murder.
5 I don't know whether our tests ............................................ (**mark**) yet or not.
6 Radio waves ............................................ (**discover**) by Marconi.
7 You wouldn't think it to look at him now, but Jack ............................................ (**bully**) when he was at school.
8 Your application ............................................ (**consider**) and we will let you know as soon as we've made a decision.
9 The roof of the car can ............................................ (**lower**) by pressing this button here.
10 Our tent ............................................ (**blow**) over in the night by the wind.
11 Chess ............................................ (**play**) for around two thousand years now.
12 Two men ............................................ (**question**) at this moment by police in connection with the burglary.

## C Write sentences in the passive.

1 Our car / service / a mechanic / at the moment.

..........................................................................................................................................................

2 A man / shoot / an air gun / outside the petrol station last night.

..........................................................................................................................................................

3 Gunpowder / invent / the Chinese.

..........................................................................................................................................................

4 At the surgery yesterday, I / examine / Dr Peterson / and I / give / a prescription.

..........................................................................................................................................................

5 I went to see it because I / tell / it was a good film / all my friends.

..........................................................................................................................................................

6 This photograph / take / my grandfather.

........................................................................................................

7 It looked like the window / break / a hammer / some time before.

........................................................................................................

8 Our dog / give / an injection / a special syringe / the vet.

........................................................................................................

9 The winning goal in last night's match / score / Donatello / a brilliant free kick.

........................................................................................................

10 Your cheque / send / last Friday and / should / deliver / to you tomorrow.

........................................................................................................

## D Rewrite using the phrase given.

1 They have been building the new road for a long time now. (**under construction**)

........................................................................................................

2 They had been training the horse for the race for over a year. (**in training**)

........................................................................................................

3 They have been dicusssing the issue in Parliament. (**under discussion**)

........................................................................................................

4 They had been observing the criminal for the past two weeks. (**under observation**)

........................................................................................................

5 They have been using this plane for over 25 years now. (**in use**)

........................................................................................................

6 They have been developing the Cyborg D423 robot for over ten years. (**in development**)

........................................................................................................

## E Rewrite in the passive starting with the words given.

1 People say that Bali is a beautiful island.
It ........................................................................................................

2 People generally think that life won't be found on Mars.
It ........................................................................................................

3 It is generally said that Christmas is too commercialised.
Christmas ........................................................................................................

4 People often argue that prison doesn't work.
It ........................................................................................................

5 People have suggested that the school should start to produce a magazine.
It ........................................................................................................

6 People say that crocodile tastes like squid.
Crocodile ........................................................................................................

7 It is said that the Vikings discovered America before Columbus.
The Vikings ........................................................................................................

8 People think that heart disease is caused by eating the wrong things.
Heart disease ........................................................................................................

## F Choose the correct answer.

1 We ........... a swimming pool put in this week.
A get
B are having
C have
D have got

2 Why don't you get a doctor ........... at your arm?
A to look
B looked
C look
D be looking

3 My teeth were a little yellow so I ........... by the dentist.
A had cleaned them
B have them cleaned
C was cleaned them
D had them cleaned

4 Stuart's thinking of having ........... !
A shaved his head
B his head shaving
C his head shaved
D shaved to his head

5 My sister ........... her ear pierced last weekend.
A made
B got
C did
D took

6 Mum and Dad didn't fancy cooking, so we got a pizza ........... .
A be delivered
B to be delivered
C delivered
D deliver

7 You should ........... a professional to check your house for earthquake damage.
A have
B make
C take
D get

8 Kelly wanted to have a live band ........... at her wedding.
A to be played
B play
C played
D been playing

9 Can we ........... this summer?
A get installed air-conditioning
B get air-conditioning to install
C have installed air-conditioning
D have air-conditioning installed

10 We ........... while we were on holiday.
A were burgled our house
B had our house burgled
C had burgled our house
D got burgled our house

## G Complete each second sentence using the word given, so that it has a similar meaning to the first sentence. Write between two and five words in each gap.

1 Someone has scratched my car on the door! **been**
My car ........................................................................ on the door!

2 Tommy is having an operation right now. **being**
Tommy ........................................................................ right now.

3 Has Fiona invited you to her party? **been**
Have ........................................................................ party?

4 Shakespeare probably wrote this play in 1587. **written**
This play ........................................................................ Shakespeare in 1587.

5 The government is considering a new law to ban smoking following new research. **considered**
A new law to ban smoking ........................................................................ following new research.

6 My mum told me to go to Megagrocers. **sent**
I ........................................................................ my mum.

7 I didn't understand a word so I asked my teacher and she explained it to me. **got**
I didn't understand a word so I ........................................................................ it to me.

## H Find the extra word in each line.

### Wedding disaster

1 ........................ My wedding had been being arranged for months. I knew exactly what I
2 ........................ wanted for that special day. I had the caterers to give me a menu and
3 ........................ have got them to provide me with samples so that I could be sure we
4 ........................ would have the best food. I also wanted to have us a string quartet play
5 ........................ classical music and I arranged that, too. My dress was been being made
6 ........................ specially and I had told the dressmaker put silver thread in it. Finally, the
7 ........................ big day got arrived. My dress was being delivered in the morning, but by
8 ........................ ten it still hadn't arrived. They called me and said it had been being
9 ........................ damaged! I was furious! I had my best friend quickly to pop out and get
10 ........................ a new dress. I had got my lawyer to call to get my money back.

## I Rewrite with the indirect object at the end of the sentence.

1 My dad got me a great computer game!
*My dad got a great computer game for me.*

2 Dave sent Jill a really nice letter.
................................................................................

3 I threw Colin the ball.
................................................................................

4 The waiter offered us a menu.
................................................................................

5 The hotel provides its guests with satellite television.
................................................................................

6 My grandma taught me this song.
................................................................................

## J Write one word in each gap.

### The European Diet

It's hard for us to imagine what (**1**) ........................ included in the European diet before America (**2**) ........................ discovered (**3**) ........................ Columbus in 1492. So many ingredients which today (**4**) ........................ grown all over the world (**5**) ........................ unknown to medieval Europeans. Potatoes, tomatoes, maize and chocolate (**6**) ........................ all originally imported from the New World. Until then, meals had (**7**) ........................ prepared using ingredients native to Europe, such as root vegetables. Of course, spices such as pepper (**8**) ........................ been traded and added to food for centuries. When the potato (**9**) ........................ first introduced, it was surprisingly unpopular. It (**10**) ........................ considered to be poisonous and it took a long time to become common. There is a story of Parmentier, a French army officer, who (**11**) ........................ potatoes planted in the royal garden and (**12**) ........................ Marie Antoinette to wear a potato flower to make them fashionable. The poor peasants were curious about the new plants and many of them (**13**) ........................ stolen to be planted in their own gardens. It was the start of French fries!

# Unit 16 Vocabulary

## Food and drink

### Topic vocabulary in contrast

see page 192 for definitions

| | | |
|---|---|---|
| chop / slice / grate | lunch / dinner | freezer / fridge |
| bake / grill / fry / roast / boil | plate / bowl / saucer / dish | frozen / freezing |
| cook / cooker / chef | vegetable / vegetarian / vegan | mix / stir / whisk |
| oven / grill / hob | fast food / takeaway | soft drink / fizzy drink |
| kitchen / cuisine | kettle / teapot | menu / catalogue |

### Phrasal verbs

| | |
|---|---|
| **drop in (on)** visit unexpectedly | **put off** make sb not want to do or not like sth |
| **get on for** be almost a particular time, number, age, etc | **run into** meet by chance |
| **go off** be no longer fresh | **run out of** not have any left |
| **go on** continue happening or doing sth; do sth after doing sth else | **take to** begin to like; begin to do sth regularly |
| **go/come round** go/come to sb's house to visit them | **try out** experiment with |
| **keep on** continue doing sth | **turn out** develop in a particular way or have a particular result |
| **leave out** not include | **turn up** appear unexpectedly or without making a firm arrangement |

### Phrases and collocations

| | |
|---|---|
| **cook** | a good/great/etc cook; cook a meal/chicken/etc; do the cooking |
| **drink** | make (sb) a drink; have a drink (of sth); drink sth; drink to sb; drink to sb's health; drink a toast to sb |
| **feed** | feed an animal/etc; feed on sth |
| **fill** | fill sth (up); filled with sth; full of sth |
| **food** | make/prepare/cook/serve food; fast/junk food; pet food; health food |
| **meal** | make/cook/have a meal; go out for a meal |
| **note** | make/take/keep (a) note of sth; note sth (down) |
| **occasion** | on this/that occasion; on occasion; on the occasion of sth; special occasion |
| **recipe** | follow a recipe; recipe book; recipe for disaster |
| **table** | lay/set/clear the table; book/reserve a table |
| **wash** | wash the dishes; wash one's hands; do the washing-up; dishwasher; washing machine |

### Word patterns

| | |
|---|---|
| **associate** sth/sb with sth/sb | **regard** sb as (being) sth |
| **careful** with/about/of sth | **remember** to do; remember sth/sb/doing; remember that |
| **choose** between; choose to do | **suggest** sth/doing (to sb); suggest that |
| **compliment** sb on sth | **tend** to do |
| **full** of sth | **wait** for sth/sb; wait (for sth) to do; wait and see |
| **lack** sth; lack of sth; lacking in sth | **willing** to do |
| **offer** sb sth; offer sth (to sb); offer to do | |

### Word formation

| | | |
|---|---|---|
| **anxious** anxiously, anxiety | **grow** growth, grown-up, growing, grown, home-grown, grower | **safe** unsafe, (un)safely, save, safety, saviour, saver |
| **appreciate** (un)appreciative(ly), appreciation | **mix** mixed, mixture, mixer | **surprise** (un)surprising(ly), surprised |
| **contain** container, content(s) | **origin** (un)original(ly), originate, originator | **sweet** sweetly, sweetener, sweetness |
| **create** creative(ly), creation, creativity, creator | **prepare** preparation, preparatory, (un)prepared | **thorough** thoroughly, thoroughness |
| **disgust** disgusting, disgusted | | |

## Topic vocabulary in contrast

### A Write a verb from the box under each picture.

**bake • chop • fry • grate • boil • grill • mix**
**roast • slice • stir • whisk**

1 .................

2 .................

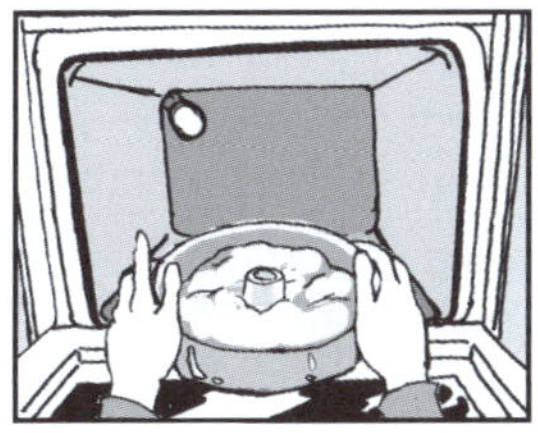
3 .................

4 .................

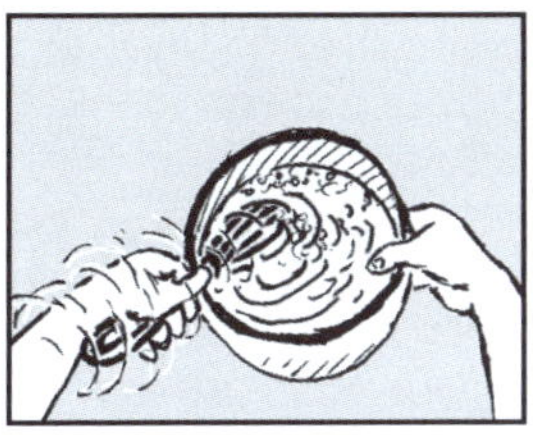
5 .................

6 .................

7 .................

8 .................

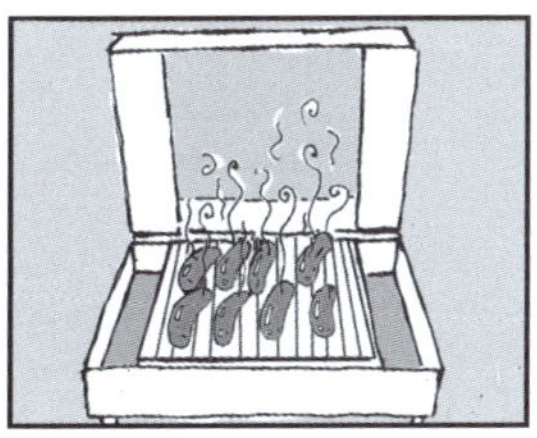
9 .................

10 .................

11 .................

### B Circle the correct word.

1 I particularly like Mexican and Indian **kitchen / cuisine**.
2 **Frozen / Freezing** fish is just as tasty as fresh fish.
3 My mum's the best **cooker / cook** in the world!
4 Once the **kettle / teapot** has boiled, pour the boiling water over the jelly cubes. They'll melt within seconds!
5 Excuse me. Could we have the **catalogue / menu**, please? We'd like to see what you have for dessert.
6 Boil the eggs for three minutes in a saucepan on the **grill / hob / oven**.
7 Any meat that's kept in the **fridge / freezer** should be defrosted thoroughly before cooking.
8 Grandma's having her new **chef / cooker** delivered next week. It's gas, so it will make cooking much easier for her.
9 Chilli con carne is one of my favourite **plates / bowls / saucers / dishes**. It's delicious!
10 Are you going to get your suit dry-cleaned for the Carlton's **dinner / lunch** party tomorrow night?
11 My friend Sally's a true **vegetable / vegetarian / vegan**, so she doesn't eat meat, fish or even any milk products like cheese!
12 Let's get a Chinese **takeaway / fast food** tonight.
13 **Fizzy / Soft** drinks are gassy because they've got carbon dioxide in them.

### Phrasal verbs

## C Write one word in each gap.

### Restaurant review: *La Clara*, Kensington

*by Celia Clarke*

I've taken (**1**) ........................ not booking a table in my real name for these restaurant reviews, as there's always the fear that I'll receive special attention if they know I'm a food critic. For Adam Carter's new restaurant, *La Clara*, on Kensington High Street, I took this one stage further by not booking a table at all.

Earlier in the evening, some friends had come (**2**) ........................ for a chat and mentioned *La Clara*. We decided just to drop (**3**) ........................ to see if there was a free table. There wasn't – always a risk if you (**4**) ........................ up without booking, of course – but we decided to wait. And wait we did. Having arrived at about 9.30, it was getting (**5**) ........................ for eleven before we were finally seated. Incidentally, while we were having a drink at the bar, we ran (**6**) ........................ the food critic of a rival newspaper. She said this was one of her favourite restaurants at the moment. I'd like to be able to report that I now agree, but unfortunately our meal turned (**7**) ........................ to be far from wonderful.

I ordered mushroom troubadour as a starter. The sauce tasted like the cream had (**8**) ........................ off. It was practically inedible. My friend Jane ordered salmon sentinale. Fifteen minutes after my mushrooms had arrived, the waiter came over to say that they had (**9**) ........................ out of salmon. He went (**10**) ........................ to say that they would be closing at midnight. It was already 11.30. The head chef of *La Clara* likes to try (**11**) ........................ one new dish every day. This is called the Chef's Special. I decided to have this – a not-particularly-exciting pasta dish – for the main course. It wasn't bad, but the waiter kept (**12**) ........................ coming over to see if we had finished. We hadn't.

I'll leave (**13**) ........................ a description of the dessert. We had to eat it so quickly I can't even remember what it tasted like.

I don't want to (**14**) ........................ anyone off trying *La Clara* – all new restaurants have problems at the start – but I for one shan't be going back any time soon.

### Phrases and collocations

## D Read ten different ways of explaining things (what something is, how to do something, etc) and decide where these texts appear.

- **A** in the instructions for a dishwasher
- **B** in the instructions for a washing machine
- **C** in the instructions for an electric cooker
- **D** in a recipe book
- **E** on a sign in a health food shop
- **F** on a menu
- **G** in an advertisement for a restaurant
- **H** in a toast at a celebration
- **I** in an article on dieting
- **J** in an article on organising a dinner party

1. Only heat-resistant ceramic and glass dishes should be used for oven baking/roasting. ............
2. A homemade chunky and succulent beefburger, filled with mozzarella cheese and served with a side salad and baked potato. ............
3. Wash the carrots and slice. Set to one side. Boil the potatoes for six minutes or until slightly soft to the touch. ............
4. Open seven days a week. Ideal for wedding receptions, birthday parties and other special occasions. ............
5. Large plates, dishes and bowls should be loaded into the bottom rack (1). Glasses should be placed upside down on the top rack (2). Cutlery should be placed in the cutlery container (3). ............
6. Are you fed up with trying to lose weight and failing? Doreen Brown asks top nutritionists how we can lose that fat, and not put it back on again. ............
7. Make a note of all the things you have to do before your guests arrive (laying the table, getting changed, etc), and when you have to do them. If you're planning to cook the meal yourself (rather than having catering), make sure you choose a menu you know well. Do not experiment with new dishes on this kind of occasion! ............

8 Whites and delicate items should be washed separately. ............
9 I ask you all to raise your glasses so we can drink to my wonderful great-grandfather, ninety-seven years young today! ............
10 Vegetarian and Vegan Products. ............

### Word patterns

## E Write one word in each gap.

1 Everyone complimented her ........................ the wonderful buffet she'd laid on.
2 The problem with drinks like that is they're full ........................ sugar.
3 I can't choose ........................ Death by Chocolate or fruit salad.
4 I'm not going to tell you what's for supper. You'll just have to wait ........................ see.
5 She's generally regarded ........................ being the best cookery book writer of her generation.
6 Most people associate English food ........................ fish and chips and shepherd's pie.
7 Karen's very careful ........................ how much salt she has.
8 There's a lack ........................ good restaurants round here.
9 The meat was well cooked, but the sauce was totally lacking ........................ flavour.

## F Complete using the correct form of the verb in brackets.

1 I tend not ................................................ (**cook**) very often during the week as I don't have time.
2 Do you remember ................................................ (**go**) to that wonderful little taverna on Skiathos last summer?
3 I must remember ................................................ (**buy**) some bread on the way home.
4 Why don't you offer ................................................ (**help**) with the washing-up?
5 I'd suggest ................................................ (**get**) a takeaway rather than cooking.
6 Would you be willing ................................................ (**lend**) me a hand with the pudding?

### Word formation

## G Use the word given in capitals at the end of each line to form a word that fits in the gap in the same line.

### Creating your own dishes

Good cooking is always a strange (**1**) .............................. of science and art and you **MIX**
certainly have to be fairly (**2**) .............................. if you want to come up with your **CREATE**
own recipes. All cooking also demands a fair amount of (**3**) .............................. , and **PREPARE**
this is doubly true when you're producing (**4**) .............................. dishes. You also have **ORIGIN**
to be thick-skinned. You'll be (**5**) .............................. by how honest people can be **SURPRISE**
when it comes to food. I've had people tell me my latest dish is (**6**) .............................. **DISGUST**
and (**7**) .............................. inedible! Sometimes, they were right! But don't get upset. **THOROUGH**
Just smile (**8**) .............................. and thank them for their valuable opinion. And **SWEET**
never forget that when you're waiting (**9**) .............................. to hear whether or not **ANXIOUS**
your 'masterpiece' is a success and they suddenly show their (**10**) .............................. , **APPRECIATE**
you'll realise it was all worth it. My tips: home-(**11**) .............................. vegetables **GROW**
are always the tastiest. Every good cook needs a top-quality (**12**) .............................. . **MIX**
It's an essential piece of kitchen equipment, not a luxury. Make sure you've
got lots of good-quality food storage (**13**) .............................. . And, finally, remember **CONTAIN**
that designing a new dish is not about (**14**) .............................. . It's about taking risks, **SAFE**
and learning from your mistakes. Have fun in the kitchen!

## A Write one word in each gap.

### Cultural differences at the dinner table

In some cultures, when you are invited to (**1**) ........................ a meal at someone's house, you might be considered rude if you don't say how nice the food is. In Britain, for example, it's normal for someone to compliment the cook (**2**) ........................ the tastiness of the meal. You can say something like, 'That was delicious. Do, please, write the recipe down (**3**) ........................ me!'

In other cultures, however, people tend not (**4**) ........................ be so full (**5**) ........................ enthusiasm for the meal. You might be regarded (**6**) ........................ being rude, as the cook might associate your praise (**7**) ........................ surprise. He or she might think, 'So, they're shocked I can cook well, are they?'

If you're not sure how to react, the best advice is to wait and (**8**) ........................ how other people at the table react. If that doesn't help, be very careful (**9**) ........................ what you say! I would suggest (**10**) ........................ one solution could be to say, 'That was delicious, but then I knew it would be!'

(1 mark per answer)

## B Complete the sentences by changing the form of the word in capitals when this is necessary.

**11** My dad never has sugar in coffee or tea but he does sometimes like to add artificial .............................. (**SWEET**).

**12** I don't know how anyone could eat eyeballs. That's .............................. (**DISGUST**)!

**13** Jenny stood .............................. (**ANXIOUS**) in the kitchen, hoping that her soufflé would rise.

**14** Did you know that tomatoes .............................. (**ORIGIN**) from South America?

**15** Donald is so .............................. (**CREATE**) in the kitchen. I think he should be a professional chef.

**16** There are sandwiches for you in a plastic .............................. (**CONTAIN**) in the fridge.

**17** It's important to observe basic health and .............................. (**SAFE**) precautions when you're handling uncooked meat.

**18** That was .............................. (**THOROUGH**) delicious! Thank you!

(1 mark per answer)

## C Complete the second sentence using the word given, so that it has a similar meaning to the first sentence. Write between two and five words in each gap.

**19** You have to stir the soup every five minutes or so. **stirred**
The soup .............................................................................. every five minutes or so.

**20** A baker delivered the cake for us this morning. **had**
We .............................................................................. a baker this morning.

**21** Elaine tasted the curry for me to see how hot it was. **got**
I .............................................................................. the curry for me to see how hot it was.

**22** Many people say that olive oil is good for the heart. **said**
Olive oil .............................................................................. good for the heart.

**23** Some people have said that red wine is good for the heart too. **been**
It .............................................................................. that red wine is good for the heart too.

24 They've been building that new supermarket for months. **construction**
That new supermarket ........................................................................................ for months.

25 These cucumbers came from our garden! **grown**
These cucumbers ........................................................................................ our garden!

26 Why don't you ask an electrician to fit your cooker? **get**
Why don't you ........................................................................................ an electrician?

27 I don't think there's enough salt in the sauce. **lacking**
I think ........................................................................................ salt.

(2 marks per answer)

## D Match to make sentences.

**28** I think this milk has gone ............
**29** I ran ............
**30** We've run out ............
**31** Mum's trying ............
**32** It must be getting ............
**33** We'd love you to come ............
**34** This lasagne hasn't turned ............

**A** out a new recipe tonight!
**B** of bread so could you go and get some?
**C** on for dinner time.
**D** off so let's throw it away.
**E** out quite how I expected.
**F** into Bob in the supermarket yesterday.
**G** round for dinner sometime.

(1 mark per answer)

## E Choose the correct answer.

**35** There's a pack of ............ vegetables in the freezer, I think.
A freezing C iced
B frozen D icy

**36** There are no vegetarian dishes on the ............ !
A leaflet C catalogue
B brochure D menu

**37** ............ the onions in cooking oil until they're golden brown.
A Boil C Fry
B Bake D Grill

**38** Pre-heat the ............ to 200°.
A oven C cuisine
B kitchen D cook

**39** I'll ............ the washing-up tonight!
A make C do
B take D have

**40** The problem with most fizzy drinks is that they're ............ sugar.
A full up C filled with
B filled up with D full of

**41** Susie and Fran ............ in on us last night, so I had to quickly defrost a pizza.
A turned C came
B dropped D went

(1 mark per answer)

**Total mark: ...... / 50**

# ● -ing form or infinitive / prefer, would rather, had better / infinitives of purpose

## verb/noun/adjective phrase + -ing form

Some verb, noun and adjective phrases are usually followed by the *-ing* form.
✓ *I've finished* ***writing*** *my essay.*
These include:

| | | | | | | |
|---|---|---|---|---|---|---|
| admit | delay | dislike | fancy | involve | miss | resist |
| appreciate | deny | enjoy | feel like | keep (on) | postpone | risk |
| avoid | detest | escape | finish | mention | practise | suggest |
| can't help | discuss | face | give up | mind | put off | understand |

**Watch out!**

- Some of the verbs, nouns and adjectives in the list above can also be followed by an object before the *-ing* form.
  ✓ *I can't stand* ***people*** *cheating in exams.*
- When we put a verb after a preposition, we almost always use an *-ing* form.
  ✓ *I'm interested* ***in hearing*** *more about that course.*

## verb/noun/adjective phrase + full infinitive

Some verb, noun and adjective phrases are usually followed by the full infinitive.
✓ *Your answer appears* ***to be*** *wrong.*
These include:

| | | | | | | | |
|---|---|---|---|---|---|---|---|
| able | arrange | choose | fail | manage | prepare | seem | would like |
| afford | ask | decide | happen | offer | pretend | tend | |
| agree | attempt | encourage | help | plan | promise | want | |
| appear | beg | expect | hope | pleased | refuse | wish | |

**Watch out!**

- Some of the verbs, nouns and adjectives in the list above can also be followed by an object before the full infinitive.
  ✓ *I didn't want to take the exam.*
  ✓ *My mum didn't want* ***me*** *to take the exam.*

## verb + bare infinitive

Some verbs can be followed by an object + the bare infinitive.
✓ *You never let me* ***say*** *the answer.*
These include:

| | | | | | | |
|---|---|---|---|---|---|---|
| feel | hear | let | make | notice | see | watch |

**Watch out!**

- The verbs *feel, hear, notice, see* and *watch* can also be followed by the *-ing* form.
  We often use the bare infinitive for a completed action (from start to finish).
  We often use the *-ing* form for an action in progress at the time.
  ✓ *I heard Miss Jenkins* ***tell*** *Julie not to do that.* ( = I heard all of it.)
  ✓ *I heard Miss Jenkins* ***telling*** *Julie not to do that.* ( = I heard part of it.)
- In the passive, *hear, make* and *see* are followed by the full infinitive.
  ✓ Active: *The teacher* ***made*** *me* ***stand*** *in the corner.*
  ✓ Passive: *I* ***was made to stand*** *in the corner.*

## verb + full infinitive or -ing form with little or no change in meaning

Some verbs can be followed by the full infinitive or the *-ing* form with little or no change in meaning.

✓ *We continued **to do** experiments in the lab all afternoon.*

✓ *We continued **doing** experiments in the lab all afternoon.*

These include:

| | | | | | | | |
|---|---|---|---|---|---|---|---|
| begin | can't bear/stand | continue | hate | intend | love | prefer | start |

## verb + full infinitive or -ing form with a change in meaning

Some verbs can be followed by both the full infinitive and the *-ing* form. The choice depends on the meaning.

✓ *I **remember** teachers at my school **hitting** children when they were naughty!*

✓ *Did you **remember to do** your homework?*

These verbs include:

| | | |
|---|---|---|
| consider | learn | remember |
| forget | like | stop |
| go on | mean | teach |
| imagine | regret | try |

See page 196 in the Reference Section for a full list of verbs and definitions.

## prefer, would rather, had better

| Form | Use | Example |
|---|---|---|
| *prefer* + noun/*-ing* + *to* + noun/*-ing* | expressing general preference | *I **prefer** biology **to** history.*<br>*I **prefer** read**ing** English texts **to** speak**ing** in English.* |
| *would prefer* + full infinitive + *rather than* (+ bare/full infinitive) | expressing specific preference (on this occasion) | *I**'d prefer to have** the lesson on Wednesday **rather than** ([**to**] **have** it) on Tuesday, if that's possible.* |
| *would rather* + bare infinitive + *than* (+ bare infinitive) | expressing general or specific preference | *I**'d rather have** the lesson on Wednesday **than** (**have** it) on Tuesday, if that's possible.* |
| *would rather* + sb + past simple/ past continuous | expressing general or specific preference (about someone else) | *I**'d rather you didn't sit** next to Brian.* |
| *had better* + bare infinitive | giving advice | *You**'d better ask** your parents if you can come on the school trip.* |

**Watch out!**

- We don't usually say *I don't prefer…* . We use *I prefer not to…* .
  ✓ *I **prefer not to** have music on when I'm studying.*

## infinitives of purpose

When we want to talk about someone's purpose (the reason they do something), we can use:

| | |
|---|---|
| the full infinitive | *I went to university **to avoid** getting a job!* |
| *in order* + full infinitive | *I went to university **in order to avoid** getting a job!* |
| *so as* + full infinitive | *I went to university **so as to avoid** getting a job!* |

**Watch out!**

- We can also express the same idea using *so (that).*
  ✓ *I went to university **so (that) I could avoid** getting a job!*
- With a negative purpose we don't normally use the full infinitive on its own.
  ✓ *I went to university **in order not to get** a job!*
  ✓ *I went to university **so as not to get** a job!*
  ✗ ~~*I went to university **not to get** a job!*~~

## A Circle the correct word or phrase.

1 I really don't feel like **going / to go** out tonight. Do you?
2 Everyone expected his business **failing / to fail** within the first few months.
3 What would you like **doing / to do** this evening?
4 We discussed **turning / to turn** the attic into a spare bedroom with the architect.
5 She wasn't able **speaking / to speak** very clearly after her accident.
6 Do you mind **moving / to move** your car, please? You're blocking the road.
7 They're going to postpone **making / to make** a decision until next month.
8 Are you planning **of getting / to get** a new DVD player?
9 Are you thinking **of getting / to get** a PlayStation?
10 I'm very pleased **telling / to tell** you that you've passed!
11 Sarah's offered **putting / to put** us up for the weekend.
12 I'm really looking forward **to going / to go** on the cruise.

## B Complete using the correct form (*-ing* form or full infinitive) of the verb in brackets. You may need to use the passive voice.

1 I'll never forgive June for .................................................. (**lie**) to me like that.
2 Daniel's not very good at .................................................. (**make**) friends.
3 I can't resist .................................................. (**buy**) things when they're in the sales.
4 We've got to encourage students .................................................. (**study**), not blame them for not studying.
5 I don't know how you managed .................................................. (**persuade**) the bank manager to lend you so much money!
6 Does Jessica dislike .................................................. (**walk**) so much that she's not going to come with us?
7 Do you deny .................................................. (**steal**) the money? Yes or no?
8 The kids were pretending .................................................. (**be**) asleep but they didn't fool me for a second.
9 I refuse .................................................. (**accept**) that there's no alternative.
10 No one understands how Jill can afford .................................................. (**go**) on so many holidays each year.
11 He only just escaped .................................................. (**send**) to prison. Next time, the judge won't be so forgiving.
12 He expected .................................................. (**give**) a brand new computer for Christmas, but all he got was a second-hand watch!

## C Read the text in Exercise D and decide whether each gap should be filled with the *-ing* form, a bare infinitive or a full infinitive. Write *ing*, *BI* or *FI* for each gap.

| | | | | | |
|---|---|---|---|---|---|
| 1 | ............ | 7 | ............ | 13 | ............ |
| 2 | ............ | 8 | ............ | 14 | ............ |
| 3 | ............ | 9 | ............ | 15 | ............ |
| 4 | ............ | 10 | ............ | 16 | ............ |
| 5 | ............ | 11 | ............ | 17 | ............ |
| 6 | ............ | 12 | ............ | | |

## D Complete using the correct form (*-ing* form, bare infinitive or full infinitive) of the verbs in the box. Use each verb only once.

**achieve • be • behave • come • do • hope • improve • learn • listen • make • play • sit down • take • tell • try • use • work**

**Report: William Watson**

William Watson sometimes seems to be afraid of **(1)** .............................................. hard. He can't help **(2)** .............................................. to avoid **(3)** .............................................. anything that involves **(4)** .............................................. his brain, particularly on Friday afternoons. He seems to detest **(5)** .............................................. life seriously, and pretends he isn't capable of **(6)** .............................................. anything of worth. This is unfortunate as, with a little more effort, William could succeed in **(7)** .............................................. great progress.
However, at present he frequently just wants **(8)** .............................................. the fool. He enjoys **(9)** .............................................. jokes. Presumably, he imagines this **(10)** .............................................. the best way to make friends, but in fact he often just ends up preventing the other students from **(11)** .............................................. . He has promised on several occasions **(12)** .............................................. his behaviour in class, but then he just keeps on **(13)** .............................................. in exactly the same way. Recently, I have had to beg him **(14)** .............................................. and be quiet in the classroom, but it's difficult to know how to make him **(15)** .............................................. to his senses. He just doesn't seem interested in **(16)** .............................................. to my opinion. I'm tempted to give up even **(17)** .............................................. that he might improve. Having said that though, Mr Watson is an extremely good maths teacher!

**Julie Cross – 5A**

## E For each pair of sentences, put a tick (✓) if both sentences mean the same thing. Put a cross (✗) if they have different meanings.

**1** a I can't bear being tickled!
b I can't bear to be tickled! ............

**2** a My boss went on saying that he was very proud of all of us.
b My boss went on to say that he was very proud of all of us. ............

**3** a Have you stopped having lunch yet?
b Have you stopped to have lunch yet? ............

**4** a Have you started having lunch yet?
b Have you started to have lunch yet? ............

**5** a They continued climbing the mountain
b They continued to climb the mountain. ............

**6** a We all saw the reporter interviewing the witness.
b We all saw the reporter interview the witness. ............

**7** a I love playing practical jokes on my younger brother.
b I love to play practical jokes on my younger brother. ............

**8** a Why don't you try holding your breath for a minute or two?
b Why don't you try to hold your breath for a minute or two? ............

**9** a I hate being cheated by taxi drivers.
b I hate to be cheated by taxi drivers. ............

## F Complete each second sentence using the word given, so that it has a similar meaning to the first sentence. Write between two and five words in each gap.

1 I should have taken my medicine this morning but I didn't remember. **forgot**
I .......................................................................... my medicine this morning.

2 I'll always remember the time when I went up Mont Blanc. **never**
I'll .......................................................................... Mont Blanc.

3 I must hang up the washing later. **remember**
I .......................................................................... up the washing later.

4 Darren thinks that wearing a suit to work is appropriate. **likes**
Darren .......................................................................... a suit to work.

5 Jackie wishes she hadn't said that to Allie. **regrets**
Jackie .......................................................................... that to Allie.

6 I'm sorry but your credit card has been cancelled by the bank. **regret**
I .......................................................................... your credit card has been cancelled by the bank.

7 Crashing the car wasn't my intention, you know! **mean**
I .......................................................................... the car, you know!

8 If I take that job, I'll have to do a lot more travelling. **mean**
Taking that job .......................................................................... to do a lot more travelling.

9 Jim's mum made him tidy his room before he could go and play in the park. **made**
Jim .......................................................................... his room before he could go and play in the park.

10 I don't suppose you watched that film last night on BBC2, did you? **happen**
You .......................................................................... that film last night on BBC2, did you?

11 People often think that learning Latin is a waste of time. **considered**
Learning Latin .......................................................................... a waste of time.

## G Each of the words or phrases in bold is incorrect. Rewrite them correctly.

1 I generally prefer coffee **from** tea. ........................
2 Do you prefer watching a DVD at home to **go** to the cinema? ........................
3 I **had** prefer to meet you a bit later, if that's all right with you. ........................
4 He'd **prefer** not have to get up so early tomorrow, but he will if he has to. ........................
5 I'd rather you **write** your essay in a notebook, to be honest. ........................
6 Would you prefer to get a pizza rather **from** go out tonight? ........................
7 You **would** better see a doctor if you're not feeling well. ........................
8 I **had** rather be poor and happy than rich and lonely. ........................
9 I'd prefer **having** an early night tonight, if that's okay with you. ........................
10 She'd **rather** start revising if she wants to do well in the exam next week. ........................
11 Shona prefers **to not** wear make-up to work. ........................

## H Write one word in each gap.

1 I prefer pop music ........................ rock, to be honest.
2 I would prefer to go to the concert tomorrow ........................ than on Saturday.
3 I ........................ playing the piano on my own to performing.
4 I'd rather ........................ to that jazz club than a nightclub.
5 I'd ........................ you didn't practise playing the trumpet while I'm trying to study.
6 You'd ........................ get tickets soon as they're running out.
7 We queued up early in ........................ to get good seats.
8 We waited for hours so ........................ not to miss the VIPs arriving.
9 I called the theatre ........................ find out what time the concert started.
10 I actually prefer ........................ to listen to music through speakers; it sounds so much better through headphones.
11 Don't you think we ........................ better turn the music down a bit?

## I Choose the correct answer.

### Approaches to learning

People appear (**1**) ............ in different ways. Some people expect (**2**) ............ mistakes in their studies and are capable of (**3**) ............ from their mistakes. They don't mind (**4**) ............ by their teacher and indeed often ask (**5**) ............ corrected.
Others, however, dislike (**6**) ............ mistakes. They try to avoid (**7**) ............ anything which they might do badly. They would rather (**8**) ............ something in small steps and be sure they have got it right (**9**) ............ attempt to do a task based on a subject they don't feel they have finished (**10**) ............ yet.
Both ways of learning seem (**11**) ............ equally valid, but a combination of the two may be the best solution. In (**12**) ............ to learn effectively, students have to remember (**13**) ............ risks sometimes. But they also have to feel comfortable and secure with what they're doing so (**14**) ............ not to become demotivated. All students should at least think about (**15**) ............ the way that they approach learning.

| | | | | |
|---|---|---|---|---|
| 1 | A learning | B to learn | C learn | D having learnt |
| 2 | A making | B to make | C make | D having made |
| 3 | A benefiting | B to benefit | C benefit | D to have benefited |
| 4 | A correcting | B being corrected | C to correct | D to be corrected |
| 5 | A being | B be | C to have been | D to be |
| 6 | A making | B to make | C to be making | D make |
| 7 | A doing | B to do | C having done | D to have done |
| 8 | A to perfect | B perfecting | C perfect | D be perfected |
| 9 | A to | B from | C that | D than |
| 10 | A explore | B to explore | C exploring | D being explored |
| 11 | A that | B to be | C as | D being |
| 12 | A desire | B demand | C need | D order |
| 13 | A to take | B taking | C to have taken | D having taken |
| 14 | A that | B much | C as | D many |
| 15 | A to question | B questioning | C question | D to be questioned |

## Education and learning

### Topic vocabulary in contrast

see page 193 for definitions

| | | |
|---|---|---|
| take / pass | prefect / pupil / student | lesson / subject |
| read / study | qualifications / qualities | achieve / reach |
| test / exam | count / measure | task / effort |
| primary / secondary / high | degree / certificate / results | know / recognise |
| colleague / classmate | speak / talk | teach / learn |

### Phrasal verbs

| | |
|---|---|
| **catch on** understand | **get on with** continue doing |
| **come (a)round (to)** be persuaded to change your mind (about) | **give in** stop making an effort to achieve sth difficult |
| **cross out** draw a line through sth written | **keep up with** stay at the same level as |
| **dawn on** if something dawns on you, you realise it for the first time | **sail through** do something or deal with something very easily |
| **deal with** handle, cope with | **set out** explain, describe or arrange sth in a clear and detailed way |
| **drop out (of)** leave school, etc before you have finished a course | **think over** consider |
| **get at** try to express | |

### Phrases and collocations

| | |
|---|---|
| **attention** | pay attention (to sth/sb); attract (sb's) attention; draw (sb's) attention to sth |
| **break** | have/take a break (from sth/doing); lunch break; tea break; commercial break; give sb a break |
| **discussion** | have a discussion (with sb) about/on sth/doing |
| **exam** | take/do/have/pass/fail an exam; sit (for) an exam |
| **homework** | do your homework; have homework (to do) |
| **idea** | question an idea; have an idea; bright idea; have no idea (about) |
| **learn** | have a lot to learn about sth/doing; learn (how) to do |
| **lesson** | go to/have a lesson; double lesson; learn a/your lesson; teach sb a lesson |
| **mind** | make up your mind (about sth/doing); bear (sth) in mind; in two minds about sth/doing; change your mind (about sth/doing); cross your mind; to my mind; (not) mind if |
| **opinion** | in my opinion; give/express your/an opinion (of/about sth/doing); hold/have an opinion (of/about sth/doing) |
| **pass** | pass sth (over) to sb; pass an exam/test/etc; pass a building/etc |
| **point** | see/take sb's point (about sth/doing); (see) the point in/of sth/doing; there's no point in sth/doing; make a point (of doing) |
| **sense** | make sense of sth; it makes sense (to do); sense of humour/taste/sight/etc |
| **suggestion** | make/accept a suggestion |

### Word patterns

| | | |
|---|---|---|
| **able** to do | **fail** to do | **similar** to sth/sb/doing |
| **admire** sb (for sth/doing) | **hope** to do; hope that | **study** sth; for sth |
| **boast** of/about sth/doing (to sb) | **learn** about sth/doing; learn to do; learn by doing | **succeed** in sth/doing |
| **capable** of doing | **settle** for/on sth | **suitable** for sth/doing; suitable to do |
| **congratulate** sb on sth/doing | | |

### Word formation

| | | |
|---|---|---|
| **academy** academic, academically | **improve** improvement, improved | **solve** solution, (un)solvable |
| **attend** attention, (in)attentive(ly), attendance, attendant | **intense** intensity, intensify, intensely | **study** student, studies, studious |
| **behave** behaviour | **literate** illiterate, (il)literacy, literature | **teach** teacher, taught |
| **certify** certificate, certified | **reason** (un)reasonable, (un)reasonably, reasoning | **think** thought, (un)thinkable, thoughtful, thoughtless |
| **educate** education, educator, educational(ly) | **revise** revision, revised | **understand** (mis)understanding, (mis)understood, understandable, understandably |
| **fail** failure, failing | **scholar** scholarship, scholarly, scholastic | |

## Topic vocabulary in contrast

### A Complete using the correct form of the words in the box.

| prefect<br>pupil<br>student |
|---|

1 In our school, most classes have about 35 ........................ in them.
2 Every year, two new ........................ are chosen from the best students in each class.
3 The university accepts around 2000 new ........................ every year.

| achieve<br>reach |
|---|

4 When he finally graduated, Victor felt he had ........................ everything he set out to do.
5 The work we're doing now will make more sense when you ........................ the sixth

| teach<br>learn |
|---|

6 Who ........................ you how to play the drums like that?
7 I would love to ........................ a new language I don't know anything about, like Swedish.

| high<br>primary<br>secondary |
|---|

8 Children in England go to ........................ school from the ages of five to eleven.
9 In Britain, grammar schools, public schools and comprehensives are often referred to as ........................ schools.
10 Americans usually refer to their secondary school as a ........................ school, and there are often separate junior and senior schools.

| degree<br>certificate<br>results |
|---|

11 The exam ........................ come out today and I'm really nervous. I hope I've passed.
12 I was so proud when my exam ........................ finally arrived in the post.
13 I would prefer to go to university and do a ........................ in astronomy, rather than start work.

### B Circle the correct word.

1 I made a few mistakes in the exam and I don't think I **passed / took** it.
2 It's not always easy to **count / measure** how intelligent someone is.
3 Did you know that our French teacher can **speak / talk** four languages?
4 My **qualifications / qualities** include a degree and an MA in chemistry.
5 Our headteacher had had her hair cut and I didn't **know / recognise** her at first.
6 In design and technology, we were given the **effort / task** of designing a stadium.
7 You'll find plenty of books on the **subject / lesson** of business studies in the library.
8 You have to **read / study** hard in order to do well at university.
9 Look at what we did in today's lesson and we'll have a quick **exam / test** tomorrow morning.
10 Our teacher asked us to choose one of our **colleagues / classmates** to be our partner for the next exercise.

## Phrasal verbs

### C Write one word in each gap.

1 Just get ........................ with Exercise C and I'll be back in a minute.
2 My teacher says that I should sail ........................ the exam, but I'm not so sure.
3 Dave didn't understand what Miss Smith was getting ........................ so he asked her to explain it again.
4 We all tried to convince our teacher to change his mind about the school trip and he finally came ........................ .
5 If you make a mistake, just cross it ........................ with a single line.
6 Belinda missed a few months of school because of illness and found it difficult to keep ........................ with her classmates.
7 The other kids were making fun of me, but I didn't catch ........................ until I heard them laughing.

## D Complete each second sentence using the word given, so that it has a similar meaning to the first sentence. Write between two and five words in each gap.

1 The ideas in your essay need to be organised better. **set**
You need to ................................................................................ in your essay better.

2 Why don't you consider the college's offer for a few days and then call them? **over**
Why don't you ................................................................................ for a few days and then call them?

3 You'll never pass the exam if you just stop trying like that. **in**
You'll never pass the exam if you just ................................................................................ like that.

4 When he was at university, Nick just couldn't handle all the work. **deal**
Nick just couldn't ................................................................................ at university.

5 I suddenly realised that I had left my homework at home. **dawned**
It ................................................................................ that I had left my homework at home.

6 Ed was very lonely at university and he left after only one month. **out**
Ed ................................................................................ after only one month because he was very lonely.

### Phrases and collocations

## E Choose the correct answer.

1 If you need to ........... the teacher's attention, just put your hand up.
A pull B attract C capture D draw

2 Make sure you ........... your homework before you go out.
A make B solve C write D do

3 Could I ........... a suggestion? Why not have piano lessons?
A have B do C put D make

4 I really don't ........... the point of taking the exam when you're not ready for it.
A take B see C have D mind

5 I'll meet you at the school gates during the lunch ........... .
A break B gap C interval D pause

6 Do you think you could pass that book ........... to me, please?
A under B through C over D in

7 Mrs Dawson said that we are ........... our lesson in the library next Monday.
A having B making C reading D going

8 In English yesterday, we had a discussion ........... different cultures.
A around B about C for D from

9 ........... my opinion, maths shouldn't be a compulsory subject.
A From B To C At D In

10 When you ........... the exam tomorrow, try to stay calm and relaxed.
A make B write C take D answer

11 My dad wants me to go to university, but I'm in ........... minds about it.
A my B two C some D different

12 I still have a lot ........... about the English language.
A learning B to learn C for learning D of learning

13 If the examiner can't ........... sense of your writing, you'll get a low mark.
A make B bring C take D understand

14 I hadn't studied, so when the teacher asked me I had ........... idea.
A none B no C even D not

### Word patterns

## F Each of the words in bold is incorrect. Rewrite them correctly.

1 I've always admired our music teacher **from** being so patient. ........................
2 My new school is quite similar **with** my old one. ........................
3 Mr Wilkins congratulated me **for** passing the exam. ........................
4 I'd better go home and study **on** tomorrow's test. ........................
5 Ian is capable **for** doing very well this year if he works hard. ........................
6 This course is suitable **to** students who are considering a career in the media. ........................
7 If you don't get into university, you'll have to settle **with** art college. ........................
8 After six attempts, Bill finally succeeded **with** passing his driving test. ........................

## G Water has damaged part of this text from a diary. Read it and decide what you think each of the original words was. Write the words in the blank spaces.

**Dear Diary**

| | |
|---|---|
| Well, my first day at the new school is over. I was able ____ make | 1 ........................ |
| a few friends, although I hope ____ I meet more people tomorrow. | 2 ........................ |
| I met one girl I didn't like, who just boasted ____ her exam results | 3 ........................ |
| and succeeded ____ annoying everyone. The teacher asked me | 4 ........................ |
| what I'd been learning ____ at my other school and when I told | 5 ........................ |
| her she said she failed ____ see how I would be able to catch up | 6 ........................ |
| with the others. I'll show her! I'm just as capable ____ doing the | 7 ........................ |
| work as the others. I'm really going to study hard ____ the test. | 8 ........................ |

### Word formation

## H Complete the sentences by changing the form of the word in capitals when this is necessary.

1 I wonder if you could tell me who was awarded the ............................ (**SCHOLAR**)?
2 Do you think that you pay enough ............................ (**ATTEND**) in class?
3 Could you tell me what the ............................ (**SOLVE**) to number seven is?
4 My dad said I'd better spend more time on my ............................ (**STUDY**).
5 I would like to know what qualifications ............................ (**TEACH**) require in your country.
6 Joshua was suspended from school for a week for bad ............................ (**BEHAVE**).
7 I did six hours of ............................ (**REVISE**) for the test, and I still failed!
8 Please send photocopies of all your ............................ (**CERTIFY**) to us at the address below.

## I Complete the text by changing the form of the word in capitals.

### Being unable to read

It seems (**1**) ............................ (**THINK**) today not to provide children with a decent (**2**) ............................ (**EDUCATE**). There is such an emphasis on (**3**) ............................ (**ACADEMY**) achievement these days that it's easy to forget what a problem (**4**) ............................ (**LITERATE**) used to be. Being unable to read can be (**5**) ............................ (**INTENSE**) embarrassing and can make someone feel like a complete (**6**) ............................ (**FAIL**). Someone who can't read is often (**7**) ............................ (**UNDERSTAND**) afraid of certain situations. The problem can seem (**8**) ............................ (**SOLVE**). However, given the right teacher, a lot of hard work and a (**9**) ............................ (**REASON**) amount of time, anyone can learn. Being able to read can lead to an (**10**) ............................ (**IMPROVE**) quality of life.

## A Write one word in each gap.

### The Exam

It may sound strange, but Ben was looking forward to the English exam. Now, don't imagine that Ben was a great student. He was always slow to catch (**1**) ........................ in class and couldn't really keep (**2**) ........................ with the other students. And he hadn't even studied (**3**) ........................ the exam. The real reason he thought he was going to sail (**4**) ........................ was that he had all the answers!

Two days before, he had found a piece of paper with all the questions and answers on it on his teacher's desk. It suddenly (**5**) ........................ his mind that maybe for once he could pass the exam. 'What's the point (**6**) ........................ studying?' he asked himself. After thinking it (**7**) ........................ for a second, he (**8**) ........................ his mind up. He copied the piece of paper and his teacher (**9**) ........................ no idea what had happened.

When the exam started, Ben sat down and turned the question paper over. He looked, and then looked again. It was the wrong paper! It dawned (**10**) ........................ Ben that he had copied the wrong exam paper! His teacher was looking at him, so Ben thought he'd better get (**11**) ........................ with it. He knew he would never succeed (**12**) ........................ passing the exam. Not all of it (**13**) ........................ sense to him, but he did his best.

The next day, his teacher gave him his paper back and said 'Well done, Ben. Much better.' Ben couldn't believe it! He had passed with a B! He realised he had (**14**) ........................ an important lesson. With a little work, who knew what he would be capable (**15**) ........................ ?

(1 mark per answer)

## B Complete the sentences by changing the form of the word in capitals when this is necessary.

**16** I passed the exam, but I'm still waiting to get my .............................. (**CERTIFY**).
**17** Have you done any .............................. (**REVISE**) for the test?
**18** Please pay .............................. (**ATTEND**), Rita, when I'm explaining what your homework is.
**19** I spent a long time on the maths problem but I still came up with the wrong .............................. (**SOLVE**).
**20** One of my classmates was suspended for a week for bad .............................. (**BEHAVE**).
**21** Well, Mrs Turner, you'll be pleased to hear that Georgia has made a big .............................. (**IMPROVE**) in geography.
**22** I'm hoping to study English .............................. (**LITERATE**) at university.

(1 mark per answer)

## C Complete the second sentence using the word given, so that it has a similar meaning to the first sentence. Write between two and five words in each gap.

**23** The headmaster made the pupil wait outside his door. **made**
The pupil ........................................................................ outside the headmaster's door.

**24** Please don't leave your books on my desk. **rather**
I ........................................................................ leave your books on my desk.

**25** I didn't understand what my teacher was trying to express so I asked her again. **getting**
I didn't understand what my teacher ........................................................................ so I asked her again.

**26** Counting the words in your composition is a waste of time. **point**
There ................................................................................ the words in your composition.

**27** I just can't decide whether to go to university or not. **minds**
I'm ................................................................................ whether to go to university or not.

**28** My cousin has decided that he isn't going to finish his engineering course. **drop**
My cousin has decided ................................................................................ his engineering course.

**29** All Emma's teachers say that she is able to do much more. **capable**
All Emma's teachers say that she ................................................................................ much more.

**30** I was really pleased that I managed to pass the exam. **succeeded**
I was really pleased that I ................................................................................ the exam.

(2 marks per answer)

## D Choose the correct answer.

**31** I didn't expect our history teacher ............ us so much homework.
A giving C to give
B give D to giving

**32** Do you remember ............ to school for the very first time?
A go C of going
B to go D going

**33** I started doing my homework when I got home from school but I stopped ............ my favourite show.
A watch C watching
B to watch D from watching

**34** Please don't forget ............ your essays during Friday's lesson.
A handing in C hand in
B to hand in D to handing in

**35** Our teacher made the whole class ............ after the lesson because we had been so noisy.
A staying C for staying
B to stay D stay

**36** 'What was Derek's reaction to the accusation?'
'Well, he denied ............ anywhere near the house at the time.'
A being C be
B to be D of being

(1 mark per answer)

## E Choose the correct answer.

**37** I was very proud when I was told that I'd been made into a ............ .
A pupil C prefect
B student D classmate

**38** With a little hard work, I'm sure you'll ............ a lot this year.
A reach C achieve
B succeed D qualify

**39** Who ............ you how to cook so well?
A taught C made
B learned D explained

**40** Lee didn't do so well in the test because he hadn't ............ .
A written C read
B studied D learned

**41** I think you need to ............ your ideas more clearly so that the reader doesn't get confused.
A dawn on C set out
B get on with D give in

**42** Oh, no! We've got a double maths ............ next!
A subject C lesson
B interval D task

(1 mark per answer)

**Total mark: ...... / 50**

# Unit 19 Grammar

## ● Questions / question tags / indirect questions

### Questions

| Form | |
|---|---|
| With *be* as a main verb | ***Am/Was*** *I on time?*<br>***Are/Were*** *you/we/they tired?*<br>***Is/Was*** *he/she/it cold?* |
| With *be* as an auxiliary verb | ***Am/Was*** *I interrupt**ing** you?*<br>***Are/Were*** *you/we/they go**ing** on a picnic?*<br>***Is/Was*** *he/she/it work**ing**?* |
| With *have* as an auxiliary verb | ***Have/Had*** *I/you/we/they got any money?*<br>***Has/Had*** *he/she/it finished?* |
| With *have* as a main verb and with all other verbs | ***Do/Did*** *I/you/we/they have enough time?*<br>***Does/Did*** *he/she/it need anything?* |
| With modals | ***Should*** *I wait?*<br>***Could*** *you help me?*<br>***Will*** *she be here soon?*<br>***Might*** *they be lost?* |
| With *who, whose, whom, what, which, where, when, why* and *how* | ***Who*** *is taking the rubbish out?*<br>***Whose*** *book is this?*<br>*To **whom** did you speak?*<br>***What*** *is the weather like?*<br>***Which*** *do you want?*<br>***Where*** *did you go on holiday?*<br>***When*** *is Terry starting work?*<br>***Why*** *did they leave?*<br>***How*** *do you spell 'environment'?* |

**Watch out!**

- With the question words *who* and *what*, whether we use *do* or not depends on whether the question word refers to the **subject** or **object** of the verb.
  - ✓ Subject: *Who **saw** you?* (= Someone saw you. Who?)
  - ✓ Object: *Who **did** you **see**?* (= You saw someone. Who?)
- Remember that after *do* or *does*, we use the bare infinitive.
  - ✓ *Did you **go** to the talk on the environment?*
  - ✗ ~~*Did you **went** to the talk on the environment?*~~
  - ✓ *Does Tom **want** a glass of orange juice?*
  - ✗ ~~*Does Tom **wants** a glass of orange juice?*~~
- Remember that the verb *mean* forms questions just like other main verbs.
  - ✓ *What **does** 'environmental' **mean**?*
  - ✗ ~~*What **means** 'environmental'?*~~

### Question tags

| Form | |
|---|---|
| With *be* as a main verb | *You **are** Canadian, **aren't** you?*<br>*She **is** beautiful, **isn't** she?* |
| With auxiliary verbs and modals | *You **haven't** lost my CD, **have** you?*<br>*We **are** having the lesson early tomorrow, **aren't** we?*<br>*People **should** recycle things, **shouldn't** they?*<br>*There **will** be lots of people there, **won't** there?* |

| | |
|---|---|
| With *have* as a main verb | *Tom* ***has*** *a lovely voice,* ***hasn't/doesn't*** *he?* |
| With other verbs | *You play the guitar,* ***don't*** *you?*<br>*Frank lives in Germany now,* ***doesn't*** *he?*<br>*Your friends really enjoyed themselves at the party,* ***didn't*** *they?* |
| With *Let's* | *Let's get a DVD tonight,* ***shall we****?* |
| With imperatives | *Pass me that book,* ***will/would/could you****?*<br>*Don't forget tonight,* ***will you****?* |

| Use | Example |
|---|---|
| To ask someone to agree with us (falling intonation) | *It's really hot,* ***isn't it****?* |
| To check whether something is true (rising intonation) | *You're Spanish,* ***aren't you****?* |

**Watch out!**

- In sentences with *I am*, we use *aren't I?* as the question tag. In sentences with *I am not*, we use *am I?*
  - ✓ *I'm the best student in the class,* ***aren't I****?*
  - ✓ *I'm not very tall,* ***am I****?*
- With *everyone, no one* and *someone*, we use questions tags with a plural verb and *they*.
  - ✓ *Everyone's going to be there,* ***aren't they****?*
  - ✓ *No one wants to come,* ***do they****?*
  - ✓ *Someone's been in here,* ***haven't they****?*
- Usually, when we have a positive verb in a sentence, we use a negative question tag. When we have a negative verb in a sentence, we use a positive question tag. In sentences with a negative word like *no, little, never, nobody, no one, hardly*, etc, we use a positive question tag.
  - ✓ *You have got* ***no*** *manners,* ***have*** *you?*
  - ✓ *We* ***never*** *enjoy our holiday,* ***do*** *we?*
- In sentences where the subject is *there*, we repeat *there* in the question tag.
  - ✓ *There's no point calling Tim now,* ***is there****?*

**US vs UK Grammar**

- In American English, a question tag with *do* can be used after a sentence with *have got*. This is not usually done in British English.
  **US**: *They've got a lot of money,* ***don't*** *they?*
  **UK**: *They've got a lot of money,* ***haven't*** *they?*

## Indirect questions

| | |
|---|---|
| **Form** | introductory phrase or question + clause with normal word order |
| **Use** | We use indirect questions when we want to ask questions politely. |

| Some introductory phrases and questions | Example |
|---|---|
| *Can/Could you tell me ... ?* | *Could you tell me what time it is?* |
| *Could you let me know ... ?* | *Could you let me know when it starts?* |
| *Do you know ... ?* | *Do you know who that woman is?* |
| *I wonder if you could tell me ...* | *I wonder if you could tell me how much this costs.* |
| *I wonder if you know ...* | *I wonder if you know what the starting salary is.* |
| *I would like to know ...* | *I would like to know what your company is going to do about it.* |

**Watch out!**

- We **do not** use question word order in the second part of the sentence.
  - ✓ *I would like to know when* ***the next train to London leaves****.*
  - ✗ ~~*I would like to know when* ***does the next train to London leave****.*~~
- Some indirect questions, which begin with a question word, need a question mark at the end.
  - ✓ ***Could*** *you tell me where the library is?*
- If a direct question is a 'yes/no' question, the equivalent indirect question uses *if* or *whether*.
  - ✓ *I wonder* ***if/whether*** *you have read this book.*

## A Choose the correct answer.

1 Oh, I'm sorry! .......... disturbing you?
A Do I C Should I
B Have I D Am I

2 Did Dorothy .......... you about the meeting on Friday?
A told C has told
B tell D tells

3 .......... hot when you were in Spain?
A Was it C Did it
B It was D It made

4 Tony, .......... got time to call Mrs Roberts?
A do you have C are you
B you have D have you

5 When your boss arrived, .......... finished the report?
A you had C had you
B did you have D were you

6 I know Jane's pretty, but .......... seen someone spend so much time in front of the mirror?
A do you ever C have you ever
B you have never D ever have you

7 It's raining, so .......... cancel the concert?
A will they C do they will
B they will D are they

8 .......... pass me the salt, please?
A You could C You are
B Are you D Could you

9 Sir, .......... repeat what the homework is, please?
A do you C you
B are you D can you

10 .......... the couple you met in France last year staying at the same hotel?
A Did C Were
B Have D Could

11 I know how to pronounce 'controversy', but what .......... ?
A does it mean C is it mean
B it means D means it

12 It's a great idea, but .......... it will work?
A are you think C you think
B do you think D you do think

## B Write questions.

1 you / wash / your hair / when I rang?

..........................................................................................

2 Julie / give / you / her e-mail address / yesterday?

..........................................................................................

3 you / always / have / lunch / this late?

..........................................................................................

4 Jack and Tom / come / to the party / tonight?

..........................................................................................

5 you / can / give / me / a hand / later?

..........................................................................................

6 how / you / spell / your name?

..........................................................................................

7 why / the government / can't / do / something / about the situation?

..........................................................................................

8 where / you / go / for your honeymoon / last year?

..........................................................................................

9 what / your house / look like / when / it is finished?

..........................................................................................

10 which / flavour of ice cream / your favourite / be?

..........................................................................................

**C** Complete using the words in the box. Use each word only once. There is one extra word you do not need to use.

**who • where • which • whose • what • whom • how • when • why**

## HELP US HELP THE ENVIRONMENT

**(1)** ........................ responsibility is it to look after the environment? Yours! And **(2)** ..................... should you start? Right now is the answer! But **(3)** ........................ is going to help you? We are! We are GreenWarriors, the environmental protest group, and we know the answers to all your questions. We've put together this factsheet to get you started.

**(4)** ........................ me?
*We all have a responsibility to the world around us. Ordinary people like you can make a big difference.*

But **(5)** ........................ can I make a difference?
*By recycling your paper, glass and plastic and by taking part in GreenWarrior demonstrations and protests in your area.*

**(6)** ........................ 's the first step?
*The first step is to come along to the GreenWarrior offices and speak to one of our officers. They will let you know about the next protest in your area.*

**(7)** ........................ other organisations are you connected to?
*GreenWarriors is a completely independent protest organisation.*

**(8)** ........................ is GreenWarriors based?
*We are a national organisation, with our headquarters in Northampton.*

**D** Circle the correct phrase.

1 'Who **asked you / did you ask** to the party?'
'Maria, but she told me she couldn't come.'

2 'Who **saw you / did you see** at the supermarket?'
'Just Ben, but I don't think he saw me.'

3 'What **gave you / did you give** the impression that Greg was depressed?'
'Oh, I don't know. He just seemed a bit down.'

4 'Who **thought you / did you think** had stolen the money?'
'Jenny, but she believed me when I told her I hadn't done it.'

5 'Which programme **taught you / did you teach** the most?'
'Well, I learned a lot from *Extreme History*.'

6 'Who **borrowed you / did you borrow** this book from?'
'Tracy, and I need to give it back to her tomorrow.'

7 'What **brought you / did you bring** to this part of the world?'
'Work, really, and I've always loved this country.'

8 'Who **accused George / did George accuse** of starting the fight?'
'He says that John started it by calling him names.'

9 'Which person **admires you / do you admire** the most?'
'I think I would say my grandmother because she's worked hard all her life.'

10 'Who **told Dave / did Dave tell** your secret?'
'I'm not sure, but I think Simone probably told him.'

## E Write one word in each gap.

### Early humans and the weather

(1) ........................ you think you understand the weather? For early humans, the weather was a constant source of questions. (2) ........................ is it raining? What (3) ........................ this storm mean? Where (4) ........................ the wind go when it blows? People came up with many explanations for the weather, usually involving gods or ancestors. (5) ........................ you explain what a rainbow is? The Cherokee people of America believed that it was the hem of the sun god's coat.

The weather has also been used to explain other things. What would you say if someone asked you (6) ........................ kangaroos come from? You'd probably say Australia, but (7) ........................ did the Aborigines explain these strange animals? They told a story about a great storm. A group of Aboriginal hunters watched in amazement as the wind blew large creatures over their heads. (8) ........................ could they be? Finally, the wind died down and the kangaroos landed on the ground. The storm had brought them a new animal to hunt.

## F Match to make sentences.

1 You've sent that letter I gave you, ...........
2 You catch the bus to school, ...........
3 You won't tell anyone about this, ...........
4 You're a friend of Charlie's, ...........
5 You were living in Hong Kong then, ...........
6 You never work more than you have to, ...........
7 You made no effort to make friends with Darren, ...........
8 You got Jimmy a cap for his birthday, ...........

A don't you?
B didn't you?
C will you?
D haven't you?
E do you?
F did you?
G weren't you?
H aren't you?

## G Complete the question tags.

1 Get me some chewing gum when you go to the shop, ........................ you?
2 Let's watch that new DVD you bought today, ........................ we?
3 There's not really much point waiting, ........................ there?
4 Tonia will put us up for the weekend, ........................ she?
5 Nobody seems to like Jessica, ........................ they?
6 I'm not making much sense now, ........................ I?
7 Let's go because it's getting late, ........................ it?
8 If you borrow my coat, don't get it dirty, ........................ you?
9 Bill should be here by now, ........................ he?
10 I'm making you feel uncomfortable, ........................ I?
11 Someone left the door open, ........................ they?
12 Nobody knows about this, ........................ they?

## H Rewrite the sentences correctly.

1 I wonder if you could tell me what time does the plane from Frankfurt arrive?

..........................................................................................................................................

2 Could you let me know when would you like me to come for an interview.

..........................................................................................................................................

3 I wonder if you know what bus should I catch for the town centre.

..........................................................................................

4 Do you think you could tell me how do you work this ticket machine?

..........................................................................................

5 I wonder you have seen George?

..........................................................................................

6 I would like to know do you have any double rooms?

..........................................................................................

7 Can you tell me what were you doing in my office?

..........................................................................................

8 Do you know where is this address?

..........................................................................................

## I Complete each second sentence using the word given, so that it has a similar meaning to the first sentence. Write between two and five words in each gap.

1 When does Tina get back from Berlin? **know**
Do .................................... back from Berlin?

2 What time does the film start tonight? **starts**
Could you tell me .................................... tonight?

3 Is service included in the price? **know**
I would like to .................................... in the price.

4 What is the salary? **let**
Could you .................................... the salary is?

5 Have you been to Brussels before? **wonder**
I .................................... to Brussels before.

6 Did Gail pass her exam? **passed**
Do you know .................................... her exam?

7 I wonder if you know where Mary went after the party last night. **go**
Where .................................... after the party last night?

8 I would like to know how many days holiday we get each year. **given**
How many days holiday .................................... each year?

## J Circle the extra word in each sentence.

1 Do you have much free time these days or are you be quite busy?
2 I would like to know it when I can expect my order to be delivered.
3 Do you think whether you could possibly let me know how soon you will have the work finished?
4 I wonder if you know who it is responsible for cleaning the building.
5 Tell Roger who did you saw when you were at the police station the other day.
6 Did Dad mention who he sold him the car to?
7 You shouldn't leave your homework to the very last minute if you want to get a good mark, should not you?
8 I wonder it if you know where I can buy something to eat.

# Unit 20 Vocabulary

## Weather and the environment

### Topic vocabulary in contrast

see pages 193-94 for definitions

| | | |
|---|---|---|
| urban / suburban / rural | clean / clear | thunder / lightning |
| smog / fog / smoke / mist | pour / drizzle / flood | global / worldwide |
| weather / climate | environment / surroundings | plain / land / field / desert |
| forecast / prediction | wind / air | extinct / endangered |
| waste / litter / rubbish | reservoir / lake / puddle / pond | recycle / reuse |

### Phrasal verbs

| | |
|---|---|
| **call for** require; need; demand | **get (sb) down** make sb feel sad or lose hope |
| **call off** cancel | **put down to** suggest that sth is the result of |
| **clear up** become brighter and better (for weather) | **put out** make something stop burning |
| **cut off** make a place difficult or impossible to enter, leave or communicate with; disconnect | **set in** start and be likely to continue for a while (for rain, winter, an economic depression, etc) |
| **die down** become less noisy, powerful or active | **stand for** represent (for abbreviations and symbols); put up with |
| **do up** repair, paint or improve | **tear down** destroy or remove (for buildings, statues, etc) |
| **face up to** accept sth and try to deal with it | **throw away** get rid of, discard |

### Phrases and collocations

| | |
|---|---|
| **control** | lose/take/have control (of sth); in control; out of control |
| **effect** | have an effect (on sth/sb); take effect |
| **end** | in the end; at the end (of sth); come to an end; come to/reach the end (of sth); happy ending |
| **floor** | on the floor; on the ground/first/second/etc floor |
| **fuss** | make/cause a fuss (about sth/doing) |
| **long** | (for) as long as; (for) a long time; take a long time (to do); long to do; long for sth (to do) |
| **look** | have/take a look at sth/sb; look like sth/sb; look at/for sth/sb |
| **mess** | make a mess (of sth); in a mess |
| **responsibility** | have/take (the) responsibility for sth/doing |
| **shower** | take/have a shower; a rain shower; a light/heavy shower of rain |
| **sight** | catch/lose sight of sth/sb; in sight of sth; at first sight |
| **waste** | a waste of time; waste your time; industrial/household waste |
| **weather** | weather forecast; under the weather |
| **world** | all over the world; around the world; throughout the world; the whole world; in the world; world record |

### Word patterns

| | | |
|---|---|---|
| **aware** of sth; aware that | **expect** sth/sb (to do); expect that | **hard** to do; hard doing |
| **covered** in/with sth | **familiar** with sth; familiar to sb | **prevent** sth; prevent sb from doing; prevent sth from happening |
| **disappointed** with/by sth; in sb | **famous** for sth/doing | **short** of sth; short on sth |
| **except** (for) sth/doing | **glance** at sth/sb | **warn** sb about/against sth/doing; warn sb of sth; warn sb not to do; warn (sb) that |

### Word formation

| | | |
|---|---|---|
| **accurate** accurately, inaccurate(ly), (in)accuracy | **globe** global(ly) | **nature** (un)natural(ly) |
| **danger** dangerous(ly); endanger; endangered | **great** greatly, greatness | **neighbour** neighbourly, neighbouring, neighbourhood |
| **develop** (un)developed, developing, developer, development | **harm** harmful(ly), harmless(ly), (un)harmed | **pollute** (un)polluted, pollution, pollutant |
| **environment** environmental(ly), environmentalist | **likely** unlikely, likelihood | **reside** residential, resident, residence |
| **extreme** extremely, extremity, extremist | **low** lower, lowness | **sun** sunny, sunshine |
| **freeze** froze, frozen, freezing, freezer | | |

### Topic vocabulary in contrast

## A Circle the correct word.

# Local news in brief

**Thresham Valley under water?**

Plans to turn much of the Thresham Valley into a large (**1**) **puddle** / **reservoir** to provide drinking water for the local area have received mixed reactions. Local councillors have praised the scheme, arguing that the environmental and economic benefits of (**2**) **flooding** / **pouring** the valley will far outweigh the disadvantages. Several small (**3**) **rural** / **urban** communities – two villages, three hamlets and two farms – in the valley will disappear, however.

**Lucky escape for farmer**

A farmer was struck by (**4**) **lightning** / **thunder** on Thursday evening, while mending a fence in one of his (**5**) **plains** / **fields**. The farmer, Jack Dobson, received treatment for slight burns at Meldew Hospital. Talking about the incident later, he said: 'It was (**6**) **drizzling** / **showering** slightly when I went out, but I'd checked the weather (**7**) **prediction** / **forecast** and it hadn't said there was going to be a thunderstorm. It was lucky I was wearing my wellington boots!'

**Save bags and save money**

Shoppers at a local supermarket are being urged not to throw away the supermarket's plastic shopping bags. A spokesperson for Asdo said: 'For every new bag we make, the factory has to pump out industrial (**8**) **waste** / **litter** and that's increasing pollution in the (**9**) **suburban** / **surrounding** area. We want to reduce the number of bags we make each year. We're offering a financial incentive to our customers to (**10**) **reuse** / **repeat** their bags by bringing them with them every time they shop with us rather than getting new ones each time.'

**Local academic causes a stir**

An academic from Davington University has caused controversy by claiming that (**11**) **global** / **worldwide** warming is not caused by human disregard for the (**12**) **weather** / **environment**. In her new book entitled *Are We to Blame?*, Professor Angela Lucini argues that large-scale changes in the Mediterranean (**13**) **land** / **climate**, for example, have taken place ever since the world was formed. 'People weren't responsible for the Ice Ages, or their coming to an end, and we certainly weren't responsible for the fact the dinosaurs became (**14**) **extinct** / **endangered** so it's a bit presumptuous of us to think we're responsible for all the problems were facing now, isn't it?' she said.

**Councillor calls for an end to the fireplace**

Local councillor Davina Forrest is calling for a ban on the use of coal fires at home. 'There's no doubt that if domestic chimneys stopped pumping out (**15**) **smoke** / **fog** into the atmosphere, the (**16**) **air** / **wind** we'd all be breathing would be much (**17**) **cleaner** / **clearer**,' she said.

### Phrasal verbs

## B Complete using the correct form of the phrasal verbs in the box.

**call for • call off • clear up • cut off • die down • do up • face up to • put out**

1 The weather should have ........................................ by this evening, shouldn't it?
2 Do you think the wind has ........................................ enough for us to go sailing without any danger?
3 Environmentalists are ........................................ stricter controls on the use of leaded petrol.
4 Why can't they ........................................ the fact that their products are bad for the environment?
5 Firefighters managed to ........................................ the forest fire before it destroyed any houses.
6 We'll have to ........................................ the demonstration if the weather's really bad, won't we?
7 The town was totally ........................................ for three days because of the floods.
8 It didn't take us long to ........................................ the old barn, did it?

## C Write one word in each gap.

1 Don't throw those batteries .......................... . They're not biodegradable!
2 Rainy days always .......................... me down.
3 Could you tell me what the letters 'CJD' stand .......................... ?
4 They're planning to tear .......................... the old cinema and build a new shopping centre on the land.
5 I think the rain's set .......................... for the day, don't you?
6 Some scientists put the extinction of the dinosaurs down .......................... changes in the world's climate.

### Phrases and collocations

## D Complete each second sentence using the word given, so that it has a similar meaning to the first sentence. Write between two and five words in each gap.

1 Josh isn't feeling very well today. **weather**
Josh is feeling a bit .......................................................................... today.
2 CFC's have badly affected the ozone layer. **effect**
CFC's have .......................................................................... the ozone layer.
3 Would you mind quickly looking at the engine? **look**
Would you mind .......................................................................... the engine?
4 Cleaning the beach took ages. **long**
It .......................................................................... clean the beach.
5 It's Carl's job to read the barometer every morning. **responsibility**
Carl .......................................................................... the barometer every morning.
6 There's no point trying to persuade him to recycle bottles and paper. **waste**
It .......................................................................... trying to persuade him to recycle bottles and paper.
7 We'll soon be able to see land, won't we? **sight**
We'll soon be .......................................................................... land, won't we?
8 I couldn't steer the boat because the waves were so high. **control**
I .......................................................................... the boat because the waves were so high.

## E Circle the correct word.

1 The days of Athens being one of the most polluted cities in the world have **come / gone** to an end.
2 Their office is **at / on** the fifteenth floor.
3 The government's **made / done** a complete mess of its environmental policy.
4 It's so hot, I think I'm going to **do / have** a cold shower to cool down.
5 As usual, so-called nature lovers are **making / taking** a fuss about nothing.
6 I can't believe there's anyone in the **complete / whole** world who wants the hole in the ozone layer to get any bigger.
7 It looks **like / as** a large number of species will become extinct over the next decade.
8 You used to believe there really was a pot of gold **at / in** the end of every rainbow, didn't you?

### Word patterns

## F Write one word in each gap.

**SAN FRANCISCO**

Tourists to San Francisco are rarely disappointed (**1**) ........................ the famous range of cultural and artistic attractions the city has to offer. But San Francisco is more famous (**2**) ........................ being on the San Andreas fault, a notorious source of earthquakes. Over seven hundred people died in San Francisco in the great earthquake of 1906, and more than 70 perished in another large quake in 1989. It's hard (**3**) ........................ imagine why anyone would want to live in such a dangerous area, but millions of people choose to do so. They are all familiar (**4**) ........................ the faultline, and are aware (**5**) ........................ the potential danger if there's another powerful quake. Yet nothing, it seems, will prevent people (**6**) ........................ building in San Francisco. A quick glance (**7**) ........................ a photo of the city shows a large number of modern skyscrapers, many of them completely covered (**8**) ........................ glass.

Seismologists are constantly warning residents (**9**) ........................ the possibility of 'the next big quake'. They expect it (**10**) ........................ happen sooner rather than later. But San Franciscans are not short (**11**) ........................ courage. Except (**12**) ........................ making doubly sure that their buildings are built to the highest safety standards, they carry on with their daily lives as if nothing could ever disrupt them.

### Word formation

## G Each of the words in bold is in the wrong form. Rewrite them correctly.

1 Most scientists accept that **globe** warming is a reality. ..............................
2 The weather was **freeze**. I was wearing two pairs of gloves and my fingers were still cold! ..............................
3 What can we do to protect **danger** species like the giant panda? ..............................
4 Meteorologists can forecast tomorrow's weather with incredible **accurate** these days. ..............................
5 **Develop** are planning to build a water park on the site of the old airport. ..............................
6 All our products are **environment** friendly. ..............................
7 Everyone should be **extreme** worried about the hole in the ozone layer. ..............................
8 We live in a **resident** area about twenty minutes from the town centre. ..............................
9 There's not much **likely** of environmental groups stopping the building of the new factory, is there? ..............................
10 Don't worry! This snake is completely **harm**. ..............................
11 Let's go outside and enjoy the **sunny** while it lasts. ..............................
12 What kind of **neighbour** did you grow up in? ..............................
13 I hope they don't **low** the price of petrol. ..............................
14 The **great** of solar power lies in its simplicity. ..............................
15 A number of different **pollute** in the river have caused the death of all the fish. ..............................
16 It's **nature** dark for this time of day. They didn't say there was going to be an eclipse, did they? ..............................

**A** If a line is correct, put a tick (✓) next to the number. If there is an extra word in a line, write it next to the number.

### Weather control

1 ........................ Forecasts might warn to us about threats posed by the weather,
2 ........................ but imagine if we could take out control of the weather and
3 ........................ prevent dangerous weather conditions from in the first place.
4 ........................ Controlling the weather may be the biggest technological
5 ........................ challenge we face. For a long of time, scientists have dreamed
6 ........................ of creating artificial clouds to bring rain to areas hit by drought,
7 ........................ but it's much harder to do than they expected that. The global
8 ........................ weather system is very complicated, with each part having an
9 ........................ effect taken on all the others. The scientists may feel they are
10 ........................ wasting up their time, but success could save millions of lives.

(1 mark per answer)

**B** Complete the sentences by changing the form of the word in capitals when this is necessary.

**11** The forecast said there was a high .............................. (**LIKELY**) of rain this weekend.
**12** We all know that using our cars causes .............................. (**POLLUTE**), but we still do it.
**13** Forecasting the weather .............................. (**ACCURATE**) takes a great deal of training.
**14** Litter is often a problem in .............................. (**RESIDENT**) areas.
**15** According to .............................. (**ENVIRONMENT**), we could be facing a crisis within fifty years.
**16** It was a wonderfully .............................. (**SUN**) day, so we decided to go to the beach.
**17** The giant panda is .............................. (**DANGER**) because its habitat is being destroyed.
**18** We didn't enjoy our walk because it was absolutely .............................. (**FREEZE**)!

(1 mark per answer)

**C** Complete the second sentence using the word given so that it has a similar meaning to the first sentence. Write between two and five words in each gap.

**19** Did you see the documentary about the ozone layer? **saw**
I wonder ........................................................................................ the documentary about the ozone layer.

**20** I saw a badger for a moment before it disappeared into the woods. **sight**
I ........................................................................................ a badger before it disappeared into the woods.

**21** I hope the weather gets better for our trip to the mountains this weekend. **up**
I hope ........................................................................................ for our trip to the mountains this weekend.

**22** Did you hear that the greenhouse in the park had been demolished ? **torn**
Did you hear that they ........................................................................................ the greenhouse in the park?

**23** Everything we do affects the environment in one way or another. **effect**
Everything we do ........................................................................................ the environment in one way or another.

**24** I don't really know a lot about the work that Greenpeace does. **familiar**
I ........................................................................................ the work that Greenpeace does.

**25** The builders have spoiled our garden. **mess**
The builders have ........................................................................................ our garden.

**26** Dr Trent said the problems were caused by rubbish in the streets. **put**
Dr Trent ........................................................................................ rubbish in the streets.

**27** Most people know that wasting water causes problems. **aware**
Most people ........................................................................................ the problems caused by wasting water.

(2 marks per answer)

## D Choose the correct answer.

**28** No one seems to care about the environment, ............ ?
A does he
B are they
C is he
D do they

**29** Do you know where ............ a book about insects?
A can I find
B I find
C I can find
D do I find

**30** The new law prevents people ............ their rubbish in certain areas.
A to leave
B from leaving
C of leaving
D leave

**31** Let's walk to the shops instead of taking the car, ............ ?
A shall we
B don't we
C will we
D won't we

**32** There isn't much point in trying to save electricity, ............ ?
A is it
B isn't there
C isn't it
D is there

**33** Don't drop your sweet wrapper on the floor, ............ ?
A do you
B aren't you
C will you
D won't you

**34** 'I went to the exhibition at the natural history museum.'
'Oh, yes? What ............ there?'
A saw you
B you did see
C you saw
D did you see

(1 mark per answer)

## E Choose the correct answer.

**35** There's been a ............ in Germany and a village was completely destroyed.
A flood C shower
B drizzle D smog

**36** Do you know what CFC ............ ?
A sets in C stands for
B does up D gets down

**37** Dinosaurs have been ............ for millions of years.
A endangered C threatened
B extinct D disappeared

**38** It's sunny, but there's a very cold ............ so don't forget your coat.
A blowing C wind
B air D gas

**39** If you ask me, ............ waste is a much bigger problem than ordinary household waste.
A industrial C working
B business D employer

**40** As towns grow, they tend to destroy the surrounding ............ areas.
A urban C land
B commercial D rural

**41** Jill put her wellington boots on and, as soon as it stopped raining, went out to play in the ............ .
A reservoirs C puddles
B lakes D ponds

(1 mark per answer)

**Total mark: ...... / 50**

# Reported speech / reported questions / reporting verbs

## Reported speech: tense and modal changes

- We use reported speech when we want to say what someone else said.
  eg *Jason said he was going to buy a new pair of trainers.*
- If the reporting verb is in the past (eg *said*), we usually have to change the tense of what the person actually said.

| Direct speech | Reported speech | Example |
|---|---|---|
| present simple | past simple | *'I **need** a credit card,' said Tim.* ➡ *Tim said he **needed** a credit card.* |
| present continuous | past continuous | *'I'**m taking** Lizzie shopping,' said Tim.* ➡ *Tim said he **was taking** Lizzie shopping.* |
| present perfect simple | past perfect simple | *'I'**ve bought** Tom a present,' said Tim.* ➡ *Tim said he'**d bought** Tom a present.* |
| present perfect continuous | past perfect continuous | *'I'**ve been thinking** about buying a car,' said Tim.* ➡ *Tim said he'**d been thinking** about buying a car.* |
| past simple | past perfect simple | *'I **spent** six euros,' said Tim.* ➡ *Tim said he'**d spent** six euros.* |
| past continuous | past perfect continuous | *'I **was hoping** to find a new top,' said Tim.* ➡ *Tim said he'**d been hoping** to find a new top.* |
| past perfect simple | past perfect simple (no tense change) | *'I'**d looked** everywhere for my credit card before I found it,' said Tim.* ➡ *Tim said he'**d looked** everywhere for his credit card before he found it.* |
| past perfect continuous | past perfect continuous (no tense change) | *'I'**d been looking** for that book for weeks before I found it,' said Tim.* ➡ *Tim said he'**d been looking** for that book for weeks before he found it.* |
| *am/is/are going to* | *was/were going to* | *'I'**m going to** go shopping,' said Tim.* ➡ *Tim said he **was going to** go shopping.* |
| *will* | *would* | *'I'**ll** need a credit card,' said Tim.* ➡ *Tim said he **would** need a credit card.* |
| *can* | *could* | *'I **can** take Lizzie shopping,' said Tim.* ➡ *Tim said he **could** take Lizzie shopping.* |
| *must / have to* | *had to* | *'I **must** go to the supermarket,' said Tim.* ➡ *Tim said he **had to** go to the supermarket.* |
| *may* | *might* | *'I **may** go shopping later,' said Tim.* ➡ *Tim said he **might** go shopping later.* |

**Watch out!**

- We do not need to make any changes to the verb tense or modal when we are reporting a scientific fact or when something is still true.
  ✓ *'Most banks **charge** interest,' said Tim.* ➡ *Tim said most banks **charge** interest.*

## Reported speech: pronoun and determiner changes

- With reported speech, we also usually have to change some pronouns and determiners. These changes include:

| Direct speech | Reported speech | Example |
|---|---|---|
| *my* | *his / her* | *'I've lost **my** credit card,' said Tim.* ➡ *Tim said he had lost **his** credit card.* |
| *this / that* + noun | *the / that* | *'I love **this** sweater,' said Tim.* ➡ *Tim said he loved **the / that** sweater.* |
| *this / that* + verb | *it* | *'**This** is a lovely sweater,' said Tim.* ➡ *Tim said **it** was a lovely sweater.* |
| *these / those* + noun | *the / those* | *'I love **those** sweaters,' said Tim.* ➡ *Tim said he loved **the / those** sweaters.* |
| *these / those* + verb | *they* | *'**These** are lovely sweaters,' said Tim.* ➡ *Tim said **they** were lovely sweaters.* |
| verb + *these / those* | *them* | *'I'm going to buy **these**,' said Tim.* ➡ *Tim said he was going to buy **them**.* |

## Reported speech: time and place changes

- With reported speech, we also usually have to change words and phrases connected to time and place. These changes include:

| Direct speech | Reported speech | Example |
|---|---|---|
| *here* | *there* | *'I usually shop **here**,' said Tim.* ➡ *Tim said he usually shopped **there**.* |
| *now / at the moment* | *then / at that moment* | *'I'm shopping **at the moment**,' said Tim.* ➡ *Tim said he was shopping **then / at that moment**.* |
| *tomorrow* | *the next/following day* | *'I'm going shopping **tomorrow**,' said Tim.* ➡ *Tim said he was going shopping **the next/following day**.* |
| *tonight* | *that night* | *'I'm going shopping **tonight**,' said Tim.* ➡ *Tim said he was going shopping **that night**.* |
| *next week/month/ year* | *the following week/ month/year* | *'I'm going shopping **next week**,' said Tim.* ➡ *Tim said he was going shopping **the following week**.* |
| *yesterday* | *the day before / the previous day* | *'I went shopping **yesterday**,' said Tim.* ➡ *Tim said he'd been shopping **the day before / the previous day**.* |
| *last week/month/ year* | *the week/month/year before / the previous week/month/year* | *'I went shopping **last week**,' said Tim.* ➡ *Tim said he'd been shopping **the week before / the previous week**.* |
| *ago* | *before / previously* | *'I went shopping two days **ago**,' said Tim.* ➡ *Tim said he'd been shopping two days **before / previously**.* |

**Watch out!**

- We do not need to make any changes to time words/phrases when the information is still true at the moment of speaking/writing.
  ✓ *'**I'm** going shopping **tomorrow**,' said Tim to Ben.* ➡ *Ben immediately called Lizzie and said, 'Tim said he**'s** going shopping **tomorrow**.'*

## Reported questions

- We use reported questions when we want to say what someone else asked.
  eg *Tim asked Tom if he wanted to go shopping with him.*
- We use the same rules regarding tense, pronoun and time and place word/phrase changes with reported questions as we do with reported speech.

| Direct speech | Reported speech | Example |
|---|---|---|
| *have, do, be* or modal (ie yes/no questions) | use *if* or *whether* | *'**Can you get me** an ice cream, Tom?' asked Tim.* ➡ *Tim asked Tom **if / whether he could get him** an ice cream.* |
| *what, who, which, when, where, why* and *how* | *what, who, which, when, where, why* and *how* | *'**Why did you buy these** shoes?' asked Tim.* ➡ *Tim asked **me why I had bought those** shoes.* |

**Watch out!**

- In direct questions we use the question form and question marks (*Can you ... ?*).
  In reported questions we don't use the question form or question marks (*asked if he could ...*).

## Reporting verbs

- Different reporting verbs take different grammatical patterns. Some verbs can take more than one pattern.
  ✓ **deny** (verb + noun) *Katie **denied the accusation**.*
  ✓ **deny** (verb + *that* clause) *Katie **denied (that)** she was a shoplifter.*
  ✓ **deny** (verb + *-ing* ) *Katie **denied stealing** the chocolate biscuits.*
  See page 197 for a full list of verbs and patterns.

## A Complete using the correct form of the verb in brackets.

1 Stewart said he ............................................ (**not / want**) any dessert as he was full.
2 Derek said that he and Belinda ............................................ (**see**) Adam recently.
3 When I called, Susie said she ............................................ (**give**) the dog a bath so she asked me to phone back in half an hour.
4 Marcus said he ............................................ (**try**) to find a flat for ages before he finally found one he liked.
5 Debbie says she ............................................ (**decide**) to quit her job but I don't believe her.
6 Our English teacher said that Shakespeare ............................................ (**be**) probably the greatest writer in the English language ever.
7 Richard said he and Patricia ............................................ (**be going to**) invite her parents for the weekend, but I don't know if they went or not.
8 Charlotte said last night that she really ............................................ (**love**) me, even if she doesn't always show it.
9 Ollie said to Linda that he ............................................ (**ask**) me to be his best man on Monday but in fact he asked Grant.
10 Pete told Francis he ............................................ (**bring up**) by his grandparents but in fact he hadn't at all.

## B If a word or phrase in bold is correct, put a tick (✓). If it is incorrect, rewrite it correctly.

1 On Monday, my boss said I **can** take Wednesday off, but he changed his mind today for some reason. ............................................
2 The receptionist said that if I wanted to have breakfast, I **will** have to pay extra. ............................................
3 A lot of people at school have said that Andrew **may** get the lead in the school play. ............................................
4 Colin said **he'd been planning** to ask Rich to move in with him for ages. ............................................
5 Lucy says she **would** let us know as soon as she gets the tickets. ............................................
6 Jordan said that she **has to** get up at five thirty every morning. ............................................
7 Before he got his results, Philip said that he **may** have to retake some exams, but now he knows he doesn't have to. ............................................
8 Did Mrs Morgan say why **she'd called**? ............................................
9 Paul said he **should** be here tomorrow night at about nine. ............................................
10 Dan said he **must** drive to Liverpool that night, but apparently he didn't go in the end. ............................................

## C Write one word in each gap.

1 Tonya said ...................... TV was broken and asked if she could come around to watch the football with us.
2 Your father said that ...................... old newspapers in the garage might be collector's items.
3 Dana told the kids she had no option but to punish ...................... .
4 Wendy said to thank you for the tomatoes and that ...................... were the tastiest ones she'd ever eaten.
5 Before he left, Carsen told his hosts that ...................... had been a lovely evening.
6 As soon as he saw the jeans, Bob told us that he had to have ...................... .

7 The Pattersons said that ........................ eldest daughter has just got a job working at the White House.

8 Grandpa said that ........................ picture over there was painted by his great-grandfather.

## D Complete each second sentence using the word given, so that it has a similar meaning to the first sentence. Write between two and five words in each gap.

1 'We'll be travelling round Europe next month,' said Jerry. **following**
Jerry said that ........................................................................................ be travelling round Europe.

2 'I had Evan and Christie over for dinner last night,' said Liz. **before**
Liz said that ........................................................................................ had Evan and Christie over for dinner.

3 'Daz came here two days ago and then suddenly left,' said Barry. **gone**
Barry said that Daz had ........................................................................................ and then suddenly left.

4 'We're going on our yearly diet tomorrow,' said Jessie and Sandy together. **starting**
Jessie and Sandy said together that ........................................................................................ yearly diet the next day.

5 'I can pick you two boys up from school this afternoon,' said their father to George and Kevin. **that**
George and Kevin's father told his sons ........................................................................................ up from school that afternoon.

6 'I'll buy these as they're so cheap!' said Toby. **going**
Toby said he ........................................................................................ as they were so cheap.

7 'You must study harder, Dave,' said Dave's mum. **him**
Dave's mum ........................................................................................ study harder.

8 'I think you may be coming down with flu,' Greg said to me. **thought**
Greg said that ........................................................................................ be coming down with flu.

9 'I don't know why they haven't contacted me recently,' said Tine. **been**
Tine said she didn't know why ........................................................................................ recently.

10 'Everything was different yesterday,' said Ben. **been**
Ben said everything ........................................................................................ before.

## E Write one word in each gap.

### The Excuses

The office was silent. 'So, let me get this right,' (**1**) ........................ Alison calmly. 'Not one of you is willing to donate some money towards Mr Bartlett's leaving present.' There was silence again for a moment, then Deidre (**2**) ........................ up, saying that she (**3**) ........................ love to give a donation, but unfortunately her house (**4**) ........................ being painted that week and she (**5**) ........................ not have any spare cash at all. Alec was next. He was very apologetic and said that he (**6**) ........................ meant to bring some money to work (**7**) ........................ morning, but had forgotten. Perhaps tomorrow? Betty said she (**8**) ........................ completely broke at (**9**) ........................ moment in time, and said she (**10**) ........................ not give anything until she (**11**) ........................ her pay cheque at the end of the week. Alison stared at them all. She (**12**) ........................ them how disappointed she (**13**) ........................ with all of them, and that she (**14**) ........................ remember their excuses when it was time for (**15**) ........................ to retire. She slammed the door behind her as she left the room.

## F Rewrite as reported questions, beginning with the words given.

1 'Have you had your ear pierced?'
My mum asked me if ..............................

2 'Can I meet you there at six o'clock tonight, Doug?'
Julian wanted to know whether ..............................

3 'Are you still moving to Blackpool next week?'
Fiona asked Rod and Jenny whether ..............................

4 'Does Graham have to wear a suit to work?'
I asked Mrs Daley if Graham ..............................

5 'Do you want someone to feed your cat while you're away?'
Jan asked me if ..............................

6 'Can you guess what I've given Lindsay for her birthday?'
Daisy asked Wendy if ..............................

7 'Do you love me or not, Gloria?'
Fred asked Gloria whether ..............................

8 'Will Simon be coming to the party tomorrow night'
Adrian wondered whether ..............................

9 'Tell me if you were anywhere near 34 Aylesford Street last night!'
The police officer demanded to know whether Sykes ..............................

## G Rewrite as direct questions.

1 She asked me why I was thinking of quitting the gym.
..............................

2 He asked her what the difference was between a refugee and an asylum seeker.
..............................

3 They asked us how we had got on with Peter three days before.
..............................

4 I asked them when they had last been on holiday.
..............................

5 She asked him which of them he preferred.
..............................

6 I asked you how you were going to get to Manchester tomorrow.
..............................

7 Carl asked Megan who she had been out with the weekend before.
..............................

8 Megan asked Carl what gave him the right to ask questions like that.
..............................

## H Complete using the correct form of the words in the box.

**agree • apologise • ask • claim • deny • order • refuse • state • suggest • tell**

1 If you want ............................................ me a question, put your hand up.

2 I ............................................ very clearly several times already that this government is not going to be blackmailed by terrorists.

3 The general ............................................ the soldiers to retreat, which they did as quickly as they could!

4 Isabelle, ............................................ that story about the giraffe. I love that story!

5 Glenda still ............................................ to me for losing my CD player.

6 If you ............................................ to cooperate with the police, you would have been in big trouble!

7 I'd like ............................................ waiting a few more days before we make a final decision.

8 The politician ............................................ having done anything wrong, despite the evidence against him.

9 I ............................................ to help you with your homework, not do it all for you!

10 Some thieves ............................................ to be electricity meter readers so they can gain access to people's houses.

## I Circle the extra word in each line.

### Getting a mortgage

1 Someone told to me a few months ago that getting a mortgage would be easy. How
2 wrong they were! When I first went into the bank, I asked if them how much I could
3 borrow. They refused that to answer even such a simple question, saying that I had to
4 actually find a house before they could tell me whether they would have lend me the
5 money or not. I thought this was ridiculous and so told it a white lie, saying that
6 I had been already found a house. They finally said they would lend me the money, so
7 that was great. Then the problems started. A few weeks later a friend told me that about
8 a wonderful flat that was for sale. He suggested to our buying it together because it was
9 so large and I agreed. When I went back to the bank and said so I was planning to
10 buy a flat with a friend, the bank manager denied doing that he had ever said the bank
11 would give me a mortgage and claimed that he has had looked at my finances and knew
12 I wasn't earning enough to borrow money. I begged with him to have another look at my
13 records as I knew he was wrong. Finally, he agreed me to reconsider my case and
14 eventually sent me a letter which stated that the bank would was quite happy to give me
15 a mortgage. By then, though, it was said too late as someone else had bought the flat!

# Unit 22 Vocabulary

## Money and shopping

### Topic vocabulary in contrast

see page 195 for definitions

| | | |
|---|---|---|
| economic / economical | discount / offer | till / checkout |
| receipt / bill | price / cost | products / goods |
| make / brand | change / cash | refund / exchange |
| bargain / sale | wealth / fortune | fake / plastic |

### Phrasal verbs

| | |
|---|---|
| **bank on** depend on sth happening | **give away** give free of charge; reveal sth you are trying to hide |
| **come across** find sth or meet sb by chance | **live on** use as a source of money |
| **come by** get sth, especially sth that is hard to get | **look round** examine (a place) |
| **come into** inherit | **make out** write all the necessary information on a cheque, etc |
| **do without** live without (sth you can't afford) | **make up for** provide sth good, so that sth bad seems less important |
| **get by** manage to survive (financially) | **put by** save an amount of money for the future |
| **get through** use all of; finish | **save up (for)** save money little by little (for a specific purpose) |

### Phrases and collocations

| | |
|---|---|
| **amount** | an amount of sth; in large/small/etc amounts; amount to |
| **charge** | charge sb (an amount of money); pay a charge; take charge (of sth/doing); in charge (of sth/doing) |
| **debt** | in debt (to sb); get in/into debt; clear a debt; owe sb a debt of gratitude |
| **demand** | in demand; on demand; a demand for sth |
| **enough** | have enough (of sth); have enough sth (to do); enough is enough |
| **expense** | at sb's/your own expense; go to the expense of; business expense; expense account |
| **fortune** | make/earn/win/spend a fortune; cost (you) a fortune; make your fortune |
| **increase** | an increase in sth (of a certain amount); a wage/price increase |
| **least** | at least; at the very least; last but not least; to say the least |
| **money** | make/earn/win/save/have money; spend money (on sth/doing); short of money; do sth for the money |
| **notice** | notice sb doing/do; take notice of sth; at short notice; give sb notice of |
| **profit** | make a profit (from sth) |
| **save** | save money/time; save sth for later |
| **shopping** | do the shopping; go shopping; shopping centre; window shopping |

### Word patterns

| | |
|---|---|
| **afford** to do | **forget** to do; forget doing; forget about sth/doing; forget if/whether |
| **argue** with sb; argue about sth/doing; argue that | **lend** sth to sb; lend sb sth |
| **beg** sb (for sth); beg sb to do | **pay** sb (for sth/doing); pay sth (to sb) |
| **belong** to sb/sth | **profit** from sth/doing |
| **borrow** sth (from sb) | **save** sb from sth/doing; save sth (for sth/sb) |
| **charge** sb (for sth/doing) | **spend** sth (on sth/sb/doing) |
| **demand** sth (from sb); demand that | |

### Word formation

| | | |
|---|---|---|
| **accept** acceptance, accepting, (un)acceptable, (un)acceptably | **expense** (in)expensive(ly), expenses | **poor** poorly, poverty |
| **assist** assistance, assistant | **finance** financial(ly), finances | **real** unreal, really, realise, realisation, reality, realistic(ally) |
| **day** daily, everyday | **invest** investment, investor | **value** (in)valuable, (in)valuably, valueless, valuation |
| **economy** economic, (un)economical(ly), economics, economist | **luxury** luxuries, luxurious(ly) | **wealth** wealthy |
| **end** endless(ly), ending, unending | **pay** paid, payment, payable | |

## Topic vocabulary in contrast

### A Circle the correct word.

1 My grandfather made a **wealth / fortune** by investing at the right time.
2 I think you'll find that the Microcar is really very **economic / economical** to drive.
3 I'm afraid we can only accept the return of the item if you still have the **receipt / bill**.
4 If you show this coupon at the **checkout / discount**, you'll receive a free gift.
5 I'm not keen on Justin Timberlake so I'll try to **refund / exchange** this CD for one by Blue.
6 The assistant called the manager when the note I gave her turned out to be **plastic / fake**.
7 This unbeatable special **offer / bill** is only available until the end of the week, so hurry!
8 Excuse me, but I don't suppose you have **make / change** for a fifty, do you?
9 I went back to the shop a week later, and the **price / cash** had gone up by 50%!

### B Complete the crossword.

**Across**

3 Nine out of ten shoppers who tried our washing powder preferred it to any other leading .... . (5)
6 If the .... situation continues to worsen, the government may have to take steps. (8)
7 You only paid €30 for such a gorgeous hat? That's a real .... ! (7)
9 Businesses are complaining that the .... of labour is rising. (4)
10 This is a robbery! Put all the money from the .... in this sack. Now! (4)
11 I need to find a bank because I didn't bring enough .... out with me. (4)
12 Come to Barons summer .... ! Everything is down 30%! (4)

**Down**

1 If you buy an extra battery at the same time as the digital camera, we can offer you a .... of 10%. (8)
2 Our supermarket stocks over a thousand household .... at low, low prices! (8)
4 When I checked the .... on my way out of the supermarket, I noticed that I had paid twice for the fruit. (7)
5 If you take something back to the shop, you might get a .... or be offered another item instead. (6)
7 Waiter! Do you think you could bring us the .... , please? (4)
8 There's very little heavy industry in my country, so we import a lot of .... from abroad. (5)

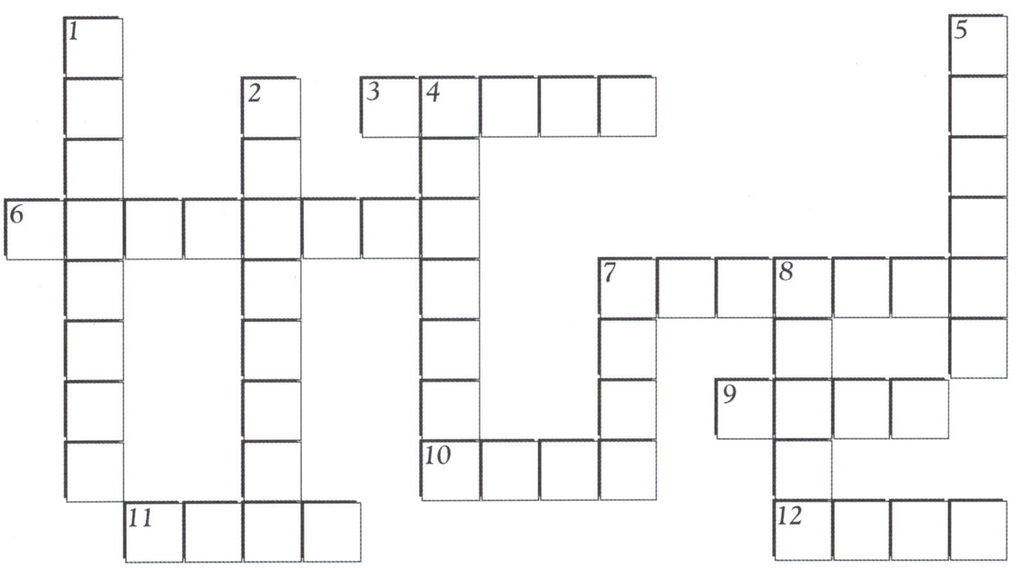

### Phrasal verbs

## C Complete using the correct form of the phrasal verbs in the box.

**look round • come by • make out • put by • get through • bank on • give away**

1 Of course I'll pay you back next week. You can .............................................. it.
2 Would you please .............................................. the cheque to Mr P. Edwards?
3 I try to .............................................. a little money each year to spend on a nice holiday.
4 We .............................................. a lot of butter in our family every week.
5 Do you fancy coming into town on Saturday to .............................................. the shops?
6 The robber couldn't explain how he .............................................. such a large amount of money when the police caught him.
7 Did you hear about the millionaire who .............................................. his entire fortune to charity?

## D Write one word in each gap.

**A lucky find**

When I was young, we always had to do (**1**) ........................ a lot of things that other kids had. We lived (**2**) ........................ my dad's wage, which wasn't much, but we managed to get (**3**) ........................ . If we needed anything, we would (**4**) ........................ up for it, but there was never very much for luxuries. Then, one day, I was helping my mum clean out my great-aunt's attic after she died when we came (**5**) ........................ my great-aunt's will! In it, she had left all her money to my mum, and my great-aunt had been very rich! We had suddenly come (**6**) ........................ a fortune! Life changed after that, I can tell you. We bought a new house and a new car and went on a great holiday to (**7**) ........................ up for all the times we hadn't been able to afford it. They say money isn't everything, but having money is a lot more fun than not having it!

### Phrases and collocations

## E Complete each second sentence using the word given, so that it has a similar meaning to the first sentence. Write between two and five words in each gap.

1 I suggest not spending all your money now so that you'll have some later. **for**
What about .................................................................................. later?
2 Did your mum gain any money when she sold her business? **profit**
Did you mum .................................................................................. when she sold her business?
3 Not many people want this type of bank account. **demand**
There is .................................................................................. this type of bank account.
4 I didn't want to owe Sue money, so I didn't borrow any. **debt**
I didn't want .................................................................................. Sue, so I didn't borrow any money.
5 You must have paid a lot of money for such a nice engagement ring, Jim! **fortune**
A nice engagement ring like that must .................................................................................., Jim!
6 Inflation has gone up by 3% this year. **increase**
There has been an .................................................................................. 3% this year.
7 You won't have any money if you keep buying CDs. **it**
You won't have any money if you keep .................................................................................. CDs.
8 Don't spend money on hiring a limousine at the airport. **expense**
Don't go .................................................................................. hiring a limousine at the airport.
9 I had to pay £50 for breaking the vase in the shop! **charged**
They .................................................................................. £50 for breaking the vase in the shop!

**10** A lot of money was stolen from the bank in the robbery. **amount**
The bank lost .................................................................................... in the robbery.

**11** I can't afford a holiday this year. **enough**
I don't have .................................................................................... on holiday this year.

**12** I succeeded through hard work, clever decisions and, finally but importantly, luck. **least**
I succeeded through hard work, clever decisions and, .................................................................... , luck.

**13** The shoplifter took a packet of crisps without the shopkeeper seeing. **notice**
The shopkeeper didn't .................................................................................... a packet of crisps.

**14** I'll go and buy what we need and you start cooking. **shopping**
I'll go and .................................................................................... and you start cooking.

### Word patterns

## F Match to make sentences.

1 I can't believe they charged me ...........
2 The old lady begged me ...........
3 I'll never forget ...........
4 My dad and my uncle always argue ...........
5 I was shocked when the bank demanded ...........
6 We really can't afford ...........
7 Debra paid the money ...........

A about the economy.
B that I pay back my loan immediately.
C learning that I had the winning ticket.
D to the girl at the desk and left.
E for using the hotel pool.
F to buy a new fridge.
G to give her some money.

## G Write one word in each gap.

**FINANCIAL CRISIS?**

Europe is heading for a financial crisis, or so some analysts believe. Although we are spending more money (**1**) ........................ luxury items and recreation than ever before, it is often money we have borrowed (**2**) ........................ a bank. Banks are willing to lend more and more money (**3**) ........................ us because they profit (**4**) ........................ it by charging us interest. We are spending money that doesn't really belong (**5**) ........................ us, and few of us save much (**6**) ........................ our old age.

### Word formation

## H Each of the words in bold is in the wrong form. Rewrite them correctly.

1 I'd really like to study **economy** at university. ........................
2 Making lots of money from gambling is a great dream, but the **real** is that most people lose everything. ........................
3 One of the biggest problems in the developing world is **poor**. ........................
4 The actress was very **expense** dressed in an outfit. ........................
5 That current affairs programme was so boring – it seemed **end**. ........................
6 You can make your **pay** at any of over 2000 cash machines around the country. ........................
7 The bank manager offered us some financial **assist** just when we needed it. ........................
8 All employees receive a **day** allowance to cover the cost of meals. ........................
9 The company is doing much better **finance** this year than last. ........................
10 There are many problems connected to being extremely **wealth**. ........................
11 I told the manager I thought the increase in prices was totally **accept**. ........................
12 I thought the painting was worth a lot of money, but it turned out to be completely **value**. ........................
13 I'd like to be able to afford the little **luxury** that make life enjoyable. ........................

**A** Use the word given in capitals at the end of each line to form a word that fits in the gap in the same line.

### Developing Countries

| | |
|---|---|
| Although too many people in the West do still live in (**1**) ............................. , on | **POOR** |
| the whole, Westerners are far more (**2**) ............................. than those who live in | **WEALTH** |
| developing countries. Things that are essential to our (**3**) ............................. lives, | **DAY** |
| and which we take for granted, such as electricity, are (**4**) ............................. to | **LUXURY** |
| millions of people around the world. Is this situation (**5**) ............................. or | **ACCEPT** |
| should the West be giving more (**6**) ............................. to developing countries? | **ASSIST** |
| Some politicians and (**7**) ............................. believe that Western financial | **ECONOMY** |
| (**8**) ............................. in developing countries would be in everyone's interest. | **INVEST** |
| As those countries get richer, they will become (**9**) ............................. trading | **VALUE** |
| partners with the West. The (**10**) ............................. is, however, that there is | **REAL** |
| an enormous amount of work to be done before people in developing | |
| countries can enjoy the kind of lives that most people lead in the West. | |

(1 mark per answer)

**B** Match to make sentences.

**11** Sharon came ............
**12** I manage to put ............
**13** You can bank ............
**14** I don't know how they can get ............
**15** If you could make ............
**16** The shop's giving ............
**17** I'm saving ............
**18** I don't know what we're going to live ............

**A** a little money by each month.
**B** out the cheque to Peardrop Limited, that would be fine.
**C** up to buy a new DVD player.
**D** into some money when her aunt died.
**E** away free software with every computer.
**F** by on such a low salary.
**G** on now I've lost my job.
**H** on house prices coming down soon.

(1 mark per answer)

**C** Complete the second sentence using the word given, so that it has a similar meaning to the first sentence. Write between two and five words.

**19** I had to pay to park in the supermarket car park! **charged**
I ........................................................................ parking in the supermarket car park!

**20** Is this credit card yours? **belong**
Does ........................................................................ you?

**21** I haven't got much money in the bank. **amount**
I've only got ........................................................................ money in the bank.

**22** Getting the car repaired was so expensive! **fortune**
It ........................................................................ to get the car repaired!

**23** Sophie demanded that the shop assistant apologise to her. **apology**
Sophie demanded ........................................................................ the shop assistant.

**24** Buying things online means I don't have to go into town so often. **saves**
Buying things online ........................................................................ to go into town so often.

**25** Don't pay attention to what Dan says; your new shoes are lovely! **notice**
Take ........................................................................ what Dan says; your new shoes are lovely!

**26** I haven't got much cash at the moment. **short**
I ........................................................................... cash at the moment.

**27** Can you lend me some money? **borrow**
Can ........................................................................... you?

(2 marks per answer)

## D Choose the correct answer.

**28** The shop assistant finally agreed ............ a full refund.
A giving me
B to give me
C give to me
D to me to give

**29** Bill asked me why ............ to go shopping with me.
A I hadn't invited him
B hadn't I invited him
C I hadn't him invited
D hadn't I him invited

**30** Ellie asked Stan ............ to look at the new catalogue.
A did he want
B do you want
C whether he wants
D if he wanted

**31** Stephen ............ me he'd bought that suit in a sale.
A said
B spoke
C told
D claimed

**32** 'What did the man say when you challenged him?'
'He said he ............ pay for the things in his bag, but I didn't believe him!'
A is going to
B has been going to
C goes to
D was going to

**33** When I last saw Carrie, she told me she ............ of buying a house, but now she's changed her mind.
A thought
B is thinking
C was thinking
D has been thinking

**34** 'What did they say when they realised you weren't a shoplifter?'
'They apologised ............ me.'
A to doubt
B they had doubted
C for doubting
D the doubt of

(1 mark per answer)

## E Choose the correct answer.

**35** This car is very ............ as it goes so far on one tank of petrol.
A financial C costly
B economical D endless

**36** I can't believe how cheap these shorts were. They were a real ............ !
A bargain C discount
B sale D offer

**37** What ............ of car does your mum drive?
A name C make
B brand D form

**38** Could you tell me who's in ............ here, please?
A charge C rule
B responsibility D organisation

**39** I paid the assistant and took the books but then stupidly left the bookshop without waiting for my ............ .
A cash C refund
B fee D change

**40** I think she ............ her fortune in the shipping industry.
A took C won
B made D saved

**41** I didn't find a new top but at ............ I got some new jeans.
A less C least
B the less D the least

(1 mark per answer)

**Total mark: ...... / 50**

# Relative clauses / participles

## Relative clauses

Relative clauses give us extra information about something/someone or identify which particular thing/person we are talking about. They are often introduced by the following words.

| Use | Example |
|---|---|
| *which* (for things and animals) | *Did you see the film* ***which*** *was on TV last night?* |
| *who* (for people, and animals when we want to give them a personality) | *Tom Davies,* ***who*** *is appearing in concert in Reading this week, is with me in the studio.* |
| *when* (for times) | *Do you remember the day* ***when*** *we met?* |
| *where* (for places) | *This is the place* ***where*** *they filmed* Citizen Kane. |
| *why* (for reasons) | *That's the reason* ***why*** *he's so popular.* |
| *whom* (for people as the object of the relative clause) | *Is that the man* ***whom*** *we saw at the cinema yesterday?* |
| *whose* (for possession) | *My next guest on the show is John Travolta,* ***whose*** *career goes back to the early seventies.* |

**Watch out!**

- When the relative pronoun (*who, which*, etc) is the subject of the relative clause, you do **not** need another subject.
  ✓ *I admire Jude Law,* ***who*** *always works hard on his films.*
  ✗ ~~*I admire Jude Law,* ***who he*** *always works hard on his films.*~~
- *Whom* is quite formal. It is natural in informal English to use *who* instead of *whom*, even when it is the object of the relative clause. After a preposition, however, we always use *whom*. Informally, we usually put the preposition at the end of the clause and use *who*.
  ✓ *Is that the man* ***who*** *we saw at the cinema yesterday?*
  ✓ *Charlie Chaplin was a comic genius* ***to whom*** *all comedians owe a great deal.*
  ✓ *Charlie Chaplin was a comic genius* ***who*** *all comedians owe a great deal* ***to****.*
- *Where* can be replaced by a preposition + *which*. Less formally, we can put the preposition at the end of the clause.
  ✓ *The theatre* ***where / in which*** *I first acted is somewhere around here.*
  ✓ *The theatre* ***which*** *I first acted* ***in*** *is somewhere around here.*
- We can do the same thing with *when*.
  ✓ *Do you know the year* ***when / in which*** *the first western was made?*
  ✓ *Do you know the year* ***which*** *the first western was made* ***in****?*

## Non-defining relative clauses

Non-defining relative clauses simply give us more information about something/someone. The sentence makes complete sense without the relative clause.

| Use | Example |
|---|---|
| To give extra information about something/someone | *Ray Watson,* ***who starred in*** **Bandits**, *is considering making a film based on the life of Einstein.* |

**Watch out!**

- Non-defining relative clauses are separated from the rest of the sentence by commas.
  ✓ Megamonsters, *which was filmed in New York, is a very disappointing film.*
- We cannot leave out the word which introduces the relative clause and we cannot use the word *that* instead.
  ✗ ~~Megamonsters, *was filmed in New York, is a very disappointing film.*~~
  ✗ ~~Megamonsters, ***that*** *was filmed in New York, is a very disappointing film.*~~
- *Which* can refer back to the whole of the sentence.
  ✓ *We finally got tickets for the concert,* ***which*** *was very lucky.*
  (It doesn't mean the concert was lucky. It means getting tickets for the concert was lucky.)

## Defining relative clauses

Defining relative clauses tell us which one of a group of things/people we are talking about. The sentence doesn't usually make complete sense without the relative clause.

| Use | Example |
|---|---|
| To tell us which one of a group of things/people we are talking about | *The book which I've read was the best of all.*<br>*The one **who** is wearing a blue shirt is Justin Timberlake, isn't it?* |

**Watch out!**

- Defining relative clauses are not separated from the rest of the sentence by commas.
  ✓ *This is the DVD which I told you about the other day.*
- We can also use *that* to introduce the relative clause.
  ✓ *This is the DVD **that** I told you about the other day.*
- We can often leave out the word which introduces the relative clause when it is the object of the clause.
  ✓ *This is the DVD I told you about the other day.*
- Notice that we do not need a preposition when we use *where* or *when*.
  ✓ *The theatre **where** I first acted is somewhere around here.*
  ✗ ~~*The theatre **where** I first acted **in** is somewhere around here.*~~
  ✓ *Do you know the year **when** the first western was made?*
  ✗ ~~*Do you know the year **when** the first western was made **in**?*~~

## Participles

Present participles end in *-ing*.
Past participles usually end in *-ed*, although there are many irregular verbs.
Perfect participles are formed using *having* + past participle.

| Use | Example |
|---|---|
| To follow prepositions and conjunctions (present and perfect participles) | *By **appearing** in that cigarette advert, he damaged his acting career.*<br>*After **playing / having played** video games all morning, I was really tired.* |
| To explain the reason for something (present and perfect participles) | ***Being** quite good looking, Ralph decided to make a career as a model.*<br>***Having seen** the film before, I knew what was going to happen.* |
| To talk about actions happening at the same time (present participles) | ***Waiting** for the show to begin, I felt really nervous.* |
| To replace some relative clauses (present and past participles) | *Imagine being the person **directing** a big budget film! (= Imagine being the person **who is directing** a big budget film!)*<br>*The person **chosen** for the part will be contacted by phone. (= The person **who is chosen** for the part will be contacted by phone.)* |
| To talk about past actions happening in sequence (perfect participles) | ***Having finished** my homework, I decided to go to the cinema.* |
| As an alternative passive form (past participles) | ***Made** to wait, the actor began to get very annoyed.* |

**Watch out!**

- You have to be careful that the participle and the rest of the sentence both refer to the same subject.
  ✓ *Watching TV, I saw a news report about Hollywood.*
  ✗ *Watching TV, a news report came on about Hollywood.*

## A Circle the correct word.

1. The minister, **which / who** was appointed just last week, made no comment on the situation.
2. Isn't that the spot **which / where** the accident happened last night?
3. The human brain, **which / who** weighs about 1400 grammes, is ten times the size of a baboon's.
4. There are several reasons **which / why** I don't want to see Michael tonight.
5. This is the office **which / where** I work.
6. The new girl in our class, **who's / whose** name is Alexandra, seems really nice.
7. The *Titanic*, **which / that** people said was unsinkable, sank on her maiden voyage.
8. All the people to **who / whom** the e-mail was sent replied.
9. April 1st, **which / when** we play tricks on people, is known as April Fools' Day.
10. Harry Hill, **who / whose** new series starts next week, is one of my favourite comedians.
11. A very popular breed of dog is the German Shepherd, **which / who** is often used as a guard dog.
12. Blackpool Tower, **which / that** was modelled on the Eiffel Tower, is a very well-known landmark.

## B If a word in bold is correct, put a tick (✓). If it is incorrect, rewrite it correctly.

1. November 5th was the day **which** Guy Fawkes tried to blow up Parliament. when
2. There were none of my favourite biscuits left when I had a cup of tea, **that** was really annoying. which
3. I've just got a new webcam **that** takes really clear pictures. ✓
4. *The Godfather* was made by Francis Ford Copolla, **who's** daughter is also a film director. whose
5. Can you think of any reason **which** Cathy should be angry with me? why
6. Here's a photo of the hotel **where** we stayed in when we were in Beijing. which
7. How do you think the first man **whom** walked on the moon felt? who
8. This is the first occasion on **which** the leaders of these two countries have met. ✓
9. He is a person for **who** very few people feel much sympathy. whom
10. The moment **which** the hero suddenly appears from behind a tree is the best moment in the whole film. when
11. I met a man **which** had a dog with only three legs. who
12. My new school, **who** I moved to about a month ago, seems like quite a friendly place. which

## C Rewrite as one sentence using a relative clause.

1. My friend, Simon, plays the guitar. He has just released a CD.
   My friend, Simon, who has just released a CD, plays the guitar.
2. Prince Charles is heir to the throne of England. His wife was Princess Diana.
   Prince Charles whose wife was Princess Diana is heir to the throne of England
3. Microsoft has a lot of power in the world of computers. That annoys some people.
   Microsoft has a lot of power in the world of computers which annoys some people
4. The euro replaced a number of national currencies. It was introduced in January 2002.
   The euro which was introduced in January 2002 replaced a number of national currencies

5 *Friends* ran for ten years. It is one of my favourite series.
Friends which is one of my favourite series, ran for ten years

6 Venus is a very hot place. It is much closer to the Sun than the Earth is.
Venus which is much closer to the Sun than the Earth is, is a very hot place

7 Cricket is popular in many countries around the world. It is played between two teams of eleven.
Cricket which is played between two teams of eleven is popular in many countries of the world

8 Parts of Buckingham Palace are open to the public. It is where the queen lives.
Parts of Buckingham Palace where the queen lives, are open to the public.

9 The greyhound is the fastest dog. It can reach speeds of over 65 kilometres an hour.
The greyhound which can reach speeds of over 65 kilometers an hour is the fastest dog

10 *1984* was written by George Orwell. His real name was Eric Blair.
1984 was written by George Orwell whose real name was Eric Blair

## D Write one word in each gap. Do not write *that* and do not leave any gaps blank.

### Find me a show that works

*by our TV reviewer, Jeremy Platt*

I'm sure there was a reason **(1)** ...why... I became a TV reviewer. Maybe it was my love of classic shows **(2)** ...which... kept me entertained as a child. Or maybe it was the presenters **(3)** ...who... seemed to promise an exciting world of glamour and showbiz. To be honest, I've watched so many shows lately **(4)** ...which... have bored me to tears that I've forgotten. Take *Kid Swap*, for example, the new show **(5)** ...which... Channel 7 hopes will revive their viewing figures. The show takes kids **(6)** ...whose... parents have had enough and swaps them with kids from other families for two weeks. The problem with this show is that I'm just not sure at **(7)** ...whom... it's aimed – parents or teenagers. Parents **(8)** ...who... watch this show will find it childish, particularly at the moment **(9)** ...when... one of the teenagers does nothing but complain. Teenage viewers **(10)** ...who... watch more than the first five minutes will soon get bored of the parents, **(11)** ...who... blame anybody but themselves for the situation. This is definitely one idea **(12)** ...which... should be put exactly where it belongs – in the bin!

## E Tick (✓) the gaps in Exercise D which could be completed using *that*. Put a cross (✗) where *that* could not be used.

| | | | |
|---|---|---|---|
| 1 ✓ | 4 ✓ | 7 ✗ | 10 ✓ |
| 2 ✓ | 5 ✓ | 8 ✓ | 11 ✗ |
| 3 ✓ | 6 ✗ | 9 ✓ | 12 ✓ |

## F Choose the correct answer.

**1** 'Who's that over there?'
'Oh, it's our new teacher, ............ just started work today.'
A that C which he
B who he D who

**2** 'Which CD did you get Marcus in the end?'
'I got him the one ............ said he really wanted to hear.'
A that C which
B who he D which he

**3** 'Who did you send a Valentine's card to?'
'I'm not telling you, but it was someone ............ name begins with "B".'
A which C whose
B who her D whose her

**4** 'Have you seen Jason Green's latest film?'
'Is that the one in ............ joins the FBI?'
A which he C whom he
B that he D which

**5** 'Why do you like Tania so much?'
'Well, she's one of the few people to ............ I can really talk.'
A which C that
B whom D who

**6** 'Why don't we go to Lionel's for dinner tonight?'
'Is that the new restaurant ............ has just opened on the other side of town?'
A which C where
B that it D which it

**7** 'Could you lend me some money?'
'I'd like you to give me one good reason ............ I should.'
A that C which
B why D who

**8** 'What do you want to do this summer?'
'I think we should go somewhere ............ has plenty of sun and sand.'
A who C when
B where D that

## G Circle the words in bold which are *not* necessary.

The number of options (**1**) **that** are available to us with (**2**) **which** to fill our leisure time is increasing all the time. While previous generations, (**3**) **who** lived before the electronic age, had musical instruments and card games (**4**) **that** they played to pass the time, we have PlayStations, computers, televisions and stereos. Although parents (**5**) **whose** teenagers spend a lot of time on these activities might worry about the effect (**6**) **which** it is having on them, for most of us they provide harmless fun, (**7**) **which** is becoming more important as life becomes more stressful. The television programmes (**8**) **which** we watch and the computer games (**9**) **that** we play all entertain us and, although there will always be people to (**10**) **whom** they seem a complete waste of time, the effect (**11**) **that** they have on society cannot be ignored. Entertainment is something (**12**) **which** we all need and, as long as we're willing to pay, there will always be someone (**13**) **who** is willing to provide it.

## H Circle the correct word or phrase.

1 Before **meeting / met** Harriet, I never knew what real love was.
2 I'm sure that after **passing / passed** your exam, you'll feel a lot better.
3 Having **finishing / finished** the letter, Peter printed it out.
4 **Looking / Looked** through the window, I saw a strange man at the door.
5 I cooked dinner and, **doing / having done** that, I sat down to watch TV.
6 **Hearing / Heard** a noise outside, Janice went to investigate.
7 **Having lost / Losing** my notes, I couldn't revise properly for the test.
8 **Having been / Being** quite intelligent, Matt hopes to get into a good university.
9 **Having missed / Missing** the start of the film, I decided not to bother watching the rest of it.
10 After **making / made** her bed, Cherie had a shower.

## I Complete the sentences so that the meaning remains the same.

1. I suddenly remembered where I'd left my keys when I was waiting for the bus.
   Waiting for the bus I suddenly remembered where I'd left my keys
2. I slipped because I was trying to run in the rain.
   Trying to run in the rain, I slipped.
3. I felt quite sorry for Tim when I saw him cry.
   Seeing Tim cry, I felt quite sorry for him
4. John was depressed because he knew he was going to fail the exam.
   Knowing that he was going to fail the exam, John was depressed
5. The reason I'm quite good at basketball is that I'm quite tall.
   Being quite tall, I'm quite good at basketball
6. Georgia didn't know any Japanese so she used a phrase book when she was there.
   Not knowing any Japanese, Georgia used a phrase book when she was there.
7. Ed can afford three holidays abroad each year because he has a lot of money.
   Having a lot of money, Ed can afford three holidays abroad every year.
8. Maria began to worry when she realised she was lost.
   Realising that she was lost, Maria began to worry

## J Tick (✓) the correct sentences. If a sentence is incorrect, rewrite it correctly.

1. Looking through the window, a plane was passing overhead.
   Looking through the window I saw a plane passing overhead
2. Realising that it was late, I ran all the way home.
   ✓
3. Having examined me, I was given a prescription by the doctor.
   Having examined me, the doctor gave me prescription
4. Turning on the television, the newsreader said there had been an explosion.
   Turning on the television, I heard the newsreader say there had been an explosion.
5. Dropping the shopping bags on the kitchen floor, Mrs Moorcroft sighed and sat down heavily.
   ✓
6. Having practised the piano, I decided to call one of my friends.
   ✓

## K If a line is correct, put a tick (✓) next to the number. If there is an extra word in a line, write it next to the number.

1 who 'Hello, viewers, and welcome to *Easy Money*, the game show who you
2 ✓ voted the best on TV! Now, remember yesterday when our current champion,
3 been Pat Barber, having been won ten thousand euros, decided to carry on? Well,
4 it she's here tonight and she's going for the star prize, which it is a brand new
5 her sports car! That's right. Having got her this far, if Pat can answer three more
6 ✓ questions correctly, then she could be driving home in this car, ladies and
7 not gentlemen. Having not seen the programme before, you will know just how
8 which difficult which it can be. I know Pat's a little nervous, but I'm sure she'll be
9 ✓ fine and there's one person for whom tonight is very special and that's Pat's
10 he husband, Frank, who he is sitting in the audience. So, let's play *Easy Money*!

## Entertainment

### Topic vocabulary in contrast

see page 195 for definitions

| | | |
|---|---|---|
| enjoy / entertain | scene / scenery / stage | novel / fiction |
| play / act / star | band / orchestra / group | comic / cartoon / comedian |
| audition / rehearsal | review / criticism | watch / see / look |
| rehearse / practise | ticket / fee | listen / hear |

### Phrasal verbs

| | |
|---|---|
| **come (a)round** happen again (for regular events) | **grow on** if sth grows on you, you start to like it more |
| **count on** rely on; trust | **let down** disappoint |
| **drop off** fall asleep | **name after** give sb or sth the same name as sb or sth else |
| **drown out** prevent a sound from being heard by making a louder noise | **put on** hold; perform (a show, play, etc) |
| **fall for** believe that a trick or joke is true | **show off** try to attract people's attention and make them admire you (usually used negatively) |
| **get along (with)** have a good relationship (with) | **take after** look or behave like an older relative |
| **go down (as)** be remembered for having done something | **take off** become successful or popular very fast |

### Phrases and collocations

| | |
|---|---|
| **fun** | have/be fun; make fun of sb |
| **funny** | find sth funny |
| **home** | make yourself at home; be/stay at home; go/get/leave home; make your way home |
| **impression** | give sb the impression; do an impression of sb; have the impression; make an impression (on sb) |
| **joke** | joke about sth/doing; joke with sb; tell/make/hear/get/understand a joke |
| **laugh** | laugh at/about sth/sb; laugh out loud; roar with laughter; have a laugh |
| **part** | take part in sth/doing; be a part of sth; part with sth; have a part (in a play, etc) |
| **party** | have/throw a party (for sb); give sb a party; go to a party; dinner/birthday/etc party |
| **play** | play a part/role (in sth); play with sth/sb; play sth; have a part/role to play (in sth); be/act/star in a play; watch/see a play |
| **queue** | join a queue; in a queue; queue up; stand/wait in a queue |
| **show** | put on a show; show appreciation (for sth/sb); show sth to sb; show sb sth; on show; steal the show; TV/radio/quiz/game show; show business |
| **silence** | in silence |
| **voice** | in a low/deep/high/etc voice; have a good/bad voice; voice an opinion (about sth) |

### Word patterns

| | |
|---|---|
| **apologise** (to sb) for sth/doing | **like** sth/doing; like to do; be like sth/doing; be like sb (to do) |
| **avoid** sth/sb/doing | **promise** to do; promise sb (sth); promise that |
| **bound** to do | **prove** to do; prove sth (to sb) |
| **deserve** sth/to do | **say** sth (to sb); say that |
| **enjoy** yourself; enjoy sth/doing | **supposed** to do |
| **happy** to do sth; happy for sb (to do sth); happy about sth/doing | **talented** at sth/doing |
| **instead** of sth/doing | |

### Word formation

| | | |
|---|---|---|
| **act** (in)active(ly), acting, actor, actress, action, (in)activity | **entertain** entertaining, entertainment, entertainer | **popular** unpopular, popularly, popularity |
| **amuse** (un)amusing(ly), amusement | **excite** (un)exciting, excited(ly), excitement | **say** saying |
| **bore** boring(ly), bored, boredom | **fame** (in)famous(ly) | **suggest** suggested, suggestive(ly), suggestion |
| **converse** conversation | **involve** (un)involved, involvement | **vary** (in)variable, (in)variably, varying, varied, various(ly), variation, variety |
| **current** currently | **perform** performing, performance, performer | |

## Topic vocabulary in contrast

### A Choose the correct answer.

1 I've got a/an ........... for the school play tomorrow. I really hope I get a main part!
A rehearsal B practice C audition D performance

2 Did you read that ........... of the new Lloyd-Rice musical? It said it was awful!
A review B criticism C report D summary

3 I'm going to stay in and ........... TV tonight.
A see B watch C look at D view

4 We really ........... ourselves at the party! Thanks so much for inviting us!
A entertained B had fun C enjoyed D occupied

5 Ellie does a/an ........... each week for the local newspaper. It's usually quite funny.
A comic B comedian C animation D cartoon

6 The water park we went to yesterday was fantastic, but the entrance ........... was a bit expensive.
A ticket B fee C charge D cost

7 *Vanilla Sky* ........... Tom Cruise, Pénelope Cruz and Cameron Diaz.
A acts B plays C stars D contains

8 When you're learning to play a musical instrument, it's important to ........... for an hour or two every day.
A rehearse B practise C perform D train

9 The play wasn't supposed to be a comedy, but everyone started laughing when some of the ........... fell over and hit one of the actors.
A scenery B scenes C stages D acts

10 Louis de Bernières' ........... *Captain Corelli's Mandolin*, which is set on the Greek island of Cephallonia during the Second World War, was an international bestseller.
A fiction B account C anecdote D novel

11 Have you ........... the joke about the guy who fell off a 20-metre-high ladder? He was fine – he fell off the bottom rung!
A listened to B overheard C heard D paid attention to

12 Being the conductor of a large ........... is an extremely demanding job. You have to make sure about a hundred musicians are playing in time.
A group B band C company D orchestra

## Phrasal verbs

### B Write one word in each gap.

**A future pop star?**

My little brother, Carl, takes (**1**) ........................ our dad in that they both like to sing. The difference is that Dad's got quite a good voice. Carl can't sing at all! This doesn't stop him, though. He's always singing. He starts as soon as he wakes up, and doesn't stop until he drops (**2**) ........................ at night. I usually get along very well (**3**) ........................ Carl, but he can be a bit annoying when he starts showing (**4**) ........................ . You can count (**5**) ........................ him to do this whenever we have guests. My mum and dad will be talking to some friends, and then suddenly the conversation will be completely drowned (**6**) ........................ by Carl singing at the top of his lungs. The other day, I told him he should be on the radio. For a second he fell (**7**) ........................ it, until I told him that that if he was on the radio, we could turn it off!

## C Complete using the correct form of the phrasal verbs in the box.

| come (a)round • go down • grow on • let down • name after • put on • take off |
|---|

1 Marlon Brando will ............................................ in history as one of the greatest actors of all time.
2 Our class is going to ............................................ a play at the end of term.
3 I didn't really like Madonna's new single when it came out, but it's starting to ............................................ me now.
4 Did you know that the sandwich is ............................................ the Earl of Sandwich?
5 The band have really ............................................ since appearing on the Video Music Awards show last month.
6 The Eurovision Song Contest is ............................................ again soon. Shall we organise a Eurovision party?
7 I felt completely ............................................ when he refused to give me his autograph. I'm never going to buy another one of his CDs!

### Phrases and collocations

## D Circle the correct word.

1 I hope you're joking **with / about** quitting your job!
2 Come in! **Make / Have** yourself at home.
3 Having taken part **in / of** several amateur karaoke competitions, Daniel was determined to get himself a recording contract.
4 Have **fun / funny** at the concert tonight, won't you?
5 What's wrong with boys playing **with / in** dolls?
6 The audience **gave / showed** their appreciation for the cast by giving them a standing ovation.
7 We're thinking of **having / giving** Dad a surprise $40^{th}$ birthday party.
8 **Voicing / Speaking** your opinion on a live TV or radio discussion programme is not as easy as it sounds.

## E Circle the extra word in each sentence.

1 What time did you get to home last night?
2 You shouldn't make the fun of Tim just because he's smaller than you.
3 A number of contemporary art installations are on the show at the moment at the Zwyborg Gallery.
4 Didn't you find out that joke funny?
5 I guess we'll have to join up the queue.
6 Everyone sat there in the silence as the comedian stumbled through his routine.
7 It's not often I laugh out loud during a movie, but *There's Something About Mary* had me roaring out with laughter the whole time.
8 I'm never going to be part with this first edition of Dickens's *Great Expectations*.
9 I have the impression of Sasha's thinking about giving up ballet classes.

### Word patterns

**F** Complete each second sentence using the word given, so that it has a similar meaning to the first sentence. Write between two and five words in each gap.

**1** Was the concert fun? **yourself**
Did ........................................................................................ the concert?

**2** I'm sure Kelly will do well in the talent contest. **bound**
Kelly ........................................................................................ well in the talent contest.

**3** Don't worry about your costume; concentrate on learning your lines! **instead**
Concentrate on learning your lines ........................................................................................ about your costume!

**4** We got there early and so we didn't have to queue. **avoid**
We managed to ........................................................................................ there early.

**5** Jason said he was sorry that he hadn't invited us to his party. **apologised**
Jason ........................................................................................ us to his party.

**6** I don't mind if you give me the money for the tickets later. **happy**
I ........................................................................................ give me the money for the tickets later.

**7** Doug isn't usually late. **like**
It ........................................................................................ be late.

**8** Sean plays the guitar very well. **talented**
Sean ........................................................................................ the guitar.

**9** You shouldn't go backstage without a pass. **supposed**
You ........................................................................................ backstage without a pass.

**10** 'I'll meet you outside the theatre at eight whatever happens,' said Dan to Kyle. **promised**
Dan ........................................................................................ outside the theatre at eight.

**11** I can't understand why he won the award for best video. **deserved**
I don't think ........................................................................................ the award for best video.

**12** In the end, it was a thoroughly enjoyable evening. **proved**
In the end, it ........................................................................................ a thoroughly enjoyable evening.

**13** I can't remember who you said had won. **say**
Who ........................................................................................ the winner?

### Word formation

**G** Complete the text by changing the form of the word in capitals.

## Reality shows

Despite the (**1**) ............................. (**SUGGEST**) by many critics that reality TV would be a very short-lived phenomenon, it is still increasing in (**2**) ............................. (**POPULAR**). Several reality shows are (**3**) ............................. (**CURRENT**) watched by millions of viewers each night, and it's clearly a form of (**4**) ............................. (**ENTERTAIN**) that's here to stay. Indeed, a number of people have become (**5**) ............................. (**FAME**) because of their (**6**) ............................. (**INVOLVE**) in reality TV shows, and have gone on to have successful careers as singers, (**7**) ............................. (**ACT**) or TV presenters. We can watch with (**8**) ............................. (**EXCITE**) each night the 'goings-on' in the house (or jungle, or bar, or school of arts). The (**9**) ............................. (**CONVERSE**) between the contestants are interesting so we don't get (**10**) ............................. , (**BORE**) and there are frequently (**11**) ............................. (**VARY**) conflicts, which provide further (**12**) ............................. (**AMUSE**). If the contestants have to give some kind of (**13**) ............................. (**PERFORM**) at the end of the week, that's even more appealing. But there's a (**14**) ............................. (**SAY**) in the TV industry: 'it's all in the editing' and this is especially true of reality shows.

**A** Use the word given in capitals at the end of each line to form a word that fits in the gap in the same line.

### My life as a clown!

| | |
|---|---|
| I've always wanted to be an (**1**) .............................. but never did anything about | **ENTERTAIN** |
| it until I lost my job last year. After a (**2**) .............................. with a friend about | **CONVERSE** |
| the (**3**) .............................. of office life, I decided not to look for another job in | **BORE** |
| management, but to earn my living from giving (**4**) .............................. at events | **PERFORM** |
| like kids' parties. So I became a clown! I'm (**5**) .............................. doing four or | **CURRENT** |
| five parties a week and I love it! I love seeing the (**6**) .............................. on the | **EXCITE** |
| kids' faces when I walk in the room. I try to have a lot of (**7**) .............................. in | **VARY** |
| my act, so I tell jokes – most of which the kids find (**8**) .............................. – and | **AMUSE** |
| bend balloons into funny animals, do impersonations of (**9**) .............................. | **FAME** |
| people and generally keep the kids (**10**) .............................. involved for an hour | **ACT** |
| or two. It's the perfect job for me! | |

(1 mark per answer)

**B** Complete the second sentence using the word given, so that it has a similar meaning to the first sentence. Write between two and five words.

**11** We didn't have a birthday party for Jake; we took him to the cinema instead. **instead**
We took Jake to the cinema for his birthday .............................................................................. a party.

**12** It doesn't surprise me that Sandra wants to live in Hollywood. **just**
It .............................................................................. want to live in Hollywood.

**13** I'm sure the audience will go wild when you come on stage. **bound**
The audience .............................................................................. wild when you come on stage.

**14** You shouldn't take food into the theatre. **supposed**
You .............................................................................. food into the theatre.

**15** At least he said he was sorry that he'd ruined my joke! **apologised**
At least he .............................................................................. my joke!

**16** My parents don't mind you staying with us after the concert. **happy**
My parents .............................................................................. stay with us after the concert.

**17** Don't tease Libby as she doesn't like it. **fun**
Don't .............................................................................. Libby as she doesn't like it.

**18** That play really affected me. **impression**
That play really .............................................................................. me.

(1 mark per answer)

**C** Write a phrasal verb in the correct form to replace the words in bold.

**19** My dad ........................ ........................ during the film, as usual! (**fell asleep**)

**20** I felt so ........................ ........................ when my parents didn't come to watch me in the school play. (**disappointed**)

**21** Although they're partners in a comedy act, apparently they don't ........................ ........................ with each other off stage. (**have a good relationship**)

**22** Let's ........................ ........................ a play at the end of term! (**perform**)

**23** Fiona ........................ ........................ her mother; they both love playing board games! (**resembles**)

**24** I told Marcie that the word 'stupid' didn't appear in the dictionary and she ...................... ...................... it! (**believed**)

**25** Laurel and Hardy will ...................... ...................... as one of the greatest double acts in comedy history. (**be remembered**)

**26** You can always ...................... ...................... Uncle Colin to cheer you up when you're feeling miserable. (**trust**)

(2 marks per answer)

## D Choose the correct answer.

**27** ........... an Oscar last year, she's now one of the most powerful movie stars in the industry.
A She won
B To win
C The winning of
D Having won

**28** 'Which cinema did you go to?' 'The one ........... they don't sell any popcorn!'
A which
B where
C whom
D who

**29** That's the actor ........... autograph I got last year!
A whose
B who
C who's
D whom

**30** ........... to change his name by his agent, John Smith became Marvo The Magnificent overnight.
A Made
B Making
C Having made
D To make

**31** The book ........... she's most famous is *Dance of the Dinosaurs*.
A in that
B to whom
C for which
D that

**32** Lyle Lovett, ........... I last saw perform over ten years ago, is on tour again.
A he who
B to whom
C who
D that

**33** And the song ........... by our listeners as their favourite of the week is *Goodbye Baby* by The Tunesmiths.
A having chosen
B chosen
C was chosen
D is chosen

**34** 'You didn't get into Harvard, did you?' 'No, and that's the reason ........... I ended up going to drama college!'
A how
B which
C for that
D why

(1 mark per answer)

## E Choose the correct answer.

**35** Could you ........... in the paper and see what's on TV tonight?
A see
B watch
C look
D examine

**36** I'm reading a ........... set in Greece during the Second World War.
A novel
B fiction
C literature
D writing

**37** Harry kept us ........... throughout the journey with his non-stop jokes.
A enjoyed
B entertained
C laughed
D pleasured

**38** I never read ........... of films as I don't trust the critics' opinions.
A reviews
B criticisms
C articles
D investigations

**39** How did your ........... go? Do you think you'll be offered the main part?
A audit
B auditorium
C audience
D audition

**40** I'd love to work in show ........... . It's so glamorous!
A industry
B business
C commerce
D trade

**41** Joe told me a joke today but I didn't ........... it at all.
A get
B bring
C fetch
D collect

**42** I didn't like this album at first but it's really starting to ........... on me now.
A grow
B raise
C develop
D increase

(1 mark per answer)

**Total mark: ...... / 50**

## Unreal past, wishes / contrast

### Unreal past

Past tenses do not always refer to past time. In some sentences and with some verbs or phrases we use a past tense to refer to the present or the future or to a general situation. These include sentences that contain:

| Structure | Example |
|---|---|
| a second conditional | *I'd buy that top if I* ***had*** *more cash on me.* |
| *suppose / what if / imagine* | *I know it's probably not going to happen but* ***suppose / imagine*** *I* ***became*** *a famous super model!*<br>*I know it's probably not going to happen but* ***what if*** *I* ***became*** *a famous super model?* |
| *would rather + you/he/she/we/ they* | ***I'd rather you didn't come*** *with me to the fashion show tomorrow.* |
| *it's (high/about) time* | ***It's (high/about) time*** *that hats* ***came*** *back in fashion.* |
| polite questions | ***Did*** *you* ***want*** *me to send you our new catalogue when it comes out?* |
| *wish / if only* | ***If only*** */ I* ***wish*** *I* ***had*** *something to wear tonight.* |

**Watch out!**

- *Suppose, what if* and *imagine* can also be followed by a present tense.
  A present tense indicates that the situation is more likely to actually happen.
  A past tense indicates that the situation is less likely to actually happen.
  ✓ *What if you* ***are*** *accepted into art college?* (more likely to happen)
  ✓ *What if you* ***were*** *accepted into art college?* (less likely to happen)

### Wishes

We use different structures with *wish / if only*, depending on exactly what we want to express.

| Use | Structure | Example |
|---|---|---|
| Expressing wishes about the present, future or generally | *wish / if only* + past simple/ continuous | *I* ***wish*** *I* ***was studying*** *history of fashion instead of biology!* |
| Expressing wishes about the past | *wish / if only* + past perfect simple/continuous | ***If only*** *I'****d known*** *Burton's was having a sale last week.* |
| Criticising other people or complaining about a situation now, in the future or generally | *wish / if only + would* | ***If only*** *Henry* ***would*** *get a haircut!* |
| Expressing hypothetical ability or permission now, in the future or generally | *wish / if only + could* | *I* ***wish*** *I* ***could*** *fit into these jeans.* |
| Expressing desires in a formal way | *wish* + full infinitive | *I* ***wish to try on*** *this ball gown.* |

**Watch out!**

- We do not usually say *If only / I wish I would …*
  ✓ ***If only / I wish I had*** *enough money to buy these shoes.*
  ✓ ***If only / I wish I could*** *afford these shoes.*
  ✗ ~~*If only / I wish I would have enough money to buy these shoes.*~~
- To express desires about the future, we often use *hope*.
  ✓ ***I hope I will*** *have enough money to buy these shoes next week.*
  ✓ ***I hope to have*** *enough money to buy these shoes next week.*
  ✗ ~~*I wish I will have enough money to buy these shoes next week.*~~

## although / though / even though

*Although*, *though* and *even though* are used to express contrast. *Even though* is more emphatic than *although* and *though*. *Though* is more informal than *although* and *even though*.

| Structure | Example |
|---|---|
| *Although / Though / Even though* + subject + verb, subject + verb | ***Although / Though / Even though*** *I wore a hat, I got sunburn.* |
| subject + verb, *although / though / even though* + subject + verb | *I got sunburn,* ***although / though / even though*** *I wore a hat.* |

**Watch out!**

- *Though* can also come at the end of a sentence.
  ✓ *I wore a hat. I got sunburn, though.*

## in spite of / despite

*In spite of* and *despite* are used to express contrast. They mean exactly the same thing and take the same grammatical structures:

| Structure | Example |
|---|---|
| *in spite of / despite* + *-ing* form, subject + verb | ***In spite of / Despite*** *wearing a hat, I got sunburn.* |
| *in spite of / despite* + *the fact (that)* + subject + verb, subject + verb | ***In spite of / Despite*** *the fact (that) I wore a hat, I got sunburn.* |
| *in spite of / despite* + noun, subject + verb | ***In spite of / Despite*** *my hat, I got sunburn.* |

**Watch out!**

- We can also put *in spite of / despite* in the middle of the sentence.
  ✓ *I got sunburn* ***in spite of / despite*** *wearing a hat.*
- We can also use the perfect *-ing* form to show that the action happened before the result.
  ✓ *I got sunburn* ***in spite of / despite having*** *worn a hat.*
- With *in spite of / despite* + *-ing* form, the subject of the main verb must also carry out the action of the *-ing* verb.
  ✗ ~~*My sunburn was terrible* ***in spite of / despite*** *wearing a hat.* (= My sunburn wore a hat!)~~

## however / nevertheless

*However* and *nevertheless* are used to express contrast. *However* is formal. *Nevertheless* is even more formal.

| |
|---|
| *The fashion show was expensive to put on.* ***However / Nevertheless****, it did make a profit.* |
| *The fashion show was expensive to put on. It did make a profit,* ***however / nevertheless****.* |
| *The fashion show was expensive to put on. It did,* ***however / nevertheless****, make a profit.* |

## while / whereas

*While* and *whereas* are used to contrast two different facts or ideas.

| Structure | Example |
|---|---|
| *while / whereas* + subject + verb, subject + verb | ***While / Whereas*** *jeans are worn by both men and women, blouses are worn only by women.* |
| subject + verb, *while / whereas* + subject + verb | *Blouses are worn only by women,* ***while / whereas*** *jeans are worn by both men and women.* |

## A Complete using the correct form of the verb in brackets.

1 Don't you think it's time you .............................................. (**tell**) Andrea the truth?
2 What if we .............................................. (**rent**) a villa by the sea for the summer?
3 I'd rather people .............................................. (**send**) me e-mails than .............................................. (**phone**) me.
4 Suppose you .............................................. (**be going to**) open a clothes shop. What kind of clothes would you stock?
5 It's time to .............................................. (**go**) now.
6 If you .............................................. (**have**) a time machine, which era would you want to go back to?
7 Shelia would come with us if she .............................................. (**not have to**) work tomorrow.
8 We'd rather you .............................................. (**not lend**) Brenda any more money – she's got to learn not to spend what she doesn't have.
9 It's high time I .............................................. (**leave**).
10 What if we .............................................. (**get**) married? Would that make you happy?

## B Each of the words or phrases in bold is incorrect. Rewrite them correctly.

1 I wish I **know** how to set the timer on this video. Where are the instructions? ..............................................
2 'If only I **listened** to Hilary,' said Warren sadly. 'Now it's too late.' ..............................................
3 I wish you **did** shut up for five minutes! ..............................................
4 If only Charlie **can** get tomorrow off work. ..............................................
5 Do you wish you **went** with Jack to the concert tomorrow night? ..............................................
6 Excuse me. I wish **speaking** with the manager of this establishment immediately. ..............................................
7 Albert wishes like anything that he **was driving** more slowly that night. ..............................................
8 I wish I **would feel** well enough to eat something. ..............................................
9 I **wish** I'll get my exam results sooner rather than later. ..............................................
10 If only you **to listen** to what your teachers tell you! ..............................................

## C Choose the correct answer.

1 It's about time you ........... thinking about setting up your own business.
A start
B have started
C started
D to start

2 I'd really rather you ........... the kids drop bits of pizza all over my new sofa.
A don't let
B aren't letting
C won't let
D didn't let

3 ........... anything particular in mind or are you just browsing?
A Did you have
B Are you having
C Can you have
D Had you had

4 I wish Karen ........... that we're not trying to interfere in her life.
A understands
B would understand
C has understood
D is going to understand

5 I'd have been able to say goodbye to Trish if only ........... to the airport in time.
A I get
B I got
C I have got
D I had got

6 Don't you sometimes wish you ........... invisible?
A could be
B would be
C will be
D are

7 Suppose we ............ we could go and live on another planet. Would you want to go?
A to hear
B hearing
C heard
D having heard

8 Do you wish ............ an official complaint?
A making
B to make
C you made
D you make

9 Adrian was ............ enough money to buy a new computer for the school.
A wishing to have raised
B wishing he will raise
C hoping to have raised
D hoping he will raise

10 Don't you wish we ............ the exam a week on Monday and not tomorrow?
A take
B will take
C would take
D were taking

## D Complete the sentences so that the meaning remains the same.

1 I don't like your criticising me all the time.
I wish ............................................................................................................
2 It's awful – Sam doesn't know how I feel about him!
If only ............................................................................................................
3 I'd love to be with you in Switzerland right now.
I wish ............................................................................................................
4 Frank regrets not taking the job when he had the chance.
Frank wishes ............................................................................................................
5 Wouldn't you like us to be standing in the middle of Times Square right now?
Don't you wish ............................................................................................................
6 It's a shame I can't play chess as well as Steve.
I wish ............................................................................................................
7 What would you do if you had a million euros?
Suppose ............................................................................................................
8 I don't really want you to smoke in here.
I'd rather ............................................................................................................
9 It's time for them to go to bed.
It's high time ............................................................................................................

## E Match to make sentences.

1 Although ............
2 Despite ............
3 Despite the ............
4 Aesop is a vegetarian, ............
5 Despite his vegetarianism, ............
6 In spite ............
7 Despite having ............
8 Aesop is a vegetarian. However, he ............
9 Aesop is a vegetarian. He does ............

A of being a vegetarian, Aesop does occasionally eat fish.
B does occasionally eat fish.
C Aesop does occasionally eat fish.
D being a vegetarian, Aesop does occasionally eat fish.
E occasionally eat fish, however.
F Aesop's a vegetarian, he does occasionally eat fish.
G been a vegetarian for years, Aesop does occasionally eat fish.
H fact that Aesop is a vegetarian, he does occasionally eat fish.
I although he does occasionally eat fish.

## F Complete using *although*, *despite*, *however* or *while*.

1 ........................ the storm, over ten thousand people took part in the marathon.
2 ........................ I wrote myself a note to remind me, I still forgot to call George tonight.
3 Most Egyptologists believe that the Sphinx is about 4000 years old. Some geologists, ........................ , argue that it must be at least 14,000 years old.
4 ........................ having taken two aspirin, I had such a bad headache that I had to go home.
5 I've never seen a UFO. ........................ , that doesn't mean that I don't believe in them.
6 There are still two million people unemployed ........................ the fact that we're in the middle of an economic boom.
7 ........................ no European country carries out capital punishment, it is widely used throughout the United States.
8 Technology has benefited humankind enormously. There are drawbacks with our reliance on technology, ........................ .
9 I couldn't find my keys ........................ searching for them everywhere.

## G Complete each second sentence using the word given, so that it has a similar meaning to the first sentence. Write between two and five words in each gap.

1 Although he was exhausted, Mike kept on climbing. **fact**
In ........................................................................ he was exhausted, Mike kept on climbing.
2 Sally had been sure she would win the music competition. She came third, however. **been**
Despite ........................................................................ would win the music competition, Sally came third.
3 Doug wasn't shortlisted for the job even though he had a great CV. **spite**
Doug wasn't shortlisted for the job ........................................................................ a great CV.
4 Planes can still take off and land but ferries have been cancelled. **whereas**
Ferries have been cancelled, ........................................................................ able to take off and land.
5 Despite having got a good degree, Sandra couldn't find a well-paid job. **even**
Sandra couldn't find a well-paid job ........................................................................ a good degree.
6 Even though he'd been robbed twice, Red still enjoyed living in the city. **having**
Red still enjoyed living in the city ........................................................................ twice.
7 It's a great film despite the plot being a little complicated. **though**
It's a great film, ........................................................................ a little complicated.
8 Despite looking everywhere, the kids failed to find the tennis ball. **although**
The kids failed to find the tennis ball ........................................................................ everywhere.
9 Pat really enjoyed the match even though she was beaten. **of**
In ........................................................................ , Pat really enjoyed the match.
10 Despite their thorough investigation of the case, the police didn't manage to catch the culprit. **investigated**
Despite ........................................................................ , the police didn't manage to catch the culprit.

**H** If a line is correct, put a tick (✓) next to the number. If there is an extra word in a line, write it next to the number.

### The school dance

1 ........................ I went to my first school dance last Saturday night and it was a disaster! If
2 ........................ only that I'd thought about what I was going to wear a bit more carefully. Although
3 ........................ being my best friend Jenny had told me it wasn't that kind of event, I'd decided
4 ........................ to look really grown-up and wear a dress and high-heeled shoes. When I got
5 ........................ there, I looked totally ridiculous and some people started laughing. Despite of
6 ........................ this slight setback, I thought I'd hit the dance floor. If I could have survive that,
7 ........................ I could survive anything. But even though that went wrong! One of my heels
8 ........................ snapped – even if though my shoes were brand new – and I had to carry them
9 ........................ to the side of the room. It was very embarrassing! Still, despite the disastrous
10 ........................ start was, Craig Fielding came up to me and asked me if I wanted to go out with
him next Saturday. Of course I said no, but he is cute! We'll see what happens!

**I** Write one word in each gap.

## On the Catwalk

with Sunny Magenta

**(1)** ........................ the fact that I try to be as upbeat as possible in this column, I have to say Milan has disappointed me. If only we **(2)** ........................ possibly go back to the glory days of fashion (ie last year) when skirts were short and pink was the new black. Pink is still in this year, interestingly enough. **(3)** ........................ , it's only being used in accessories such as buckles, belts, braces and beads. Brown – the must-have colour of the season – has never been my favourite colour, **(4)** ........................ I have to say that Belinda Steven's all-brown paper beachwear was quite stunning. That's in **(5)** ........................ of its complete impracticality, of course. It really is **(6)** ........................ time that haute couture entered the real world just a tiny bit. I know it's supposed to be more art than clothing, but suppose you actually **(7)** ........................ the mistake of buying a Diego Fernandez baseball cap made of candle wax. That's one walk in the sunshine and five thousand euros is dripping down your face! Now, I'm not saying I wish I **(8)** ........................ stayed back in dull and grey London – the after-show parties were tremendous, as always. But I do hope that next season I **(9)** ........................ be able to report that the fashion world's got a grip on itself once more, and then – **(10)** ........................ though none of us will ever be able to afford any of the items I describe in this column – at least we'll have something to dream about once more.

# Unit 26 Vocabulary

## Fashion and design

### Topic vocabulary in contrast

see page 196 for definitions

| | | |
|---|---|---|
| put on / wear | cloth / clothing | look / appearance |
| costume / suit | blouse / top | supply / produce |
| dye / paint | design / manufacture | glimpse / glance |
| fit / suit / match | current / new / modern | average / everyday |

### Phrasal verbs

| | |
|---|---|
| **catch on** become popular or fashionable | **line up** get/put into lines |
| **do away with** get rid of | **pop in(to)** visit quickly or for a short time |
| **draw up** create (plans, etc) | **show (a)round** take sb on a tour of a place |
| **dress up** put on fancy or unusual clothes | **take off** remove (a piece of clothing) |
| **go over** repeat or think about again in order to understand completely | **tear up** rip into pieces |
| **grow out of** develop from; become too big for | **try on** put on (a piece of clothing) to see how it looks and whether it fits |
| **hand down** give something valuable to your children or grandchildren, usually when you die | **wear out** become old and unusable |

### Phrases and collocations

| | |
|---|---|
| **art** | work of art; modern art; art gallery; art exhibition |
| **clothes** | put on/try on/wear/take off clothes; clothes line; clothes peg; best clothes |
| **combination** | in combination with; combination of |
| **compliment** | pay sb a compliment; compliment sb on sth |
| **example** | be/set an example; an example of; for example; follow an/sb's example |
| **fashion** | in fashion; be/go out of fashion; follow fashion; fashion model/show |
| **hair** | cut/brush sb's hair; have/get a new hairdo/hairstyle; have a haircut; let your hair down |
| **make-up** | put on/apply/wear/take off make-up |
| **pattern** | follow a pattern; a checked/striped/plain pattern |
| **style** | in style; be/go out of style; do sth/go somewhere in style; have style |
| **taste** | have/show good/bad taste (in sth); in good/bad taste |
| **tendency** | have a tendency to do |
| **trend** | a trend in sth; follow/set a trend |

### Word patterns

| | |
|---|---|
| **advise** sb to do; advise sb that; advise sb on/about sth; advise (sb) against sth/doing | **proud** of sth/sb/doing; proud to do |
| **anxious** about sth/doing; anxious to do | **refer** to sth; refer sb to sth |
| **criticise** sb (for sth/doing) | **seem** to be; it seems that |
| **insist** on sth/doing; insist that | **stare** at sth/sb |
| **plenty** of sth; plenty more sth; plenty to do | **use** sth (for sth/doing); use sth to do |
| **prepare** (sb) for sth; prepare to do | **useful** for sth/doing; useful to sb |

### Word formation

| | | |
|---|---|---|
| **advertise** advertisement, ad(vert), advertising, advertiser | **enthuse** (un)enthusiastic(ally), enthusiasm, enthusiast | **similar** dissimilar(ly), similarity |
| **attract** (un)attractive(ly), attraction | **expect** (un)expected(ly), expectation, expectancy | **style** (un)stylish(ly), stylist, stylishness |
| **beauty** beautiful(ly) | **fashion** (un)fashionable, (un)fashionably | **succeed** success, (un)successful(ly) |
| **decide** decision, (in)decisive(ly), undecided | **like** alike, dislike, unlike, likeness, (un)likeable, liking | **use** usage, useful(ly), useless(ly), user, (un)usable |
| **desire** (un)desirable | **produce** product, producer, production, (un)productive(ly) | |

### Topic vocabulary in contrast

## A Complete using the correct form of the words in the box.

| |
|---|
| **current • glimpse • fit • clothing • match • look • glance modern • suit • new • appearance • cloth** |

1 If you care about your ........................ too much, people might start to think you're vain.
2 It's quite a nice skirt, but I don't think it really ........................ my shoes.
3 My mum always looks quite ........................ and tries to keep up with the latest fashions.
4 The ancient Romans wore items of ........................ quite different from today's fashions.
5 As I went into the designer's office, I caught a ........................ of her drawings before she hurriedly put them away.
6 I know long skirts were in last year, but the ........................ fashion is to wear them quite short.
7 I've got to buy some ........................ shoes for the wedding on Saturday.
8 I didn't get the coat in the end because it didn't ........................ me under the arms.
9 The shirt is so expensive because it's made out of a special ........................ that has gold in it.
10 I don't think this jumper ........................ you because you've got blue eyes and pale skin.
11 The designer ........................ at my designs and told me that they needed more work.
12 Long dresses and high heels is quite a good ........................ for you.

## B Circle the correct word.

1 Do you think the **average / everyday** person is interested in fashion?
2 I wish Dad would get a new **costume / suit** to wear for his job interview.
3 I've got red hair, so I never **put on / wear** red clothes or I'd look silly.
4 John got a really cool **blouse / top** in town yesterday with Eminem on it.
5 India **supplies / produces** the world with cheap clothes.
6 I'm going to get my nails **dyed / painted** tomorrow.
7 During the **design / manufacture** of the clothes, lasers are used to cut the material accurately.
8 Which **costume / suit** do you think I should wear to the fancy-dress party – the cowboy or the vampire?

### Phrasal verbs

## C Write one word in each gap.

## Anti-fashion

*by Lisa Wilkinson*

If you ask me, it's high time they (**1**) ........................ away with fashion. I've had enough of it. Just when I think I've finally got it right, I pop (**2**) ........................ a clothes shop to find that they've changed all the rules! One minute it's cool to wear brand new expensive stuff, and the next you have to take all that (**3**) ........................ and wear clothes that look as if they've been handed (**4**) ........................ by your grandma. You can't win! Well, I've torn (**5**) ........................ my fashion magazines and adopted anti-fashion. It's an idea that has grown (**6**) ........................ of frustration and, to be honest, a lack of money to spend on yet another dress that I only wear once.

I started by drawing (**7**) ........................ a plan. I decided to line all my clothes (**8**) ........................ together, try them all (**9**) ........................ and give to charity anything that either didn't fit or suit me. Then, I wouldn't buy any more new clothes until something wore (**10**) ........................ . I went (**11**) ........................ my plan again, and knew that I would have to be tough with myself. After all, I'd spent a lot of money on some of that stuff. Finally, I plucked up the courage to do it. It felt a little bit like being a child again, dressing (**12**) ........................ in your mum's clothes, but I also felt a great sense of freedom.

That was a year ago and, although I occasionally see something and think, 'Oh, that's gorgeous!', I haven't bought any clothes. If you ever come over to my house and I (**13**) ........................ you around my bedroom, you might see last season's fashions, but you'll also see a woman who feels free. And that's anti-fashion. Do you think it'll catch (**14**) ........................ ?

### Phrases and collocations

## D Choose the correct answer.

1 I don't like ........... on clothes in shops because I don't want people to see me in something that doesn't suit me.
A putting B trying C wearing D handing

2 I'm not sure a green skirt ........... combination with a blue top is such a good idea.
A on B at C in D for

3 Everyone complimented Kitty ........... her new outfit.
A on B to C in D from

4 I think some modern designs are more like ........... of art.
A makes B works C objects D jobs

5 I wish people didn't ........... a tendency to follow fashion without thinking about what suits them personally.
A do B make C get D have

6 I don't think T-shirts and jeans will ever go ........... of style, do you?
A away B out C off D down

7 Make sure you ........... your make-up with a soft brush, like this one.
A apply B construct C decorate D dress

8 If you wear that shirt with the ........... pattern, you'll look like a chessboard!
A plain B striped C shiny D checked

9 You always seem to look so formal. If only you would ........... your hair down!
A get B set C put D let

10 The latest trend ........... footwear is to wear very simple, traditional shoes.
A of B on C in D from

11 My sister and I share the same taste ........... clothes and we wear each other's things all the time.
A in B of C for D on

12 Why can't you ........... Edgar's example and wear a tie to work?
A set B make C follow D do

13 My dad asked me whether his clothes were ........... fashion and I said they were – about twenty years ago!
A in B from C on D of

### Word patterns

## E Write one word in each gap.

1 It was Lia's first job as a model and she was quite anxious ........................ it.
2 Bill seems ........................ have had his hair done differently.
3 I couldn't help staring ........................ the man in the restaurant who was wearing a kilt.
4 Before starting my design, I referred ........................ some books of past designs to give me inspiration.
5 Plenty ........................ fashion designers have been successful in spite of not having any formal training in fashion.
6 I asked the shop assistant to advise me ........................ my choice of shoe.
7 Many fashion journalists criticised the actress ........................ arriving at the Oscars in a second-hand dress.
8 The supermodel insisted ........................ having a star on her dressing room door.
9 These days, most designers use a computer ........................ visualise their designs before they make any clothes.
10 Visiting fashion shows can be quite useful ........................ picking up new ideas.

## F Complete using the correct form of the verb in brackets.

1 I was very proud ............................................... (**see**) my designs up there on the catwalk.
2 My teacher advised me ............................................... (**study**) fashion at university, despite my parents' objections.
3 To be a model, you have to be prepared ............................................... (**work**) very long hours.
4 Mario knew that there was still plenty ............................................... (**do**) before his first fashion show.
5 I managed to chat to Charlie and she advised me against ............................................... (**become**) a model.
6 Westwood's designs didn't seem ............................................... (**be**) as interesting as the ones she produced last year.
7 When I first started as a fashion photographer, I was anxious ............................................... (**please**) everyone.
8 My teacher advised me ............................................... (**forget**) about becoming a fashion model and concentrate on my studies instead.

**Word formation**

## G Use the word given in capitals at the end of each line to form a word that fits in the gap in the same line.

### VISIT TO A FASHION SHOW

| | |
|---|---|
| I was really (**1**) .............................. about my first visit to a fashion show. I had | **ENTHUSE** |
| always loved fashion but had only ever seen models in (**2**) .............................. on | **ADVERTISE** |
| TV. Finally, I was going to see a real show! I got out my most (**3**) .............................. | **FASHION** |
| clothes. I wanted to look as (**4**) .............................. as the models. I don't know if I | **STYLE** |
| was completely (**5**) .............................. , but I never had much money to spend on | **SUCCESS** |
| clothes and I felt (**6**) .............................. , which is the main thing. When we got | **ATTRACT** |
| there, it was fantastic! There were so many (**7**) .............................. women! The show | **BEAUTY** |
| started and imagine my surprise when, completely (**8**) .............................. , the first | **EXPECT** |
| model was wearing clothes just like I was! Everyone saw the (**9**) .............................. | **SIMILAR** |
| and a couple of people asked me who my (**10**) .............................. was! Amazing! | **STYLE** |

## H Complete the sentences by changing the form of the word in capitals when this is necessary.

1 This designer's clothes are really quite ........................ (**LIKE**) anything I've ever seen before.
2 His clothes are very ........................ (**DESIRE**) and they sell for thousands of dollars.
3 I couldn't decide which hat to get, but then again I've always been quite ........................ (**DECIDE**).
4 We went on a school trip to a clothes factory and saw some of the ........................ (**PRODUCE**) process.
5 I'm afraid I'm completely ........................ (**USE**) when it comes to making my own clothes.
6 I don't ........................ (**LIKE**) this season's fashion – I just don't think it suits me personally, that's all.
7 These dresses are ........................ (**BEAUTY**) made – just feel the quality!
8 I'm still ........................ (**DECIDE**) about whether to go to the fashion show next week or not.

## A Write one word in each gap.

### Does what we wear matter?

In spite of there (**1**) ........................ some truth in the expression 'Never judge a book by its cover', which reminds us that appearances can be deceptive, there (**2**) ........................ to be far more truth in the expression 'You never get a second chance to make a first impression'. There are plenty (**3**) ........................ examples of people who have insisted (**4**) ........................ expressing their individuality through their clothing and have suffered for it.

If you are going to wear outrageous clothes, you've got to be prepared (**5**) ........................ the reaction of others. That reaction may not be positive. You may be stared (**6**) ........................ , criticised (**7**) ........................ wearing something unusual, or even insulted. On the other hand, you may be complimented (**8**) ........................ your style. Location and situation are very important. At a job interview, for (**9**) ........................ , you should probably be more anxious (**10**) ........................ please your potential employers than interested in showing off the latest fashions.

(1 mark per answer)

## B Complete the sentences by changing the form of the word in capitals when this is necessary.

**11** Tracy works as a .............................. (**STYLE**) for a large modelling agency.

**12** There's a .............................. (**SIMILAR**) between the fashions of the 1980s and the 1960s.

**13** I think you should lower your .............................. (**EXPECT**) a little; it's not easy to become a supermodel, you know.

**14** Let me know when you make a .............................. (**DECIDE**) about what to wear for the wedding.

**15** Fashion critics have greeted the new clothing line with .............................. (**ENTHUSE**).

**16** The factory has increased .............................. (**PRODUCE**) of its shoes in an attempt to keep up with demand.

**17** That necklace is .............................. (**BEAUTY**)!

**18** All our clothes are designed for men and women .............................. (**LIKE**).

(1 mark per answer)

## C Complete the second sentence using the word given, so that it has a similar meaning to the first sentence. Write between two and five words.

**19** You should get some new sunglasses. **about**
It .............................................................................. some new sunglasses.

**20** I hate it when you wear that silly tie! **wish**
I .............................................................................. wear that silly tie!

**21** Janice regrets wearing such formal clothes to the party. **had**
Janice .............................................................................. such formal clothes to the party.

**22** I bought the suit although it was second-hand. **despite**
I bought the suit .............................................................................. second-hand.

**23** It's a shame I can't make it to the sales this weekend! **only**
If .............................................................................. make it to the sales this weekend!

**24** In spite of my begging her for hours, Carol refused to lend me her new jacket. **though**
Carol refused to lend me her new jacket ........................................................................... for hours.

**25** I don't want you to buy exactly the same trainers as I've got. **rather**
I ........................................................................... buy exactly the same trainers as I've got.

**26** I can't go to the party as I don't have anything to wear! **something**
I'd go to the party ........................................................................... to wear!

**27** Despite being a grandmother, Edna still tries to dress fashionably. **fact**
In spite ........................................................................... is a grandmother, Edna still tries to dress fashionably.

(2 marks per answer)

## D Match to make sentences.

**28** I'm just going to pop ...........
**29** I've grown ...........
**30** I'd like to try ...........
**31** I never thought that skirts for men would catch ...........
**32** We all lined ...........
**33** I'd take ...........
**34** Let's all dress ...........

**A** on that jacket you've got hanging in the window.
**B** off my shoes but I think my feet smell!
**C** into that new boutique for a few minutes.
**D** up and they took our measurements.
**E** up for the Halloween party!
**F** out of these shoes so my mum's going to get me some new ones.
**G** on, but they have!

(1 mark per answer)

## E Choose the correct answer.

**35** Could you wipe the table with a damp ........... , please?
A clothe C cloth
B clothing D clothes

**36** I've decided to ........... my hair green for the party!
A dye C sketch
B paint D draw

**37** That top doesn't ........... me; it's just not my style.
A fit C match
B suit D go with

**38** That's the most incredible ........... of art I've ever seen!
A job C brand
B creation D work

**39** Jeans and T-shirts will never go out of ........... .
A trend C fashion
B image D tendency

**40** I need a funny ........... for the fancy-dress party. Any ideas?
A dress C suit
B uniform D costume

**41** Tim forgot to use clothes ........... and all his clean clothes fell off the line into the mud!
A pegs C hooks
B clips D pins

(1 mark per answer)

**Total mark: ...... / 50**

# Inversions / possessives

## Inversions with negative adverbial words and phrases

When we put some negative adverbial words and phrases at the beginning of a sentence for emphasis, the subject and the verb 'invert'. This means we use the question form of the verb, even though the sentence is not a question. Inversions are quite formal and are not usually used in conversation.

**Form** negative adverbial word/phrase + question form
***No sooner had I accepted*** *the job than they told me I had to work weekends.*

| Negative adverbial | Example |
|---|---|
| *Never* | ***Never have I worked*** *so hard in all my life.* |
| *Rarely* | ***Rarely have I worked*** *so hard in all my life.* |
| *Seldom* | ***Seldom have I worked*** *so hard in all my life.* |
| *No sooner (... than)* | ***No sooner had Matt started*** *work* ***than*** *he resigned.* |
| *Hardly (... when)* | ***Hardly had Matt started*** *work* ***when*** *he resigned.* |
| *Not only (... but also/too)* | ***Not only were you*** *late for work,* ***but*** *you had* ***also*** *forgotten the report.* |
| *Under no circumstances* | ***Under no circumstances are employees allowed*** *to leave the building without permission.* |
| *At no time/point* | ***At no time/point was I told*** *what the job involved.* |
| *Little* | ***Little did I realise*** *that I would become managing director just two years later.* |
| *Not until* | ***Not until the next day did I hear*** *that I had got the job.* |
| *Only* | ***Only at the end of the interview did I think*** *I had a chance of getting the job.* |

**Watch out!**

- *Little* is used with verbs of thought (*realise, know, suspect,* etc) and means *'I did not realise/etc at all ...'.*
  ✓ ***Little did I know*** *how things were going to turn out.*
  (= I did not know at all how things were going to turn out.)
- With *not until* and *only*, you have to be careful about which verb to invert.
  ✓ ***Not until I had finished*** *my homework* ***was I allowed*** *to go out.*
  ✗ ~~***Not until had I finished*** *my homework* ***I was allowed*** *to go out.*~~
  ✓ ***Only when I had finished*** *my homework* ***was I allowed*** *to go out.*
  ✗ ~~***Only when had I finished*** *my homework* ***I was allowed*** *to go out.*~~

## Other inversions

| Use | Example |
|---|---|
| In short answers and other similar structures using *so, neither* and *nor* | *'I'm a plumber.'*<br>*'Really?* ***So am I!****'*<br>*My sister doesn't like getting ready for work, and* ***neither do I / nor do I****.* |
| After *as, so* and *such* | *The manager was nervous about the director's visit,* ***as were the rest of the staff****.*<br>***So late was it*** *that there was no one in the office.*<br>***Such a hot day was it*** *that no one wanted to work.* |
| In conditional sentences | ***Were our staff*** *better trained, we might make a larger profit.* (= If our staff were better trained ...)<br>***Had I known*** *about the vacancy, I would have applied.* (= If I had known ...) |

**Watch out!**

- Remember that *'So am/do/have I'* is used to agree with a positive statement and *'Neither/Nor am/do/have I'* is used to agree with a negative statement.
  ✓ *'I really like my job.'* ***'So do I.'***
  ✓ *'I really don't like my job.'* ***'Neither do I / Nor do I.'***

## Possessive 's and s'

We can show possession by using 's and s'.

| Use | Example |
|---|---|
| We use 's with singular nouns, including names, and with irregular plurals which do not end in -s. | *That's the manager**'s** car, over there.*<br>*We are still waiting for Sarah**'s** decision about who to take on.*<br>*I think that women**'s** rights should be protected by law.* |
| We just add an apostrophe to regular plural nouns ending in -s. | *The worker**s'** pay was increased by ten percent.* |
| We use 's or s' in some time expressions. | *After an hour**'s** wait, I finally got to see the manager.*<br>*I'll be at the factory in about ten minute**s'** time.* |
| We usually use 's or s' with people (or groups composed of people) and animals. For other things, we normally use *of the/my/*etc. | *Is this John**'s** briefcase?*<br>*We held a meeting to discuss the company**'s** finances.*<br>*The vet had a close look at the cat**'s** paw.*<br>*The technician had a close look at the back **of my** computer.*<br>(not *...at my computer's back*) |

**Watch out!**

- With singular names ending in -s, some people use 's and some people just add an apostrophe. They are both correct, although using 's is more common.
  ✓ *The report is on Charles**'s** computer in the office.*
  ✓ *The report is on Charles**'** computer in the office.*
- With plural names ending in -s, we just add an apostrophe, as with other plurals.
  ✓ *The Smiths**'** business eventually closed down.*
- With phrases, the possessive 's and s' must go at the end of the whole phrase.
  ✓ *Tom, Dick and Harry**'s** office is around here somewhere.*
  ✗ ~~*Tom**'s**, Dick**'s** and Harry**'s** office is around here somewhere.*~~
  ✓ *The President of France**'s** visit to England will be good for business.*
  ✗ ~~*The President**'s** of France visit to England will be good for business.*~~

## Possessive determiners and pronouns

| Structure | Example |
|---|---|
| Possessive determiners *(my, your, his, her, its, our, their)* come before a noun and show possession | *I'm really excited about **my** new job.*<br>*Are you looking forward to meeting **your** new boss?* |
| Possessive pronouns *(mine, yours, his, hers, ours, yours, theirs)* are used instead of a noun | *My new job is great. How about **yours**?* (= ...your job)<br>*Our business is doing quite well, but I hear Simon and Julie are having problems with **theirs**.* (= ...their business) |
| Possessive pronouns can also be used after *of* to show possession | *She's a colleague of **mine**.* (= ...one of my colleagues)<br>*Are they customers of **yours**?* |

**Watch out!**

- A common mistake to be avoided is using a possessive pronoun instead of a possessive determiner or using a determiner instead of a pronoun.
  ✓ *I don't really get on so well with **my** boss.*
  ✗ ~~*I don't really get on so well with **mine** boss.*~~
  ✓ *I know your job is dangerous, but did Frank and Jenny tell you about **theirs**?*
  ✗ ~~*I know your job is dangerous, but did Frank and Jenny tell you about **their**?*~~
- Remember that there are no apostrophes in possessive pronouns.
  ✗ ~~*I know your job is dangerous, but did Frank and Jenny tell you about **their's**?*~~
- Don't get confused between *its* (possessive determiner, without an apostrophe) and *it's* (contraction for *it is* or *it has*, with an apostrophe).
  ✓ *Our company is hoping to increase **its** share of the market.*
  ✗ ~~*Our company is hoping to increase **it's** share of the market.*~~

## A Write *when* or *than* in each gap.

1 Hardly had we started ........................ the fire alarm went.
2 No sooner had we set off ........................ my brother needed the toilet.
3 No sooner were the animals caught ........................ they escaped again.
4 Hardly had I closed my eyes ........................ I dropped off to sleep.
5 No sooner do I do the washing ........................ there's another pile to be done.
6 Hardly were we in position ........................ the bomb went off.

## B Choose the correct answer.

1 No sooner ........... down than the phone rang.
A I had sat B do I sit
C had I sat D was I sitting

2 Never ........... a greater day in the history of mankind.
A did there be B was there
C there was D there has been

3 At no time ........... that he was the killer.
A I didn't suspect B was I suspect
C I had suspected D did I suspect

4 Little ........... that I knew his secret.
A did John know B John did know
C was John know D John knew

5 Not until ........... her did I realise how beautiful she was.
A I saw B did I see
C was I saw D saw I

6 Not only ........... my keys, I've lost my wallet, too.
A I have lost B are I lost
C I did lose D have I lost

7 Rarely ........... about the environment enough to give up their car.
A do people care B people care
C are people care D care people

8 Only when ........... may vehicles cross the train tracks.
A is the green light on
B the green light is on
C did the green light be on
D on is the green light

9 Seldom ........... such a rude person!
A have I met B I have met
C did I met D am I meeting

10 Only after doing his chores ........... to go to meet his friends.
A Jason was allowed
B did Jason allow
C was allowed Jason
D was Jason allowed

## C If a word or phrase in bold is correct, put a tick (✓). If it is incorrect, rewrite it correctly.

1 Hardly **Tom had opened** the door when the dog ran out into the street.
..................................................
2 Only when **I read** the book did I realise why it was so special. ..................................................
3 Not only **you passed** the exam, but you also got an A! ..................................................
4 Not until **do I see** Greg next week will I know whether he got the job.
..................................................
5 No sooner **had we found** our seats than the film began. ..................................................
6 At no point while the race is taking place **members of the public are not allowed** onto the track. ..................................................
7 Under no circumstances **do the equipment to be used** without supervision.
..................................................

8 Little **I thought** that one day my best friend would become prime minister.
..................................................

9 Never **did I be** so pleased to see someone else succeed. ..................................................

10 Hardly **I had put** the baby to bed when she started crying. ..................................................

## D Complete using the correct form of the words in brackets.

### Hacker!

No sooner (**1**) .................................................. (**I** / **start**) working at Taylforth Nielsen, the computer company, than I realised it was the perfect opportunity for my hobby: hacking! Don't get me wrong. At no point (**2**) .................................................. (**I** / **have**) ever stolen anything. I do it for the challenge. Not only (**3**) .................................................. (**I** / **like**) proving I can do it, but sometimes (**4**) .................................................. (**it** / **help**) a company to build a better security system. Rarely (**5**) .................................................. (**they** / **see**) it like that, of course. I decided I would see if I could break into the Grand Bank system. Little (**6**) .................................................. (**I** / **realise**) what was waiting for me.

The second day of working there, hardly (**7**) .................................................. (**everyone else** / **leave**) when I started to try simple passwords. Seldom (**8**) .................................................. (**this** / **is**) enough, though. You usually have to work much harder than that. Not until midnight (**9**) .................................................. (**I** / **get**) access to the Grand Bank system. Hardly (**10**) .................................................. (**I** / **have**) time to look around the system when the door to my office flew open and three men rushed in. Only when (**11**) .................................................. (**they** / **show**) me their ID (**12**) .................................................. (**I** / **realise**) that it was the police. They had been expecting something like this and had traced my computer! Not only (**13**) .................................................. (**I** / **be fired**), but (**14**) .................................................. (**they** / **keep**) all my computer records, too. Maybe it's time to find another hobby.

## E Complete the sentences so that the meaning remains the same.

1 Photographs are not permitted under any circumstances.
Under ..................................................................................................................

2 We've never faced such a serious problem as this.
Never ..................................................................................................................

3 I only realised it was Vanessa when she removed her hat.
Only ..................................................................................................................

4 The audience didn't laugh at any point during the show.
At ..................................................................................................................

5 As soon as Patrick had finished the e-mail, he sent it.
No ..................................................................................................................

6 It wasn't clear who was going to win the match until the last few minutes.
Not ..................................................................................................................

7 Dennis passed his driving test and had an accident almost immediately afterwards.
Hardly ..................................................................................................................

8 I didn't learn the result of the match until I read the evening paper.
Only ..........................................................................................................................................

9 The president will not resign under any circumstances.
Under ........................................................................................................................................

10 The accused showed no emotion at any time during the trial.
At ..............................................................................................................................................

## F Complete the responses to these statements.

1 'I wish I had more money.'
'So ................................'
2 'We never seem to spend much time together in my family.'
'Neither ........................'
3 'I'm not going to Jacob's party next Sunday.'
'Nor ...............................'
4 'I didn't do my homework last night.'
'Nor ...............................'
5 'I'll be on holiday this time next week.'
'So .................................'
6 'I had no idea Chris was getting married.'
'Neither ..........................'
7 'I should really get more exercise.'
'So ..................................'

## G Write one word in each gap.

1 Such a long way ........................ it that we decided to go by train.
2 So badly ........................ I play chess that I almost never agree to have a game.
3 Pupils are expected to behave politely, as ........................ members of staff.
4 So tired ........................ I that I decided to lie down for a while.
5 Such a threat to society ........................ you that I have no choice but to send you to prison.
6 So cold ........................ it last winter that all our pipes froze.
7 Calculators are banned from the examining room, as ........................ dictionaries and handheld computers.
8 I have been having very strange dreams lately, as ........................ my twin sister.

## H Form possessives from the nouns given.

1 (Billy): ..................Billy's.................. opinion
2 (my mum): ............................................. cooking
3 (our next door neighbours): ............................................. cat
4 (George the Fifth): ............................................. daughter
5 (people): ............................................. prejudices
6 (the Greenes): ............................................. holiday home
7 (women): ............................................. magazines
8 (the boss): ............................................. car

9 (Jack and Jill): ............................................... wedding
10 (students): ............................................... marks
11 (children): ............................................... shoes
12 (politicians): ............................................... promises

## I Complete using the words in the box. Use each word only once.

**her • hers • it's • its • mine • my • their • theirs**

1 Tell Michelle that it's my problem, not ........................ .
2 Are you sure this isn't ........................ , because it looks just like the one I was given for Christmas?
3 Thanks for the offer, but I think I'll use ........................ own money.
4 I saw a wallet on the floor next to a couple of tourists and asked them if it was ........................ .
5 Remind your sister to bring ........................ book to the lesson tomorrow.
6 I'm not sure, but I think ........................ Mark's bag, isn't it?
7 Could you make sure that your children don't leave ........................ toys in my garden again, please?
8 What secrets do you think the Moon might be hiding within ........................ craters?

## J If a line is correct, put a tick (✓) next to the number. If there is an extra word in a line, write it next to the number.

### FIRST DAY AT WORK

1 ........................ Well, Trisha, that's my own first day at my new job out of the way. I wasn't
2 ........................ sure what to expect, but it turned out okay. My manager was really nice,
3 ........................ much nicer than yours boss sounds from your letter. No sooner had I arrived
4 ........................ at work than did he made me a cup of tea! It was a really pleasant surprise.
5 ........................ Not only did he do that, but he was also kind enough to explain to me how
6 ........................ everything worked. The office is really modern and its comfortable. The other
7 ........................ people all have their own desks, but mine desk still hasn't been delivered, so
8 ........................ I am sharing with someone else for now. Little did I not realise when I took
9 ........................ the job that I was going to enjoy it so much. I have finally found a job that I
10 ........................ am happy in, and so will you have, I'm sure. Hope tomorrow's as much fun!

# Unit 28 Vocabulary

## Work and business

### Topic vocabulary in contrast

see page 197 for definitions

| | | |
|---|---|---|
| employer / employee / staff | wage(s) / salary / pay | overtime / promotion / pension |
| job / work / career | commute / deliver | company / firm / business |
| earn / win / gain | retire / resign | union / charity |
| raise / rise | fire / sack / make redundant | |

### Phrasal verbs

| | |
|---|---|
| **back out** decide not to do sth you agreed to do | **set up** start (a business, organisation, etc) |
| **bring out** produce and start to sell a new product | **slow down** decrease speed |
| **close down** stop operating (for companies) | **speed up** increase speed |
| **see through (to)** continue (or help to continue) to the end of sth unpleasant or difficult | **stand in for** do sb's job for them while they are not available |
| **see to** deal with | **take on** start to employ; accept (work or responsibility) |
| **set to** start doing sth in a determined or enthusiastic way | **take over** take control of (a business, etc) |
| **set out** start working on sth in order to achieve an aim | **turn down** not accept (an offer, request, etc) |

### Phrases and collocations

| | |
|---|---|
| **agreement** | come to/reach (an) agreement (on/about sth); in agreement (on/about/with) sth |
| **arrangement** | make an arrangement (with/for sb) (to do); have an arrangement (with sb) (to do) |
| **business** | do business (with sb); in business; go somewhere on business; business trip; small business; big business |
| **complaint** | have/make a complaint (about sth) (to sb); letter of complaint (to sb) (about sth) |
| **day** | have/take/get a day off; day job; day trip; day by day; the other/next day |
| **decision** | make/take a decision (to do sth); come to/reach/make a decision (about sth) |
| **duty** | do one's duty; a sense of duty; on/off duty; have a duty to sb/to do |
| **effort** | make an effort (to do); put effort into sth/doing |
| **experience** | have an experience; have/gain/get experience in/of sth/doing; experienced in/at sth/doing |
| **hold** | put/keep sb on hold; hold on (to sth); hold sth |
| **interest** | have/take/express an interest in sth/doing; in your interest to do; earn/get/pay interest |
| **interview** | have/go to/attend an interview; job interview |
| **job** | do a job; have a job (to do); apply for a job; take/get a job; in a job |
| **work** | do some work; have work to do; go to work; at work; work hard; out of work; place of work |

### Word patterns

| | |
|---|---|
| **absent** from sth | **good** for sb (to do sth); good at sth/doing; good to sb |
| **apply** for sth; apply in writing | **qualify** as/in sth |
| **attach** sth to sth; attached to sth | **responsible** for sth/doing |
| **begin** doing/to do/sth; begin by doing | **specialise** in sth/doing |
| **depend** on sth/sb | **train** to do |
| **experienced** in/at sth/doing | **work** as/at/in sth; work for sb |

### Word formation

| | | |
|---|---|---|
| **add** added, addition, additional(ly) | **help** (un)helpful(ly), helpless(ly), helping, helper | **profession** (un)professional(ly) |
| **apply** (in)applicable, applied, applicant, application | **industry** industrial(ly), industrious(ly) | **qualify** (un)qualified, qualifying, qualification |
| **commerce** commercial(ly) | **machine** machinery | **responsible** irresponsible, (ir)responsibly, (ir)responsibility |
| **dedicate** dedicated, dedication | **manage** managing, management, manager | **supervise** supervision, supervisor |
| **effect** (in)effective(ly) | **meet** met, meeting | **work** working, (un)workable, worker, works |
| **employ** (un)employed, (un)employable, (un)employment, employer, employee | | |

### Topic vocabulary in contrast

## A Circle the correct word.

1 The **charity / union** I'm a member of is calling for a nationwide strike next week.
2 It's **company / firm / business** policy not to allow the use of phones for personal calls during working hours.
3 The recent **raise / rise** in the cost of petrol has affected loads of small businesses round here.
4 In some professions, you have to **retire / resign** when you're 60 or 65 years old.
5 My grandfather gets a **pension / promotion** from the company he used to work for.
6 Not only did we all have to work **overtime / promotion** this weekend, but we didn't get paid for it!
7 Have you had any news about that **work / job / career** you applied for yet?
8 The starting **salary / wage** is €20 000 per year.
9 You'll get a weekly **pay / wage** of about €300 before deductions.
10 She became a full-time member of **employees / staff / employers** last year.

## B Complete using the correct form of the words in the box.

| **commute • deliver • earn • gain • make • sack • win** |
|---|

1 No sooner had Denzil .................................... the lottery than he decided to quit his job.
2 How long does it take you to .................................... to work every day?
3 How much does a state school teacher .................................... each year?
4 Over a hundred workers were .................................... redundant when the factory closed.
5 Our next-door neighbour was .................................... for stealing company property.
6 Does your local supermarket .................................... ?
7 Rarely have I .................................... so much valuable experience in such a short space of time.

### Phrasal verbs

## C Write one word in each gap.

**It just takes hard work and commitment**
Entrepreneur Jane Dickson describes how she got started

I was working as an IT Manager for a small publishing company (in fact, I was standing **(1)** .................. for the actual manager while she was away on maternity leave) when the company was taken **(2)** .................. by a large multinational media organisation. It was in the depths of the recession, and initially our new owners promised to see our small company **(3)** .................. the hard times. Things got worse, though, and they finally backed **(4)** .................. of their agreement. Our company closed **(5)** .................. . We were all made redundant – it was horrible!
I wasn't sure what I wanted to do next. I **(6)** .................. down several offers of work as I didn't want to rush into anything. Then, one day, I woke up and thought: 'I'm going to set **(7)** .................. my own business!' At first it was tough. I had to **(8)** .................. to everything myself – I was the only employee! – but I set **(9)** .................. it with dedication and refused to give up, whatever happened. Over the last five years, as the company's grown, I've taken **(10)** .................. more and more staff. Dickson's now employs over five hundred people! I set **(11)** .................. to be successful, and I've managed it. I feel very lucky, although, to be honest, luck has nothing to do with it. It just takes hard work and commitment. I don't feel satisfied yet, though. We're bringing **(12)** .................. new products all the time, and I want to continue doing that. I also want to speed **(13)** .................. our production process to make it more efficient. I'm not planning to slow **(14)** .................. any time soon!

### Phrases and collocations

## D Match to make sentences.

1 I put a lot of effort ..........
2 They've made their decision ..........
3 It's not in your interest to ..........
4 The secretary's kept me ..........
5 I don't know why you didn't apply ..........
6 I think we're all in agreement ..........
7 Dean's been out ..........
8 The shop hasn't been in ..........
9 I'm glad you're finally taking an interest ..........
10 Jason lives fairly near his place of ..........

A on hold for ages.
B about who's going to get promoted.
C of work for over two months now.
D into writing this report.
E business long.
F in your work.
G for that position.
H accept a pay cut.
I work, doesn't he?
J on this, aren't we?

## E Write one word in each gap.

1 Maybe you should write a letter .................... complaint to the manager.
2 When was the last time you had a .................... off?
3 Hardly had the police officer come .................... duty when he had to respond to an emergency.
4 My dad's .................... work at the moment, I'm afraid. Can you call back later?
5 I am available to .................... an interview at your convenience.
6 He's been .................... this job for over thirty years.
7 Our company .................... a lot of business with Altech Industries.
8 Sol's made an arrangement .................... the wholesalers to deliver more frequently in future.
9 June's got several years' experience .................... dealing with young children.

### Word patterns

## F Choose the correct answer.

1 Who is responsible .......... dealing with complaints?
A with B for C in D at

2 We began .......... looking round for advertising agencies which had experience of our market.
A to B with C by D at

3 The covering letter wasn't attached .......... the CV.
A to B with C from D by

4 Don't you think you should apply for the job .......... writing?
A with B for C at D in

5 I was only absent .......... the office for a few minutes!
A for B from C in D about

6 Success in this industry depends a lot .......... luck!
A with B from C at D on

## G Cross out the incorrect word in each sentence and write the correct word on the line.

1 Sadie's quite good ~~in~~ typing. ...at...
2 Jimmy qualified ~~at~~ a doctor a couple of years ago. ...as...
3 You need to be good at languages to work ~~in~~ an interpreter. ...as...
4 It'll be good ~~that~~ Rudy to get some work experience this summer. ...for...
5 You've got to be experienced ~~from~~ dealing with difficult authors if you want to be an editor. ...in...
6 We specialise ~~for~~ manufacturing tiles for the building industry. ...in...
7 After qualifying ~~as~~ veterinary medicine, she decided to move to Yorkshire. ...in...
8 I'd love to work ~~as~~ advertising. ...in...
9 Joanne is training ~~for~~ become a trapeze artist at the moment! ...to...

### Word formation

## H Complete the sentences by changing the form of the word in capitals when this is necessary.

1 All the heavy ...machines... (**MACHINE**) in the factory has been manufactured on site.
2 Al is a manager at the local water ...work... (**WORK**).
3 An ...industrial... (**INDUSTRY**) dispute is threatening to delay production of the new car.
4 We work under close ...supervision... (**SUPERVISE**), so there's not much opportunity for initiative.
5 Farm ...workers... (**WORK**) in Belgium have accepted a 5% pay increase.
6 There'll be an ...additional... (**ADD**) charge of €30 for delivery.
7 Supersonic planes have never been a ...commercial... (**COMMERCE**) success.
8 We couldn't have built this new train without the ...dedication... (**DEDICATE**) and expertise of the entire workforce.
9 The plan is completely ...working... (**WORK**). Let's just forget it!

## I Complete the text by changing the form of the word in brackets.

### Job fairs

Although a certain percentage of graduates will still be (**1**) ...employed... (**employ**) six months after leaving university, the majority will have found (**2**) ...employment... (**employ**) by then. Many of these will even have been offered a job while at university, as a result of visiting a job fair.

Job fairs are held at many universities each year. Companies come along to advertise jobs, which are usually in (**3**) ...management... (**manage**), and the career structures and benefit packages that go with them. Job fairs are an (**4**) ...effective... (**effect**) way for undergraduates to find out what kind of job they might be interested in.

If you go to a job fair, dress (**5**) ...professional... (**profession**). Don't wear jeans and a T-shirt. Wear a suit! You don't want to look (**6**) ...responsibility... (**responsible**) when you have your first (**7**) ...meeting... (**meet**) with your potential (**8**) ...employer... (**employ**). If you're interested in a job on offer, you may have to fill out an (**9**) ...application... (**apply**) form, so it's (**10**) ...helping... (**help**) to take along relevant information with you. You'll also need proof of all your (**11**) ...qualifications... (**qualify**), so don't forget to take photocopies of all your certificates with you.

# Review 14

## A Write one word in each gap.

Dear Sir,

I would like to (**1**) ........................ a complaint about an article that appeared in your newspaper last week. In the article, entitled 'Why they are (**2**) ........................ of work', the writer suggested that the unemployed were responsible (**3**) ........................ their own situation. If the writer had (**4**) ........................ their job properly and (**5**) ........................ a little effort to speak to local unemployed people, they might have realised that this is not the case.

Let me begin (**6**) ........................ saying that most unemployed people want to work. They apply (**7**) ........................ jobs and (**8**) ........................ a great deal of effort into changing their situation.

The truth is that local businesses are simply not taking (**9**) ........................ new staff. The government is to blame for the way in which economic growth has (**10**) ........................ down, making life difficult for many businesses.

I look forward to reading a more balanced article in the future.

Yours faithfully,

Rebecca Winterson

(1 mark per answer)

## B Complete the sentences by changing the form of the word in capitals when this is necessary.

**11** Dave left the office keys in a pub and he was sacked for being so .............................. **(RESPONSIBLE)**.

**12** 'Leave it to me. I'll find a solution,' the manager said, .............................. **(HELP)**.

**13** All .............................. **(APPLY)** are asked to send their CV to Mrs Simpson in the Personnel Department.

**14** My job is to .............................. **(SUPERVISE)** the telesales workers.

**15** Carol has worked for us for over twenty years with great loyalty and .............................. **(DEDICATE)**.

**16** All our .............................. **(EMPLOY)** receive four weeks paid holiday per year.

**17** The managing director didn't think the suggestion would ever be .............................. **(WORK)**, so we had to think of another solution.

**18** It seems that Mr Jones lied about his .............................. **(QUALIFY)** on his application form.

(1 mark per answer)

## C Complete the second sentence using the word given, so that it has a similar meaning to the first sentence. Write between two and five words.

**19** Yuri qualified and then immediately found a really good job. **than**
No ........................................................................... he found a really good job.

**20** Women don't often get promoted in some industries. **do**
Rarely ........................................................................... in some industries.

**21** I never realised that Tony was the head of Fizzyco. **realise**
Little ........................................................................... that Tony was the head of Fizzyco.

**22** I didn't know about the meeting until Tracy rang. **did**
Not until ........................................................................................ about the meeting.

**23** I think you will benefit from getting a new job. **good**
I think it will be ........................................................................................ a new job.

**24** The two companies finally agreed the deal. **reached**
The two companies finally ........................................................................................ the deal.

**25** Customers of the bank are never allowed into the basement area. **circumstances**
Under ........................................................................................ customers of the bank allowed into the basement area.

**26** I didn't think of a good answer to the interviewer's question until later. **did**
Only ........................................................................................ a good answer to the interviewer's question.

**27** It was such a boring job that no one wanted to do it. **was**
Such ........................................................................................ that no one wanted to do it.

(2 marks per answer)

## D Match to make sentences.

**28** Ironworks Limited has closed ...........
**29** Henry asked Janet to stand ...........
**30** Mr Carter asked me to see ...........
**31** I heard that Bigburger have taken ...........
**32** Roger says he never set ...........
**33** Apparently, Fatfoods are bringing ...........
**34** I'm thinking of setting ...........

**A** in for him while he went into town.
**B** out a new flavour of ice cream next month.
**C** over Cookright and plan to close some branches.
**D** down and 400 people have lost their jobs.
**E** up a business selling my own jewellery.
**F** to the orders while he spoke to a customer.
**G** out to become a millionaire – it just happened!

(1 mark per answer)

## E Choose the correct answer.

**35** The ........... for this position starts at thirty thousand euros per year.
A wage C salary
B payment D tip

**36** After working at the same factory for thirty years, my grandfather was looking forward to his ........... .
A overtime C charity
B pension D allowance

**37** Some people ........... to London every day from as far away as Leeds.
A connect C correspond
B commute D commence

**38** Most governments tax people on the amount they ........... each year.
A win C earn
B gain D benefit

**39** Shelley disagreed with the board's decision and so she ........... and went to work for another company.
A retired C sacked
B fired D resigned

**40** When the factory closed, over a hundred people were ........... redundant.
A done C given
B taken D made

**41** Here at Weatherby's, we provide all our ........... members, from senior management down, with regular training.
A staff C crowd
B crew D firm

(1 mark per answer)

**Total mark: ...... / 50**

# Progress Test 2

## A Choose the correct answer.

### Criticism

It can (**1**) ........... a long time to become successful in your chosen field, however (**2**) ........... you are. One thing you have to be (**3**) ........... of is that you will face criticism along the way. The world is (**4**) ........... of people who would rather say something negative than positive. If you've made up your (**5**) ........... to achieve a certain goal, such as writing a novel, don't let the negative criticism of others (**6**) ........... you from reaching your target, and let constructive criticism have a positive (**7**) ........... on your work. If someone says you're totally (**8**) ........... in talent, ignore them. That's negative criticism. If, however, someone (**9**) ........... you to revise your work and gives you good reasons for doing so, you should (**10**) ........... their suggestions carefully. There are many film stars who were once out of (**11**) ........... . There are many famous novelists who made a complete (**12**) ........... of their first novel – or who didn't, but had to (**13**) ........... approaching hundreds of publishers before they could get it published. Being successful does (**14**) ........... on luck, to a certain extent. But things are more likely to (**15**) ........... well if you persevere and stay positive.

| | | | | |
|---|---|---|---|---|
| **1** | A be | B have | C take | D do |
| **2** | A talented | B invested | C mixed | D workable |
| **3** | A alert | B clever | C intelligent | D aware |
| **4** | A overflowing | B full | C filled | D packed |
| **5** | A mind | B brain | C thought | D idea |
| **6** | A cease | B remove | C avoid | D prevent |
| **7** | A outcome | B result | C effect | D consequence |
| **8** | A lacking | B short | C missing | D absent |
| **9** | A suggests | B advises | C proposes | D explains |
| **10** | A think | B consider | C look round | D take |
| **11** | A career | B business | C job | D work |
| **12** | A mess | B rubbish | C trash | D garbage |
| **13** | A put off | B bank on | C keep on | D drop in on |
| **14** | A require | B need | C depend | D trust |
| **15** | A turn out | B come into | C deal with | D sail through |

(1 mark per answer)

## B Choose the correct answer.

**16** Ed ........... at the clock and realised he was late for the meeting.
A glimpsed B observed
C glanced D watched

**17** What's the entrance ........... for the outdoor music festival?
A ticket B fare
C price D fee

**18** Don't ........... the potatoes in oil; that's so unhealthy!
A fry B boil
C bake D grill

**19** I want to take these jeans back because they're too small but I can't find the ........... anywhere.
A recipe B receipt
C receiver D reception

**20** I'll pick up a ........... on the way home and then we won't have to cook.
A takeaway B fast food
C delivery D microwave

**21** Certificates provide proof of your ........... .
A qualities B diplomas
C qualifications D ambitions

**22** Living on a farm in the middle of nowhere, ours is about the most ............ lifestyle you can have!
A urban B suburban
C rural D municipal

**23** Will was made ............ three months ago and is still looking for a job.
A sacked B fired
C retired D redundant

**24** The audience showed their ............ by giving the orchestra a standing ovation.
A entertainment B review
C appreciation D audition

**25** I'd like to speak to the person in ............, please.
A charge B responsibility
C duty D obligation

(1 mark per answer)

## C Write one word in each gap.

### Lack of faith in politicians

A recent survey has shown an increase (**26**) ........................ distrust for politicians. They've always been regarded (**27**) ........................ untrustworthy, but now politicians are below estate agents and even lawyers in the public's estimations. A majority of the people who (**28**) ........................ questioned associate politicians (**29**) ........................ an inability to tell (**30**) ........................ truth. They believe they're responsible (**31**) ........................ most of the country's problems, have had a negative effect (**32**) ........................ the country's image abroad, refuse to face (**33**) ........................ to the fact that they cause more problems than they solve and never apologise for (**34**) ........................ made mistakes. The survey, (**35**) ........................ was carried out over a period of three months, also shows that politicians often give the impression (**36**) ........................ being arrogant and only (**37**) ........................ note of what the electorate believe at election time. In (**38**) ........................ of these disturbing findings, people do not believe that (**39**) ........................ is no point in voting at elections. (**40**) ........................ least politicians can take some comfort in that!

(1 mark per answer)

## D Choose the correct answer.

**41** All the flowers for the wedding ............ tomorrow.
A will be delivering
B will have delivered by
C are going to deliver
D are going to be delivered

**42** 'Have we still got lots of time?'
'No, ............ get a move on. We're going to be late.'
A you'd rather
B you'd better
C you'd prefer to
D you'd be better off

**43** Let's order a pizza, ............ we?
A should
B will
C shall
D could

**44** I wonder ............ mind watching this bag for me for a moment.
A would you
B you would
C if would you
D whether you would

**45** The prime minister denied ............ anything wrong.
A to do
B having done
C to have done
D to be doing

**46** The woman ............ purse I found has offered to give me a reward.
A whose
B who
C who's
D to whom

**47** It's high time they ........... .
A are leaving
B were leaving
C have to leave
D had been leaving

**48** I wish you ........... so rude to Rosalind last night.
A weren't
B wouldn't be
C hadn't been
D haven't been

**49** Despite ........... president, she felt totally powerless.
A being
B she was
C of having been
D to be

**50** We ........... today and I got into trouble because I hadn't done it.
A had checked our homework
B had our homework checked
C were checked our homework
D have checking our homework

(1 mark per answer)

## E Match to make sentences. There is one extra letter you will not use.

**51** When we can afford it, we're going to do ...........
**52** Jason's thinking of dropping ...........
**53** When the factory closed ...........
**54** They should do away ...........
**55** Let me take you out to dinner to make ...........
**56** I never wanted a mortgage but I'm coming ...........
**57** Cynthia's decided to set ...........

**A** round to the idea now.
**B** up for forgetting your birthday.
**C** with cheque books now that everyone has a credit card.
**D** up the attic and turn it into a spare bedroom.
**E** out of college and getting a job.
**F** out a number of different products in the next few months.
**G** up a small business producing temporary tattoos.
**H** down, hundreds of workers lost their jobs.

(1 mark per answer)

## F Complete the second sentence using the word given, so that it has a similar meaning to the first sentence. Write between two and five words in each gap.

**58** I don't think George has the ability to climb right to the top of that mountain! **capable**
I don't think George ........................................ right to the top of that mountain!

**59** Joanne, do you know anything about Chaos Theory? **familiar**
Joanne, ........................................ Chaos Theory?

**60** You shouldn't have bought presents for all of us. **expense**
You shouldn't have ........................................ buying presents for all of us.

**61** Charles often phones up TV stations to complain about programmes. **tendency**
Charles ........................................ up TV stations to complain about programmes.

**62** Alice seemed tired to me. **impression**
Alice ........................................ she was tired.

**63** Taking out a private pension scheme will benefit you. **interest**
It is ........................................ out a private pension scheme.

**64** I understand what Gary was saying but I don't agree with him. **point**
I can ........................................ but I don't agree with him.

**65** They won't allow passengers to get off the train at the next station. **prevent**
They're going ........................................................................... off the train at the next station.

**66** I want you to try really hard to pass this exam! **effort**
I want you to ........................................................................... to pass this exam!

(2 marks per answer)

**G** If a line is correct, put a tick (✓) next to the number. If there is an extra word in a line, write it next to the number.

## The secret of comedy

| | | |
|---|---|---|
| **67** | ......................... | It is often been said that the secret of good comedy is timing. |
| **68** | ......................... | As a comedian myself, I know that's not true. The secret |
| **69** | ......................... | of good comedy is to be funny! I was told that a joke the other |
| **70** | ......................... | day about a man whose his dog has no nose. When asked how |
| **71** | ......................... | it smells, the man replies 'Terrible!'. The problem here is |
| **72** | ......................... | that, despite of the joke having a fairly clever punchline, |
| **73** | ......................... | no one finds it a funny. However good your timing is, you |
| **74** | ......................... | can't make out people laugh at that joke. I get my friends to |
| **75** | ......................... | tell to me jokes all the time. If I've never heard them before, |
| **76** | ......................... | and if they make me laugh it out loud, I might consider |
| **77** | ......................... | using them in my comedy act. I am like jokes that rely on |
| **78** | ......................... | word play (even though the joke was about the noseless dog |
| **79** | ......................... | is rubbish!). 'My mum's from Cuba and my dad's from |
| **80** | ......................... | Iceland so I guess that makes me up an ice cube.' Now |
| **81** | ......................... | that's a classic joke however you tell it. Comedy is made not |
| | | just to do with timing! |

(1 mark per answer)

**H** Use the word given in capitals at the end of each line to form a word that fits in the gap in the same line.

## Memories and reality

| | |
|---|---|
| There is a well-known (**82**) .............................. ,'School days are the best days | **SAY** |
| of your life.' No (**83**) .............................. at school ever believes it though, and | **STUDY** |
| by the time you realise it's true, it's too late! It's when you're worried | |
| about your (**84**) .............................. situation and are beginning to hate the | **FINANCE** |
| (**85**) .............................. of working in an office or factory every day that you | **BORE** |
| look back fondly on the (**86**) .............................. times you had at school. When | **EXCITE** |
| you're still at school you often focus on the negatives, like having to | |
| pay (**87**) .............................. during a tedious chemistry lesson, being punished | **ATTEND** |
| for bad (**88**) .............................. (when you didn't do anything wrong anyway) | **BEHAVE** |
| or feeling (**89**) .............................. in an exam because you don't know any of the | **HELP** |
| answers (and, in fact, had completely (**90**) .............................. the questions too!). | **UNDERSTAND** |
| But it's quite (**91**) .............................. to complain about things and then have | **ACCEPT** |
| great memories afterwards. Just have a good time at the time as well! | |

(1 mark per answer)

**Total mark: ...... / 100**

| Bare infinitive | Past simple | Past participle |
|---|---|---|
| arise | arose | arisen |
| awake | awoke | awoken |
| be | was, were | been |
| bear | bore | borne |
| beat | beat | beaten |
| become | became | become |
| begin | began | begun |
| bend | bent | bent |
| bind | bound | bound |
| bite | bit | bitten |
| bleed | bled | bled |
| blow | blew | blown |
| break | broke | broken |
| bring | brought | brought |
| build | built | built |
| burn | burnt / burned | burnt / burned |
| burst | burst | burst |
| buy | bought | bought |
| catch | caught | caught |
| choose | chose | chosen |
| come | came | come |
| cost | cost | cost |
| creep | crept | crept |
| cut | cut | cut |
| deal | dealt | dealt |
| dig | dug | dug |
| do | did | done |
| draw | drew | drawn |
| dream | dreamt / dreamed | dreamt / dreamed |
| drink | drank | drunk |
| drive | drove | driven |
| eat | ate | eaten |
| fall | fell | fallen |
| feed | fed | fed |
| feel | felt | felt |
| fight | fought | fought |
| find | found | found |
| fly | flew | flown |
| forbid | forbad(e) | forbidden |
| forget | forgot | forgotten |
| forgive | forgave | forgiven |
| freeze | froze | frozen |
| get | got | got / gotten |
| give | gave | given |
| go | went | gone / been |
| grind | ground | ground |
| grow | grew | grown |
| hang | hung / hanged | hung / hanged |
| have | had | had |
| hear | heard | heard |
| hide | hid | hidden |
| hit | hit | hit |
| hold | held | held |
| hurt | hurt | hurt |
| keep | kept | kept |
| kneel | knelt | knelt |
| know | knew | known |
| lay | laid | laid |
| lead | led | led |
| learn | learnt / learned | learnt / learned |
| leave | left | left |
| lend | lent | lent |
| let | let | let |
| lie | lay | lain |

| Bare infinitive | Past simple | Past participle |
|---|---|---|
| light | lit | lit |
| lose | lost | lost |
| make | made | made |
| mean | meant | meant |
| meet | met | met |
| pay | paid | paid |
| put | put | put |
| quit | quit | quit |
| read | read | read |
| ride | rode | ridden |
| ring | rang | rung |
| rise | rose | risen |
| run | ran | run |
| say | said | said |
| see | saw | seen |
| seek | sought | sought |
| sell | sold | sold |
| send | sent | sent |
| set | set | set |
| sew | sewed | sewn |
| shake | shook | shaken |
| shine | shone | shone |
| shoot | shot | shot |
| show | showed | shown |
| shrink | shrank | shrunk |
| shut | shut | shut |
| sing | sang | sung |
| sit | sat | sat |
| sleep | slept | slept |
| slide | slid | slid |
| smell | smelt / smelled | smelt / smelled |
| speak | spoke | spoken |
| speed | sped / speeded | sped / speeded |
| spend | spent | spent |
| spill | spilt / spilled | spilt / spilled |
| spin | span / spun | spun |
| spit | spat | spat |
| split | split | split |
| spread | spread | spread |
| spring | sprang | sprung |
| stand | stood | stood |
| steal | stole | stolen |
| stick | stuck | stuck |
| sting | stung | stung |
| strike | struck | struck |
| swear | swore | sworn |
| sweep | swept | swept |
| swim | swam | swum |
| swing | swung | swung |
| take | took | taken |
| teach | taught | taught |
| tear | tore | torn |
| tell | told | told |
| think | thought | thought |
| throw | threw | thrown |
| understand | understood | understood |
| wake | woke | woken |
| wear | wore | worn |
| weep | wept | wept |
| win | won | won |
| wind | wound | wound |
| write | wrote | written |

# Verbs + full infinitive or -ing form with a change in meaning [Unit 17]

Some verbs can be followed by the full infinitive or the *-ing* form. The choice depends on the meaning.

| Verb | Meaning | Example |
| --- | --- | --- |
| **remember** + full infinitive | do something you are/were planning to do | *I'm glad I* ***remembered to do*** *my homework.* |
| **remember** + *-ing* | think of a past event | *I* ***remember*** *teachers at my school* ***hitting*** *children when they were naughty!* |
| **forget** + full infinitive | not do something you are/were planning to do | *I* ***forgot to turn up*** *for my driving test yesterday. How silly!* |
| **forget** + *-ing* | not be able to remember a past event | *I'll never* ***forget taking*** *my driving test for the first time. It was awful!* |
| **try** + full infinitive | make an effort to achieve something | *I'm really going to* ***try to pass*** *these exams.* |
| **try** + *-ing* | do something as an experiment to solve a problem | *If you don't know what that word means,* ***try looking*** *it* ***up*** *in a dictionary.* |
| **stop** + full infinitive | interrupt an action to do something else | *I was busy writing an essay but I had to* ***stop to answer*** *the phone.* |
| **stop** + *-ing* | stop an action | *Please* ***stop talking****!* |
| **go on** + full infinitive | stop one action and start another | *Jared attended Chichester Comprehensive and then* ***went on to study*** *philosophy at Cambridge.* |
| **go on** + *-ing* | continue | *The kids* ***went on laughing*** *even after the teacher had told them to stop.* |
| **learn / teach** + full infinitive | learn/teach a skill | *I'd love to* ***learn to paint*** *well.* |
| **learn / teach** + *-ing* | learn/teach a subject | *She* ***teaches painting*** *at a local adult education centre.* |
| **like** + full infinitive | be in the habit of; think it right to do | *We* ***like to interview*** *candidates in person before offering them a place on the course.* |
| **like** + *-ing* | enjoy | *Do you* ***like learning*** *foreign languages?* |
| **mean** + full infinitive | intend | *I didn't* ***mean to cheat****. I just happened to see Helen's book.* |
| **mean** + *-ing* | involve | *Being at university often* ***means learning*** *to live on your own.* |
| **regret** + full infinitive | be sorry about giving someone bad news | *We* ***regret to inform*** *you that your application has been rejected.* |
| **regret** + *-ing* | be sorry about what (has) happened | *I* ***regret leaving*** *school with no qualifications.* |
| **consider / imagine** + full infinitive | believe; think something is/was | *Everyone* ***considers*** *it* ***to be*** *the best grammar book on the market.*<br>*I* ***imagine*** *him* ***to be*** *a very good teacher.* |
| **consider / imagine** + *-ing* | think about | *I'm* ***considering going*** *to evening classes.*<br>***Imagine being*** *a graduate!* |

| | |
|---|---|
| Different reporting verbs take different grammatical patterns. Some verbs can take more than one pattern. | |
| **Pattern:** verb + noun | |
| **Verbs:** | **Examples:** |
| deny | *Katie **denied the accusation**.* |
| say | *When Angie **said the price**, I couldn't believe it!* |
| suggest | *I **suggest the blue suit** for the wedding.* |
| tell (certain phrases) | *Why don't you **tell that joke** about the merchant banker?* |
| **Pattern:** verb + *that* clause | |
| **Verbs:** | **Examples:** |
| claim | *Katie **claimed (that)** she wasn't a shoplifter.* |
| deny | *Katie **denied (that)** she was a shoplifter.* |
| say | *Katie **said (that)** she wasn't a shoplifter.* |
| state | *Katie **stated (that)** she wasn't a shoplifter.* |
| suggest | *The police **suggested (that)** Katie empty her pockets.* |
| **Pattern:** verb + *-ing* | |
| **Verbs:** | **Examples:** |
| deny | *Katie **denied stealing** the chocolate biscuits.* |
| suggest | *The police **suggested checking** the security video.* |
| **Pattern:** verb + full infinitive | |
| **Verbs:** | **Examples:** |
| agree | *Katie **agreed to empty** her pockets.* |
| claim | *Katie **claimed to be** innocent.* |
| refuse | *The police **refused to believe** Katie.* |
| **Pattern:** verb + someone + full infinitive | |
| **Verbs:** | **Examples:** |
| ask | *The police **asked Katie to empty** her pockets.* |
| beg | *Katie **begged the policewoman to believe** her.* |
| command | *The judge **commanded Katie to replace** the biscuits.* |
| order | *The judge **ordered Katie to replace** the biscuits.* |
| tell | *The judge **told Katie** never **to steal** again.* |
| **Pattern:** verb ( + *to* + someone) + for + *-ing* | |
| **Verb:** | **Example:** |
| apologise | *Katie **apologised (to everyone) for causing** so much trouble.* |
| **Pattern:** verb + someone + noun | |
| **Verbs:** | **Examples:** |
| ask | *The judge **asked Katie a question**.* |
| tell (certain phrases) | *Katie **told the judge the truth.*** |

## Unit 2

**voyage (n)** a long journey, especially on a ship: *It was a long way from London to New York by sea, but the voyage was quite relaxing.*

**journey (n)** an occasion when you travel from one place to another, especially over a long distance: *We had a long journey ahead of us.*

**trip (n)** an occasion when you go somewhere and come back again: *The whole family went on a trip to Florida.*

**travel (n)** the activity of travelling: *Foreign travel never really appealed to him until he retired.*

**excursion (n)** a short journey that you make for pleasure: *My grandmother often talks about going on excursions to the sea when she was a girl.*

**view (n)** the things that you can see from a particular place: *We had a spectacular view of the mountains from our room.*

**sight (n)** a person or a thing that you see that has a particular feature: *Windmills are a common sight in this part of the country.*

**world (n)** the planet that we live on: *It's easy these days to communicate with people who live on the other side of the world.*

**earth (n)** the land on which we live: *They felt the earth shake.*

**area (n)** a part of a place or building: *Bus services in rural areas are not very good.*

**territory (n)** an area of land that is controlled by a particular country, leader or army: *Russian troops crossed into Austrian territory in February 1849.*

**season (n)** one of the four periods into which the year is divided according to the weather: *She likes to paint the changing seasons in the garden.*

**period (n)** an amount of time: *The long dry period ended with heavy rain.*

**fare (n)** the money that you pay for a journey: *The fare from York to Leeds has gone up.*

**ticket (n)** a piece of paper that shows that you have paid to do something such as travel on a train, bus, plane, etc: *We'll send your tickets a week before your flight.*

**fee (n)** an amount of money that you pay to be allowed to do something such as join an organisation: *The gallery charges a small entrance fee.*

**miss (v)** to be too late for something such as a train or bus: *I missed the last train home again.*

**lose (v)** to no longer have something: *Mike lost his job last year.*

**take (v)** to move or carry someone or something from one place to another: *What time do you take Amy to school?*

**bring (v)** to take someone or something with you from one place to another: *Bring a coat in case it turns cold.*

**go (v)** to move or travel to a place that is away from where you are now: *We're planning to go to Spain this winter.*

**book (v)** to arrange to have or use something at a particular time in the future: *Shall I book a room for you?*

**keep (v)** to continue to have or own something: *We should keep this car and sell the other one.*

**arrive (v)** to reach a place: *What time does your plane arrive?*

**reach (v)** to arrive somewhere: *We hoped to reach the camp before dark.*

**live (v)** to have your home in a particular place: *Paris is a nice place to live.*

**stay (v)** to live or remain in a place for a while as a guest or visitor: *How long is he planning to stay with you?*

**border (n)** the official line that separates two countries or regions: *Thousands of refugees were fleeing across the border.*

**edge (n)** the part of something that is furthest from its centre: *Victoria was sitting on the edge of the bed.*

**line (n)** a long thin mark on the surface of something: *Draw a straight line.*

**length (n)** a measurement of how long something is in size: *The boat was 16 feet in length.*

**distance (n)** the amount of space between two people or things: *They started to walk the short distance to the camp.*

**guide (v)** to show someone where to go by going with them: *He guided them through the forest.*

**lead (v)** to take someone to a place by going there with them, usually in front of them: *The estate agent led us into the kitchen.*

**native (adj)** living in a particular country or area since birth: *My wife's a native New Yorker, but I'm from Atlanta.*

**home (town) (n)** the city or town where you lived as a child: *I live in Washington, but my home town is Denver, Colorado.*

## Unit 4

**pitch (n)** a flat area of ground that is used for playing sports on: *Hundreds of fans invaded the pitch at the end of the game.*

**track (n)** a piece of ground that is used for running or racing: *The cars have to go round the track eighteen times.*

**court (n)** an area marked with lines where some sports are played, including tennis and basketball: *I'll meet you at the tennis court!*

**course (n)** an area where a race or sport takes place: *It's one of the most challenging golf courses in the country.*

**ring (n)** a raised area that is surrounded by ropes where people take part in boxing or wrestling: *The boxers are just about to enter the ring.*

**rink (n)** a large flat area where people go to skate: *Jan fell over on the ice rink and hurt her knee.*

**win (v)** to defeat everyone else by being the best, or by finishing first in a competition: *Who won the race?*

**beat (v)** to defeat someone in a game, competition, election or battle: *England needed to beat Germany to get to the final.*

**score (v)** to get a point in a game or sport: *No one scored in the first half.*

**play (n)** a piece of writing that is intended to be performed by actors in a theatre or on television or the radio: *The school's going to put on a play this Christmas.*

**game (n)** an activity that you take part in for fun, usually one that has rules: *Monopoly is a game for all the family.*

**spectator (n)** someone who watches a public activity or event: *The spectators cheered as the two teams came onto the court for the final.*

**viewer (n)** someone who watches television programmes: *A number of viewers have written in to complain about last week's programme.*

**umpire (n)** someone whose job is to make sure that players obey the rules in some sports, for example tennis, baseball and cricket: *I hate it when tennis players argue with the umpire.*

**referee (n)** someone whose job is to make sure that players in a game obey the rules: *The referee blew the whistle and the most important football match of my life began.*

**final (n)** the last game, race, etc in a competition, that decides who wins the whole competition: *We played well throughout the whole tournament, but then lost in the final to Willsborough.*

**finale (n)** the last part of a performance with the most exciting music and dancing: *Everyone in the cast comes on stage and sings for the finale.*

**end (n)** the time when a situation or an event stops: *Are you going to stay till the end of the game?*

**ending (n)** the way in which a story, film or play ends: *Children usually prefer books with a happy ending.*

**bat (n)** a wooden object used for hitting the ball in games such as baseball, cricket and table tennis: *A good cricket bat can be extremely expensive.*

**stick (n)** a long thin piece of wood that is used for hitting or carrying something in a sport: *I'm not very happy with my hockey stick.*

**rod (n)** a long thin bar or stick made of metal, plastic or wood: *We got Celia a fishing rod for her birthday.*

**racket (n)** an object used for hitting the ball in games such as tennis: *Can I borrow your tennis racket?*

**amateur (adj)** done for pleasure instead of as a job: *I'm interested in amateur photography but I'd never want to be a professional photographer.*

**professional (adj)** playing a sport or taking part in an activity as a job rather than for enjoyment: *He became a professional footballer at the age of eighteen.*

**sport (n)** sports in general: *The school is keen to involve more young people in sport.*

**athletics (n)** sports such as running, throwing and jumping: *I love watching athletics, particularly the long jump and the javelin.*

**interval (n)** a short break between the parts of something such as a play or concert: *The play was so boring that we walked out during the interval!*

**half time (n)** in football and some other team sports, a period of rest between the two halves of a match: *The teams are going to swap ends at half time, so Coventry will be playing uphill in the second half.*

**draw (v)** if two teams or opponents draw, or if they draw a match, they both have the same score, so that neither wins: *They drew 1-1 with Manchester United last week.*

**equal (v)** to be as good as someone or something else: *She equalled the record with a time of 27.69 seconds.*

**competitor (n)** someone who takes part in a competition: *There were over 5000 competitors in the marathon last year!*

**opponent (n)** someone who is competing against you: *His opponent received only 36 per cent of the vote.*

## Unit 6

**artificial (adj)** not natural or real, but made by people: *The growers use both natural and artificial light.*

**false (adj)** made to look like something real: *I realised that the man was wearing a false beard.*

**natural (adj)** existing in nature, and not produced by people: *This cloth is made from natural fibres.*

**physical (adj)** real and able to be seen, touched or felt: *There was no physical evidence to connect Whitman with the crime.*

**true (adj)** based on facts or on things that really happened: *The film is based on a true story.*

**accurate (adj)** correct in every detail and without any mistakes: *We need to get an accurate estimate of what the new building will cost.*

**method (n)** a way of doing something, especially a planned or established way: *We developed new methods of pollution control.*

**way (n)** a method for doing something: *There are so many delicious ways you can prepare chicken.*

**engine (n)** the part of a vehicle that makes it move: *There was a problem with the engine, so we took the car to the garage.*

**machine (n)** a piece of equipment with moving parts that does a particular job: *Sue showed him how to operate the washing machine.*

**motor (n)** the part of a machine or vehicle that makes it work: *The pump is powered by an electric motor.*

**aim (n)** the thing that you hope to achieve by doing something: *My main aim on this course is to gain confidence.*

**cause (n)** an event, thing or person that makes something happen: *The cause of death was found to be a heart attack.*

**reason (n)** a fact, situation or intention that explains why something happened, why someone did something or why something is true: *The police asked her the reason for her visit.*

**estimate (v)** to guess or calculate an amount or value by using available information: *It is impossible to estimate how many of the residents were affected.*

**calculate (v)** to discover a number or amount by using mathematics: *He calculates that the proposal would cost 4 million.*

**electric (adj)** using or relating to electricity: *I've just got a new electric toothbrush.*

**electronic (adj)** using electricity and extremely small electrical parts, such as microchips: *Our maths teacher said that we're allowed to use electronic calculators in the exam.*

**invent (v)** to design or create something that did not exist before: *Alfred Nobel invented dynamite.*

**discover (v)** to find something that was hidden or that no one knew about before: *William Herschel discovered Uranus in 1781.*

**research (n)** the detailed study of something in order to discover new facts: *He did some research into the causes of lung cancer.*

**experiment (n)** a scientific test to find out what happens to someone or something in particular conditions: *Researchers now need to conduct further experiments.*

**progress (n)** the process of developing or improving: *Keep me informed about the progress of the project.*

**development (n)** change, growth or improvement over a period of time: *The development in the country's economy means that more people are able to buy their own homes.*

**modern (adj)** relating to or belonging to the present time: *Modern offices are usually full of computers.*

**new (adj)** recently made, invented or developed: *They are going to build a new office block here.*

**industry (n)** all the businesses involved in producing a particular type of goods or services: *The new tax will affect everyone in the fishing industry.*

**factory (n)** a building where large quantities of goods are produced using machines: *She works in a factory.*

**award (n)** a prize that is given to someone who has achieved something: *She won the Player of the Year award.*

**reward (n)** something good that happens or that you receive because of something that you have done: *You deserve a day off as a reward for working so hard.*

**take place (phr)** to happen: *The Olympics take place every four years.*

**occur (v)** to happen: *The police said that the accident occurred at about 4.30 pm.*

## Unit 8

**deny (v)** to say that something is not true: *A spokesman denied that the company had acted irresponsibly.*

**refuse (v)** to say that you will not do or accept something, or will not let someone do something: *I asked him to apologise, but he refused.*

**agree (v)** to have the same opinion as someone else: *Doreen thought that the house was too small, and Jim agreed.*

**accept (v)** to recognise that something is true, fair or right: *Most scientists accept that climate change is linked to pollution.*

**headline (n)** the title of a newspaper story, printed in large letters: *The whole of the front page of the paper was taken up with the headline 'YOU LIAR!'.*

**heading (n)** the title at the top of a page or piece of writing: *If you look at the heading, it'll tell you what the paragraph is about.*

**feature (n)** a newspaper or magazine article, or a part of a television or radio programme that concentrates on a particular subject: *This week we've got a special feature on new children's books.*

**article (n)** a piece of writing in a newspaper or magazine: *He has written several articles for* The Times.

**talk show (n)** a television or radio programme in which famous people talk about themselves and their work: *Did you see Johnny Depp on that talk show last night?*

**quiz show (n)** a television or radio programme in which people answer questions in order to win prizes: *Your general knowledge is very good; maybe you should go on a quiz show.*

**game show (n)** a television programme in which people play games or answer questions in order to win prizes: *Bruce Forsythe used to host a game show called* The Generation Game.

**announcer (n)** someone whose job is to give information about television or radio programmes between other programmes: *The announcer's just said that* Big Brother *is not going to be on tonight after all as they're showing a football match instead.*

**commentator (n)** someone whose job is to give a description of an event on television or radio as it happens: *I'd love to be a sports commentator but I don't think I can talk quickly enough!*

**tabloid (n)** a newspaper that has small pages and not much serious news: *I don't know why you waste your money on that tabloid. It's just full of gossip about minor celebrities!*

**broadsheet (n)** a serious type of newspaper that is printed on large sheets of paper: The Daily Telegraph *and* The Guardian *are both examples of broadsheets.*

**journalist (n)** someone whose job is to report the news for a newspaper, magazine, radio programme or television programme: *Enid works as a journalist for the local newspaper.*

**columnist (n)** a journalist who writes a regular series of articles for a particular newspaper or magazine: *As a columnist, I'm allowed to express my opinion in ways that other journalists are often not allowed to.*

**press (n)** newspapers and news magazines, or the journalists who work on them: *She has been criticised in the press for not speaking out on this issue.*

**media (n)** radio, television, newspapers, the Internet and magazines, considered as a group: *The story has been widely reported in the media.*

**programme (n)** a television or radio broadcast: *More people watch the news than any other programme.*

**program (n)** a series of instructions that makes a computer do something: *I'm thinking of getting a new word processing program for my laptop.*

**channel (n)** a television station and the programmes that it broadcasts: *What's on the other channel?*

**broadcast (n)** a programme that is broadcast: *We usually watch Channel 5's main news broadcast in the evening.*

**bulletin (n)** a short news broadcast: *There's a two-minute news bulletin on at eleven o'clock.*

**newsflash (n)** a short broadcast of an important piece of news in the middle of a television or radio programme: *We interrupt this programme to bring you a newsflash.*

## Unit 10

**relationship (n)** the way in which two or more people or groups behave towards each other: *What was your relationship with your mother like?*

**connection (n)** a relationship between things or people: *Some journalists are saying that there's a connection between the criminal and the bank manager.*

**blame (n)** responsibility for an accident, problem or bad situation: *Why do I always get the blame for everything?*

**fault (n)** the fact of being responsible for a bad or unpleasant situation: *It's my fault – I forgot to give him the message.*

**old (adj)** something that is old has existed or been used for a long time: *I'm meeting an old friend for lunch.*

**ancient (adj)** relating to a period of history a very long time ago: *The ancient Egyptians built pyramids for the dead bodies of the kings.*

**crowd (n)** a large number of people in the same place: *The boys disappeared into the crowd.*

**audience (n)** the people who watch or listen to a performance: *His jokes offended many people in the audience.*

**enjoy (v)** to get pleasure from something: *Did you enjoy your meal?*

**please (v)** to make someone feel happy and satisfied: *He'll do anything to please her.*

**support (v)** to provide someone with the money, food, shelter or other things that they need in order to live: *How can we support our families on such low wages?*

**assist (v)** to help someone or something: *Her job is to assist the head chef.*

**kind (adj)** behaving in a way that shows you care about other people and want to help them: *Thank you, Mark, you've been very kind.*

**polite (adj)** behaving towards other people in a pleasant way that follows all the usual rules of society: *It's not polite to talk with your mouth full of food.*

**sympathetic (adj)** willing to understand someone's problems and help them: *You're not being very sympathetic.*

**likeable (adj)** pleasant, friendly and easy to like: *I've always found Bill to be a very likeable person.*

**nervous (adj)** feeling excited and worried, or slightly afraid: *Driving on mountain roads always makes me nervous.*

**bad-tempered (adj)** made annoyed or angry very easily: *I don't like our new history teacher – she's so bad-tempered!*

**sensitive (adj)** likely to become upset very easily: *Paul was always a very sensitive little boy.*

**sensible (adj)** reasonable and practical: *This seems to be a sensible way of dealing with the problem.*

**company (n)** the activity of being with other people: *I thought you might want some company tonight.*

| | |
|---|---|
| **group (n)** | several people or things that are together or that are related to each other in some way: *Why don't you join the local drama group?* |
| **popular (adj)** | liked by many people: *Jenny is one of the most popular girls in the school.* |
| **famous (adj)** | if someone or something is famous, a lot of people know their name or have heard about them: *He dreamt of becoming a famous footballer.* |
| **typical (adj)** | behaving in a way that is usual for a particular person: *She responded with typical enthusiasm.* |
| **usual (adj)** | typical of what happens in most situations, or of what people do in most situations: *She gave us her usual polite smile.* |
| **ordinary (adj)** | normal or average, and not unusual or special: *It was just an ordinary Saturday morning.* |
| **close (adj)** | related to you directly, for example by being your parent, child, brother or sister: *All my close relatives live in Oxford.* |
| **near (adj)** | close to someone or something: *A group of students were standing near the entrance.* |
| **unknown (adj)** | if something is unknown, people do not know about it or do not know what it is: *For some unknown reason, the plane landed at the wrong airport.* |
| **infamous (adj)** | well known for something bad: *Al Capone was an infamous gangster.* |

## Unit 12

| | |
|---|---|
| **proof (n)** | information or evidence that shows that something is definitely true: *We were unable to establish proof of her innocence.* |
| **evidence (n)** | facts, statements or objects that help to prove whether someone has committed a crime: *The police didn't have enough evidence to convict him.* |
| **suspect (v)** | to believe that something is true: *Police suspected that she had some connection with the robbery.* |
| **arrest (v)** | if the police arrest someone, they take that person to a police station because they think that he or she has committed a crime: *He was arrested for possession of illegal drugs.* |
| **charge (v)** | to accuse someone of committing a crime: *The police have charged him with murder.* |
| **suspect (n)** | someone who might have committed a crime: *Have the police interviewed any suspects yet?* |
| **accused (n)** | someone who is accused of a crime in a court of law: *The accused told the judge that he was not guilty.* |
| **decision (n)** | a choice that you make after you have thought carefully about something: *The committee will make a decision by the end of the week.* |
| **verdict (n)** | an official judgment made in a court: *The jury took 16 hours to reach a verdict.* |
| **commit (v)** | to do something that is illegal or morally wrong: *The study aims to find out what makes people commit crimes.* |
| **break (v)** | to fail to obey a rule or law: *Students who break these rules will be punished.* |
| **rule (n)** | a statement that explains what you can or cannot do in a particular situation: *You can't do that, it's against the rules!* |
| **law (n)** | the system of rules that must be obeyed in society: *Failing to declare any extra income is against the law.* |
| **justice (n)** | treatment of people that is fair and morally right: *Victims are calling for justice.* |
| **right (n)** | something that you are morally or legally allowed to do or have: *We are fighting for workers' rights.* |
| **judge (n)** | someone whose job is to make decisions in a court of law: *The judge sentenced her to ninety days in prison.* |
| **jury (n)** | a group of members of the public who decide whether someone is guilty in a court case: *The jury found him guilty.* |
| **prosecute (v)** | to officially accuse someone of a crime and ask a court of law to judge them: *My neighbour is being prosecuted for driving without a valid licence.* |
| **persecute (v)** | to treat someone very badly because of their race, religion or political beliefs: *A large number of Catholics were persecuted during the war.* |
| **capital punishment (n)** | the punishment of legally killing someone who has committed a serious crime: *They still have capital punishment in the USA.* |
| **corporal punishment (n)** | punishment that consists of hitting someone: *When I was at school, corporal punishment was common.* |
| **robber (n)** | someone who steals money or property: *Why do they always glamorise bank robbers in movies?* |
| **burglar (n)** | someone who enters a building illegally in order to steal things: *Burglars broke into our office last night and stole all the telephones.* |
| **thief (n)** | someone who steals something: *How dare you accuse me of being a thief; I've never stolen anything in my life!* |
| **vandal (n)** | someone who deliberately damages or destroys things, especially public property: *Vandals have broken the public telephone outside our house again.* |
| **hooligan (n)** | someone who is noisy or violent in public places: *Football hooligans caused a lot of damage to the stadium.* |
| **sentence (v)** | if a judge sentences someone, they officially say what that person's punishment will be: *He was sentenced to 15 years in prison.* |
| **imprison (v)** | to put someone in a prison, or to keep them in a place that they cannot escape from: *He had been imprisoned for fifteen years before he managed to prove his innocence.* |

**innocent (adj)** not guilty of a crime or anything bad: *Under the law, everyone is considered innocent until proved guilty.*

**guilty (adj)** someone who is guilty has committed a crime or has done something wrong: *Patrick knew that he was guilty of lying.*

**witness (n)** someone who sees a crime, accident or other event happen: *Witnesses reported hearing two gunshots.*

**bystander (n)** someone who sees an event happen, but who is not directly involved in it: *The car crashed into the wall, nearly hitting two bystanders.*

**lawyer (n)** someone whose profession is to provide people with legal advice and services: *Mayer's lawyer spoke to the press today.*

**solicitor (n)** in the UK, a lawyer who gives legal advice, writes legal contracts, and represents people in the lower courts of law: *You'll be hearing from my solicitor.*

## Unit 14

**prescription (n)** a piece of paper that a doctor gives you that says what type of medicine you need: *The drug is only available on prescription.*

**recipe (n)** a set of instructions for cooking or preparing a particular food: *You must give me the recipe for this apple pie!*

**operation (n)** the process of cutting into someone's body for medical reasons: *She may need an operation on her knee.*

**surgery (n)** medical treatment in which a doctor cuts open someone's body: *I'm afraid you're going to need surgery on your hand.*

**sore (adj)** painful and uncomfortable, usually as a result of an injury, infection or too much exercise: *I always feel stiff and sore after gardening.*

**hurt (v)** to feel pain somewhere in your body: *Fred's knees hurt after skiing all day.*

**pain (n)** a bad feeling in part of your body when you are hurt or become ill: *An old injury was causing him intense pain.*

**illness (n)** a particular disease, or a period of being ill: *Mike's illness meant that he missed almost two months of school.*

**disease (n)** an illness that affects people, animals or plants: *Studies have revealed that vegetarians suffer less from heart disease.*

**injured (adj)** hurt in an accident or attack: *The injured man was taken to hospital.*

**damaged (adj)** harmed physically: *After the explosion, people were warned to keep away from the damaged buildings.*

**thin (adj)** someone who is thin has very little fat on their body: *Charles was thin and very tall.*

**slim (adj)** thin in an attractive way: *She had a slim youthful figure.*

**remedy (n)** a cure for pain or for a minor illness: *I know a really good herbal remedy for headaches.*

**cure (n)** a medicine or treatment that makes someone who is ill become healthy: *Doctors say there are several possible cures.*

**therapy (n)** a form of treatment for an illness or medical condition: *Since the accident, Tina's been having therapy to help her walk again.*

**effect (n)** a change that is produced in one person or thing by another: *Scientists are studying the chemical's effects on the environment.*

**result (n)** something that is caused directly by something else: *He said the argument was the result of a misunderstanding.*

**healthy (adj)** physically strong and not ill: *I feel very healthy at the moment.*

**fit (adj)** healthy, strong and able to do physical exercise: *Running around after the kids keeps me fit.*

**examine (v)** to look at something or someone carefully: *She opened the suitcase and examined the contents.*

**investigate (v)** to try to find out all the facts about something in order to learn the truth about it: *We sent a reporter to investigate the rumour.*

**infection (n)** the process of becoming infected with a disease: *There are ways to reduce your risk of infection.*

**pollution (n)** chemicals and other substances that have a harmful effect on air, water or land: *The agency is responsible for controlling air pollution.*

**plaster (n)** a thin piece of cloth or plastic that sticks to your skin to cover a cut: *Do you know where the plasters are? I've cut my finger.*

**bandage (n)** a long thin piece of cloth that you wrap around an injured part of your body: *The doctor carefully removed the bandage to have a look at my injured arm.*

**ward (n)** a large room in a hospital with beds for people to stay in: *When I was in hospital, I was put on a ward with ten other children.*

**clinic (n)** a place where people go to receive a particular type of medical treatment or advice: *My doctor sent me to an eye clinic to see a specialist.*

**dose (n)** a particular amount of a drug or medicine that has been measured so that you can take it: *The dose for children is two tablets, three times a day.*

**fix (n)** an amount of a drug that someone feels that they need to take regularly: *Many addicts steal in order to pay for their daily fix.*

**fever (n)** a medical condition in which the temperature of your body is very high: *Mrs Connors called the doctor in the middle of the night because Jenny had a fever.*

**rash (n)** an area of small red spots on your skin that is caused by an illness or a reaction to something: *I think I'm allergic to that new washing powder because I've got a rash on my legs.*

## Unit 16

**chop (v)** to cut something such as food or wood into pieces: *Chop the meat into small cubes.*

**slice (v)** to cut something into flat pieces: *I'll slice some bread.*

**grate (v)** to rub food against a grater in order to cut it into small pieces: *Could you grate some cheese, please?*

**bake (v)** to cook food such as bread and cakes in an oven: *She baked me a cake for my birthday.*

**grill (v)** to cook something by putting it close to great heat above or below it: *Do you want to grill the sausages or fry them?*

**fry (v)** to cook food in hot oil or fat, or to be cooked in this way: *Heat the oil in a large pan and fry the onion and garlic for 5 minutes.*

**roast (v)** to cook meat or vegetables in an oven: *Roast the potatoes next to the chicken.*

**boil (v)** to cook something in boiling water, or to be cooked in this way: *How long does it take to boil an egg?*

**cook (n)** someone who cooks food, either as their job or for pleasure: *Jane's a very good cook.*

**cooker (n)** a large piece of kitchen equipment that you use for cooking food. It usually includes an oven and a hob: *We bought a new electric cooker last week.*

**chef (n)** someone whose job is to cook food in a restaurant: *Aristotelis works as a chef in a big restaurant in Utrecht.*

**oven (n)** a large piece of equipment in a kitchen that you cook food in: *Preheat the oven to 220°C, Gas mark 7.*

**grill (n)** the part of a cooker where food is cooked under great heat: *Can you put the sausages under the grill?*

**hob (n)** the top part of a cooker that you put pans on: *Put the pan on the hob and heat gently.*

**kitchen (n)** a room where you prepare and cook food, and wash dishes: *We sometimes eat in the kitchen.*

**cuisine (n)** a particular style of cooking: *I love Thai cuisine.*

**lunch (n)** a meal that you eat in the middle of the day: *I'll get a sandwich for lunch.*

**dinner (n)** the main meal of the day, usually eaten in the evening: *I haven't had dinner yet.*

**plate (n)** a flat round dish that you put food on: *Let's put all the sandwiches on one plate.*

**bowl (n)** a round container that you use for eating, serving or preparing food: *In a large bowl, mix together the eggs, sugar and butter.*

**saucer (n)** a small round flat dish that you put a cup on: *I bought some matching cups and saucers.*

**dish (n)** food that has been prepared and cooked in a particular way: *Do you have any vegetarian dishes?*

**vegetable (n)** a part of a plant used as food, for example a potato, bean or cabbage: *We grow all our own vegetables.*

**vegetarian (n)** someone who chooses not to eat meat or fish: *My sister has been a vegetarian for ten years.*

**vegan (n)** someone who chooses not to eat anything made from animals or fish, including eggs, milk and cheese: *It must be quite difficult going to restaurants if you're a vegan.*

**fast food (n)** food that is made and served very quickly, and that you can take away with you: *Many people think that fast food like hamburgers is unhealthy.*

**takeaway (n)** a meal that you buy in a restaurant and take home to eat: *Let's get a Chinese takeaway on the way home.*

**kettle (n)** a container that is used for boiling water: *Put the kettle on!*

**teapot (n)** a container with a handle and a spout (=small tube for pouring) that you use for making and pouring tea: *Put three teabags in the teapot and pour in the boiling water.*

**freezer (n)** a large piece of electrical equipment that is used for freezing food: *I'll put the ice cream in the freezer.*

**fridge (n)** a piece of equipment that is used for storing food at low temperatures: *Could you get the milk out of the fridge, please?*

**frozen (adj)** preserved by being made extremely cold and stored at a very low temperature: *I usually buy frozen vegetables.*

**freezing (adj)** very cold: *It's absolutely freezing in here!*

**mix (v)** to combine two or more substances so that they become a single substance: *Mix the flour with the eggs and butter.*

**stir (v)** to move food or a liquid around using a spoon or other object: *Stir the sauce gently over a low heat.*

**whisk (v)** to mix something such as eggs or cream using a whisk or a fork: *Whisk the eggs for two or three minutes.*

**soft drink (n)** a cold drink that does not contain any alcohol: *If you'd like a soft drink, we've got some orange juice.*

**fizzy drink (n)** a fizzy drink is a sweet drink without alcohol that has bubbles: *I don't like fizzy drinks like lemonade.*

**menu (n)** a list of the food that is available in a restaurant: *Do you see anything you like on the menu?*

**catalogue (n)** a book that contains pictures of things that you can buy: *Alan bought his jeans from a mail order catalogue.*

## Unit 18

**take (v)** to perform an action: *I decided to take the exam, even though I knew I was going to fail.*

**pass (v)** to be successful in an examination or test, by achieving a satisfactory standard: *Do you think you'll pass?*

**read (v)** to look at and understand words in a letter, book, newspaper, etc: *I read a few chapters every night.*

**study (v)** to do work such as reading and homework: *You need to study hard if you want to pass.*

**test (n)** a set of written or spoken questions that is used for finding out how much someone knows about a subject: *Did you get a good mark in your physics test?*

**exam (n)** an important test of your knowledge, especially one that you take at school or university: *I'm taking the exam in June.*

**primary (adj)** relating to the education of children between the ages of about five and eleven: *I really didn't want to leave my primary school.*

**secondary (adj)** relating to the education of children between the ages of 11 and 16 or 18: *Once Ian went to secondary school, he really developed a lot of self-confidence.*

**high [school] (adj)** in the UK, a school for children between the ages of 11 and 18; in the US, a school for children between the ages of 14 and 18: *I hated high school because everyone was worried about being popular.*

**colleague (n)** someone who works in the same organisation or department as you: *Friends and colleagues will remember him with affection.*

**classmate (n)** someone who is in your class at school: *I get on well with all my classmates.*

**prefect (n)** in some schools in the UK, an older student who controls the activities of younger students and helps them to obey the rules: *At our school, the headmaster chooses the prefects at the start of each academic year.*

**pupil (n)** someone who goes to school or who has lessons in a particular subject: *All the pupils stood up as the head teacher entered the room.*

**student (n)** someone who goes to a university, college or school: *Jennifer is one of my best students.*

**qualifications (n)** something such as a degree or a diploma that you get when you successfully finish a course of study: *Simon left school with no qualifications.*

**qualities (n)** positive features of a person's character: *What qualities do you most admire in others?*

**count (v)** to calculate how many people or things there are in a group: *All the votes have been counted.*

**measure (v)** to find the exact size, amount, speed or rate of something: *We measured from the back of the house to the fence.*

**degree (n)** a course of study at a university, or the qualification that you get after completing the course: *She's doing a degree at Exeter University.*

**certificate (n)** an official document that proves that you have passed an examination or have successfully completed a course: *Doctors often put their certificates up in their offices to show that they are qualified.*

**results (n)** the mark that a student gets in an examination: *You should get your exam results next week.*

**speak (v)** to be able to talk in a particular language: *Do you speak Chinese?*

**talk (v)** to speak, or to have a conversation: *Can their baby talk yet?*

**lesson (n)** a period of time in which students are taught about a subject in school: *Don't forget to bring your books to Monday's lesson.*

**subject (n)** something that you learn or teach in a school, for example English, mathematics or biology: *I prefer science subjects, like physics and biology, to arts subjects.*

**achieve (v)** to succeed in doing or having something: *We have achieved what we set out to do.*

**reach (v)** to get to a particular point in time, or to a particular stage in a process: *The children have reached the age when they want more privacy.*

**task (n)** something that you have to do, often something that is difficult or unpleasant: *Ken began the difficult task of organising the information.*

**effort (n)** physical or mental energy needed to do something: *Writing a book takes a lot of time and effort.*

**know (v)** to be familiar with someone or something, for example because you have met someone before or been to a place before: *Do you know Terry Davis?*

**recognise (v)** to know someone or something because you have seen, heard or met them before: *I recognised the house from your description.*

**teach (v)** to help students to learn something in a school, college or university by giving lessons: *She teaches children with learning difficulties.*

**learn (v)** to gain knowledge or experience of something, for example by being taught: *What did you learn at school today?*

## Unit 20

**urban (adj)** relating to towns and cities: *People moved to the urban areas for jobs.*

| | |
|---|---|
| **suburban (adj)** | in a suburb, relating to a suburb, or typical of a suburb: *We live a suburban life in a quiet residential area on the outskirts of town.* |
| **rural (adj)** | relating to the countryside, or in the countryside: *I'd find rural life difficult after living in a city for so long.* |
| **smog (n)** | polluted air that forms a cloud close to the ground: *Smog is a serious form of pollution in many large cities.* |
| **fog (n)** | thick clouds that form close to the ground and are difficult to see through: *Driving in fog can be very dangerous.* |
| **smoke (n)** | a grey, black or white cloud that is produced by something that is burning: *A column of black smoke slowly rose above the building.* |
| **mist (n)** | a mass of small drops of water in the air close to the ground: *The whole valley was covered with mist this morning.* |
| **weather (n)** | the conditions that exist in the atmosphere, for example whether it is hot, cold, sunny or wet: *The hot weather will continue through the weekend.* |
| **climate (n)** | the climate of a country or region is the type of weather it has: *Mexico is renowned for its hot climate and spicy food.* |
| **forecast (n)** | a statement about what is likely to happen, usually relating to the weather, business or the economy: *Did you hear a weather forecast today?* |
| **prediction (n)** | a statement about what you think will happen in the future: *My prediction is that there'll be an election within six months.* |
| **waste (n)** | the useless materials, substances or parts that are left after you have used something: *Many factories have stopped pumping waste into rivers.* |
| **litter (n)** | things that people have dropped on the ground in a public place, making it untidy: *I wish the tourists here wouldn't drop so much litter on the ground.* |
| **rubbish (n)** | things that you throw away because they are no longer useful: *The streets were littered with rubbish.* |
| **clean (adj)** | not dirty or polluted: *Go and put on a clean shirt.* |
| **clear (adj)** | if the sky is clear, there are no clouds: *We were just lying on the ground looking up at the clear, blue sky.* |
| **pour (v)** | to rain very hard: *The thunder and lightning stopped, but it continued to pour.* |
| **drizzle (v)** | to rain very lightly: *It was only drizzling when I left so I didn't bother taking an umbrella with me.* |
| **flood (v)** | to cover a place with water, or to become covered with water: *Water burst through the dam and flooded local villages.* |
| **environment (n)** | the natural world, including the land, water, air, plants and animals: *Industrial development is causing widespread damage to the environment.* |
| **surroundings (n)** | a place and all the things in it: *She soon became accustomed to her new surroundings.* |
| **wind (n)** | a natural current of air that moves fast enough for you to feel it: *A cold wind blew.* |
| **air (n)** | the mixture of gases that we breathe: *She breathed in the cold air.* |
| **reservoir (n)** | a lake, often an artificial one, where water is stored so that it can be supplied to houses, factories, etc: *They're planning to build a new reservoir to supply water for the area.* |
| **lake (n)** | a large area of water surrounded by land: *There were some boys swimming in the lake.* |
| **puddle (n)** | a small pool of water that is left on the ground after it has rained: *Our dog loves jumping in puddles.* |
| **pond (n)** | an area of water that is smaller than a lake: *My grandparents have got a small pond in their garden.* |
| **thunder (n)** | the loud noise that you sometimes hear in the sky during a storm: *Carol jumped under the bed when she heard the thunder!* |
| **lightning (n)** | the bright flashes of light that you see in the sky during a storm: *The ship was struck by lightning soon after it left the port.* |
| **global (adj)** | including or affecting the whole world: *The global economy has become increasingly unstable.* |
| **worldwide (adj)** | happening or existing all over the world: *This is a worldwide network of more than 100 organisations.* |
| **plain (n)** | a large flat area of land: *There's a large, flat plain between two mountain ranges.* |
| **land (n)** | an area of ground, especially one used for a particular purpose such as farming or building: *The land around here is very fertile.* |
| **field (n)** | an area of land that is used for keeping animals or growing food: *That's a field of wheat over there.* |
| **desert (n)** | a large area of land with few plants and dry weather: *The Sahara is one of the biggest deserts in the world.* |
| **extinct (adj)** | if something such as a type of animal or plant is extinct, it no longer exists: *A number of plants and insects in the rainforests have already become extinct.* |
| **endangered (adj)** | if something such as a type of animal or plant is endangered, it may soon become extinct: *What can we do to help protect endangered species?* |
| **recycle (v)** | to treat waste materials so that they can be used again: *You should recycle those newspapers and bottles.* |

**reuse (v)** to use something again: *Once you've recorded a film onto a video cassette, you can reuse the tape by just recording over the original film.*

## Unit 22

**economic (adj)** relating to the economy, business and trade: *The project will bring great social and economic benefits to the region.*

**economical (adj)** not spending or costing much money: *The material is an economical substitute for plastic or steel.*

**receipt (n)** a document that you get from someone showing that you have given them money or goods: *Keep all your credit card receipts.*

**bill (n)** a piece of paper that shows how much money you owe after you have eaten in a restaurant: *Could we have the bill, please?*

**make (n)** a product that is made by a particular company: *This is a very popular make of car.*

**brand (n)** a product or group of products that has its own name and is made by one particular company: *I tried using a new brand of soap.*

**bargain (n)** something you buy that costs much less than normal: *Her dress was a real bargain.*

**sale (n)** an event or period of time during which a shop reduces the prices of some of its goods: *I'm sure you'll find the same dress in a sale if you wait a little.*

**discount (n)** a reduction in the price of something: *Air Canada are currently offering a 10% discount on selected airfares.*

**offer (n)** a special price that is lower than the usual price for something: *The shop had a half-price offer on CDs.*

**price (n)** the amount of money that you have to pay in order to buy something: *Oil was at its lowest price in 30 years.*

**cost (n)** the amount of money that you need in order to buy something or to do something: *The cost of basic foods has risen dramatically.*

**change (n)** coins rather than notes: *Have you got change for a five-pound note?*

**cash (n)** money in the form of notes and coins: *Do you want to pay in cash or by credit card?*

**wealth (n)** a large amount of money and other valuable things: *He was a man of immense wealth.*

**fortune (n)** a large amount of money: *They must have spent a fortune on flowers.*

**till (n)** a piece of equipment that is used in shops for adding up the amount of money that someone has to pay and for keeping the money in: *The shop assistant opened the till and put the money into it.*

**checkout (n)** the place where you pay in a supermarket or other large shop: *You don't need to weigh the vegetables – they do it at the checkout.*

**products (n)** things that are made, grown or obtained in large quantities so that they can be sold: *Come in and see our large range of software products.*

**goods (n)** objects that are produced for sale: *Wilkins was found in possession of £8000 worth of stolen goods.*

**refund (v/n)** to give money back to someone because they have paid too much for something or have decided that they do not want it / the money that you get back: *Sandra asked the shop to refund her money as the jeans were too small.*

**exchange (v)** to give someone something in return for something that they give you: *If this T-shirt doesn't fit my sister, can she exchange it for a larger one?*

**fake (adj)** made to look like something real in order to trick people: *It turned out to be a fake passport.*

**plastic (adj)** made of a very common light, strong substance that is produced by a chemical process: *I think that we should reuse all our plastic bags to help the environment.*

## Unit 24

**enjoy (v)** to get pleasure from something: *Did you enjoy your meal?*

**entertain (v)** to give a performance that people enjoy: *The children sang and danced to entertain the crowd.*

**play (v)** to have a particular part in a play or film: *She played Blanche in* A Streetcar Named Desire.

**act (v)** to perform in plays or films: *I've always wanted to act.*

**star (v)** if you star in a film, play, television programme, etc, or if it stars you, you are the main actor or performer in it: *He starred in the school play.*

**audition (n)** an occasion when you sing, dance or act so that someone can decide if you are good enough to perform: *Good luck with your audition for the play.*

**rehearsal (n)** an occasion when you practise for the performance of a play, concert, etc: *We've got rehearsals every night this week.*

**rehearse (v)** to practise a play, concert, etc before giving a performance: *How many times are you going to rehearse that song before the talent show?*

**practise (v)** to repeat an activity regularly so that you become better at it: *How many hours a day do you practise?*

**scene (n)** a part of a play, book, film, etc in which events happen in the same place or period of time: *I love the opening scene of* Macbeth.

**scenery (n)** the furniture and painted background on a theatre stage: *The play was good but the scenery wasn't very realistic.*

**stage (n)** the part of a theatre where the actors or musicians perform: *They had now been on stage for over four hours.*

**band (n)** a group of musicians who play popular music: *He used to play in a jazz band.*

**orchestra (n)** a large group of musicians who use many different instruments in order to play mostly classical music: *There are over fifty people in the school orchestra.*

**group (n)** a small set of musicians who play pop music: *Would you like to be in a pop group?*

**review (n)** an article in which someone gives their opinion of a play, book, exhibition, etc: *The film got really good reviews.*

**criticism (n)** a comment or comments that show that you think something is wrong or bad: *The new plans drew fierce criticism from local people.*

**ticket (n)** a piece of paper that shows that you have paid to do something such as go to a concert, visit a museum, or travel on a train, bus, plane, etc: *We'll send your tickets a week before your flight.*

**fee (n)** an amount of money that you pay to be allowed to do something such as join an organisation: *The gallery charges a small entrance fee.*

**novel (n)** a long written story about imaginary characters and events: *Have you read any of Martin Amis' novels?*

**fiction (n)** books and stories about imaginary events and people: *Hardy wrote poetry as well as fiction.*

**comic (n)** a magazine that contains stories told in a series of drawings: *My little brother gets a comic every Friday.*

**cartoon (n)** a film or TV programme made by photographing a series of drawings so that things in them seem to move; a humorous drawing or series of drawings in a newspaper or magazine: *There's a very funny cartoon in today's paper.*

**comedian (n)** someone whose job is to entertain people by making them laugh: *The comedian was so bad the audience didn't let him finish his act.*

**watch (v)** to look at someone or something for a period of time: *Did you watch the news last night?*

**see (v)** to watch something such as a film or television programme: *Have you seen* American Beauty*?*

**look (v)** to direct your eyes towards someone or something so that you can see them: *Dan looked at his watch.*

**listen (v)** to pay attention to a sound, or to try to hear a sound: *Do you like listening to music?*

**hear (v)** to realise that someone or something is making a sound: *Mary heard the sound of voices.*

## Unit 26

**put on (phr v)** to cover a part of your body with a piece of clothing or jewellery so that you are wearing it: *Dorothy put on her coat and went out.*

**wear (v)** to have something on your body as clothing, decoration or protection: *He was wearing jeans and a T-shirt.*

**costume (n)** clothes that the actors wear in a play or film: *I thought the costumes they were wearing in the play were fantastic.*

**suit (n)** a set of clothes made from the same cloth, usually a jacket with trousers or a skirt: *He was wearing a dark suit and a tie.*

**dye (v)** to change the colour of something such as cloth or hair using dye: *Why don't you dye your hair red?*

**paint (v)** to put paint onto something in order to change its colour: *Wash the walls before you start to paint.*

**fit (v)** if clothes fit, they are the right size for you: *It is important that children's shoes fit correctly.*

**suit (v)** if a style or something you wear suits you, it makes you look good: *The new hairstyle really suits her.*

**match (v)** if one thing matches another, or they match, they form an attractive combination: *She wore a green dress and a hat to match.*

**cloth (n)** material used for making things such as clothes and curtains: *I really like the cloth you've used on these cushions. What is it?*

**clothing (n)** clothes: *I told the hotel manager that some items of clothing had gone missing from my room.*

**blouse (n)** a shirt for women: *Women are expected to wear blouses in our office.*

**top (n)** a piece of clothing that covers the upper part of your body: *She was wearing a red skirt and a black top.*

**design (v)** to decide how something will be made, how it will work, or what it will look like, and often to make drawings of it: *The bride wore a dress that she designed herself.*

**manufacture (v)** to make goods in large quantities in a factory: *The firm manufactures women's clothing.*

**current (adj)** happening or existing now: *Production is likely to remain at current levels.*

**new (adj)** recently made, invented or developed: *They are going to build a new office block here.*

**modern (adj)** relating to or belonging to the present time: *Modern offices are usually full of computers.*

| | |
|---|---|
| **look (n)** | the appearance that someone or something has: *Let us create a stylish modern look for your home.* |
| **appearance (n)** | the way that someone or something looks: *The twins are almost identical in appearance.* |
| **supply (v)** | to provide someone or something with something that they need or want: *Two huge generators supply power to farms in the area.* |
| **produce (v)** | to make or grow something: *We are now producing the same quantity of goods with far fewer workers.* |
| **glimpse (v)** | to see someone or something for a moment or not completely: *I glimpsed a strange man through the window, and then he was gone.* |
| **glance (v)** | to look somewhere quickly and then look away: *'I must go,' Claudia said, glancing at her watch.* |
| **average (adj)** | the typical amount or level: *Unemployment here is twice the national average.* |
| **everyday (adj)** | very common or completely normal: *We all need a friend to help us with everyday problems.* |

## Unit 28

| | |
|---|---|
| **employer (n)** | a person or organisation that pays workers to work for them: *The factory is the largest single employer in the area.* |
| **employee (n)** | someone who is paid regularly to work for a person or organisation: *There are six part-time employees working here.* |
| **staff (n)** | the people who work for a particular company, organisation or institution: *The embassy employs around 50 people on its full-time staff.* |
| **job (n)** | work that you do regularly to earn money: *Andy got a holiday job at a factory in Bristol.* |
| **work (n)** | a job that you are paid to do: *It's not easy to find work.* |
| **career (n)** | a job or profession that you work at for some time: *Rosen had decided on an academic career.* |
| **earn (v)** | to receive money for work that you do: *Most people here earn about £30 000 a year.* |
| **win (v)** | to get something as a prize for defeating other people or because you are lucky: *He won £4000 in the lottery.* |
| **gain (v)** | to get more of something, usually as a result of a gradual process: *I've gained a lot of weight this winter.* |
| **raise (n)** | an increase in the amount that you are paid for work: *Why don't you ask for a raise?* |
| **rise (n)** | an increase in size, amount, quality or strength: *The proposed tax rise was not unexpected.* |
| **wage(s) (n)** | a regular amount of money that you earn for working: *I've usually spent all my wages by Tuesday.* |
| **salary (n)** | a fixed amount of money that you earn each month or year from your job: *I get an annual salary of £25 000.* |
| **pay (n)** | money that you receive for doing your job: *They were demanding higher pay.* |
| **commute (v)** | to travel regularly to and from work: *My father commutes to work every day.* |
| **deliver (v)** | to take something such as goods or letters to a place and give them to someone: *I can deliver the letter this afternoon.* |
| **retire (v)** | to stop working permanently, especially when you are old: *He retired from the army last month.* |
| **resign (v)** | to state formally that you are leaving your job: *He made it clear that he was not resigning from active politics.* |
| **fire (v)** | to make someone leave their job as a punishment: *She was fired for refusing to include the information in her report.* |
| **sack (v)** | to force someone to leave their job: *Hundreds of workers are to be sacked at the factory.* |
| **make redundant (phr)** | if someone is made redundant, they have been told that they must leave their job because they are no longer needed: *When the company closed, my dad was made redundant.* |
| **overtime (n)** | extra hours that someone works at their job, or money that is paid for working extra hours: *Do you get paid extra for doing overtime?* |
| **promotion (n)** | a move to a job at a higher level: *His main objective is to get a promotion.* |
| **pension (n)** | an amount of money that someone receives regularly when they no longer work because of their age or because they are ill: *My grandma gets a small pension from the state.* |
| **company (n)** | an organisation that sells services or goods: *Max works for a large oil company.* |
| **firm (n)** | a business, or a company: *Josh works for a law firm in Chicago.* |
| **business (n)** | an organisation that buys or sells products or services: *Sheryl's parents run a small clothing business.* |
| **union (n)** | an organisation that represents the workers in a particular industry: *We encourage all employees to join a union.* |
| **charity (n)** | an organisation that gives money and help to people who need it: *The charity helps fund projects in developing countries.* |

| | |
|---|---|
| **ask after** | ask for news about: *Tony was asking after you and I told him you were fine.* |
| **back down** | stop demanding sth, stop saying that you will do sth: *It seemed as if the man was going to start a fight with the manager, but he eventually backed down.* |
| **back out** | decide not to do sth you agreed to do: *But you promised to help me this weekend – you can't back out now!* |
| **bank on** | depend on sth happening: *I'm really banking on getting that job at the supermarket.* |
| **break down** | stop working (for a machine, etc): *That's the third time our car's broken down this month!* |
| **break out** | escape (from prison): *Reports are coming in that five prisoners have broken out of Pentonwood Prison.* |
| **break out** | start suddenly (for a war, fire, etc): *It seems that the fire broke out in the kitchen.* |
| **bring forward** | change the date/time of an event so it happens earlier: *Because of recent events, the meeting has been brought forward to the 29th.* |
| **bring in** | introduce a new law or system: *The government are planning to bring in a law banning hunting.* |
| **bring on** | cause (an illness, etc): *Being out in the fog always brings on my asthma.* |
| **bring out** | produce and start to sell a new product: *Did you hear that REM have just brought out a new album?* |
| **bring up** | look after a child until he or she becomes an adult: *Both Sarah's parents died when she was young and she was brought up by her grandmother.* |
| **bring up** | start discussing a subject: *I hate to bring it up, but do you have that money you owe me?* |
| **call for** | require, need: *The manager said that the situation called for some difficult decisions.* |
| **call for** | demand: *The farmers are calling for assistance from the government.* |
| **call off** | cancel: *I hope they don't call the concert off because of this rain.* |
| **carry on** | continue: *You carry on painting this wall and I'll go and get some more brushes.* |
| **carry out** | perform an experiment, etc: *The investigators have been carrying out tests on the pieces of plane recovered after the accident.* |
| **catch on** | become popular or fashionable: *You green hair is great, but I don't think it'll catch on!* |
| **catch on** | understand: *Greg is really clever and always catches on in class very quickly.* |
| **catch up with** | reach the same point/level as: *I ran a little faster to try to catch up with the others.* |
| **chase after** | follow sb/sth quickly in order to catch them: *The shopkeeper ran out of the shop and chased after the shoplifter as he ran down the street.* |
| **check in** | register at a hotel or an airport: *Give me your passport and I'll go to the desk to check in.* |
| **check out** | leave a hotel: *All guests must check out by midday.* |
| **check out** | investigate: *Let's check out that new website Bill was talking about.* |
| **clear up** | become brighter and better (for weather): *If it doesn't clear up, then I'm afraid we may have to cancel the race.* |
| **close down** | stop operating (for companies): *What is the government doing about the fact that dozens of local businesses are closing down every month?* |
| **come (a)round** | happen again (for regular events): *Christmas soon comes around, doesn't it?* |
| **come (a)round (to)** | be persuaded to change your mind (about): *That's a good point. Maybe I'm coming round to your way of thinking.* |
| **come across** | find sth or meet sb by chance: *I came across some old photographs while I was clearing out my desk.* |
| **come by** | get sth, especially sth that is hard to get: *How did you come by that painting?* |
| **come down with** | start to suffer from a minor illness: *After being out in the storm, Alice came down with a cold.* |
| **come forward** | offer help or information: *After the police appealed for help from the public, a number of people came forward with useful information.* |
| **come into** | inherit: *At the age of eighteen, Roger suddenly came into a fortune.* |
| **come off** | succeed: *Well, I think it's a stupid plan and I'll be amazed if it comes off.* |
| **come on** | develop or make progress: *Your piano playing is really coming on, isn't it?* |
| **come on** | start to be broadcast: *That quiz show you wanted to watch comes on in half an hour.* |
| **come out** | be published: *I can't wait until the next Harry Potter book comes out.* |
| **come round/to** | become conscious: *After a worrying few minutes, Sean started to come round and opened his eyes.* |
| **come up with** | think of (an idea, a plan, etc): *Who do you think came up with the idea of the bicycle?* |
| **count on** | rely on, trust: *Don't worry – you can count on me to help if you need it.* |
| **cross out** | draw a line through sth written: *Danny realised that he'd made a spelling mistake and crossed the word out.* |
| **cut down (on)** | do less of (smoking, etc): *If you can't give up smoking, you could at least try to cut down.* |
| **cut down (on)** | reduce an amount of: *My doctor has advised me to cut down on fat.* |
| **cut off** | make a place difficult or impossible to enter, leave or communicate with: *The snow meant that the village was cut off for over a month.* |

| | |
|---|---|
| **cut off** | stop the supply of sth: *When we move, don't forget to tell them to cut the water and electricity off.* |
| **cut off** | disconnect: *I was talking to Gordon on the phone when we were suddenly cut off.* |
| **dawn on** | if something dawns on you, you realise it for the first time: *It suddenly dawned on me that Sharon loved Oscar and that was why she was behaving so strangely.* |
| **deal with** | handle, cope with: *My job mostly involves dealing with complaints from members of the public.* |
| **die down** | become less noisy, powerful or active: *The actor waited for the laughter to die down before continuing.* |
| **do away with** | get rid of: *I think they should do away with double yellow lines and just let people park where they want to.* |
| **do up** | repair, paint or improve: *You should have your house done up before you sell it.* |
| **do without** | live without (sth you can't afford): *If there's one thing I could never do without, it's my mobile phone.* |
| **draw up** | create (plans, etc): *The architect started to draw up the plans for the new house.* |
| **dress up** | put on fancy or unusual clothes: *I used to love dressing up in my mum's clothes when I was a little girl.* |
| **drop in (on)** | visit unexpectedly: *I hope you don't mind me dropping in on you like this, only I was just passing and I thought we could have a quick cup of coffee.* |
| **drop off** | let someone get out of a vehicle: *Let's get the taxi driver to drop us off outside the supermarket.* |
| **drop off** | fall asleep: *After a long day at work, Henry dropped off in front of the TV.* |
| **drop out (of)** | leave school, etc before you have finished a course: *Dave's parents were very disappointed when he dropped out of university.* |
| **drown out** | prevent a sound from being heard by making a louder noise: *The shouts from the audience drowned the politician out and no one could hear a word he was saying.* |
| **face up to** | accept sth and try to deal with it: *You need to face up to your responsibilities.* |
| **fall for** | fall in love with: *Romeo really fell for Juliet when he first kissed her.* |
| **fall for** | believe (a lie/trick/joke, etc): *I told Sam that we had the day off school, and he fell for it!* |
| **fall out (with)** | have an argument with and stop being friends: *Pamela hasn't spoken to her father since they fell out eight years ago.* |
| **feel up to** | feel well enough to do: *I know I should go to the gym today, but I don't really feel up to it.* |
| **fill in** | add information in the spaces on a document: *Just fill in this form and then hand it in at reception.* |
| **find out** | discover information, etc: *I've always wanted to find out more about the ancient Egyptians.* |
| **flick through** | turn and look at the pages of a magazine, etc quickly: *I was flicking through a magazine when, suddenly, I saw a photograph of the man who had stolen the money!* |
| **get (sb) down** | make sb feel sad or lose hope: *This rainy weather really gets me down.* |
| **get along (with)** | have a good relationship (with): *I don't know why, but I don't really get along with my girlfriend's parents.* |
| **get at** | try to express: *The man pointed at his shoulder, but I couldn't understand what he was getting at.* |
| **get away with** | escape punishment for: *The police promised that the thieves would not be allowed to get away with the robbery.* |
| **get back** | return from a place: *When did you get back from holiday?* |
| **get by** | manage to survive (financially): *I don't make a huge amount of money, but we get by.* |
| **get on (with)** | have a good relationship (with): *I get on with most of my teachers – except Mr Mills!* |
| **get on for** | be almost a particular time, number, age, etc: *I'm not sure what time it is, but it must be getting on for midnight.* |
| **get on with** | continue doing: *Jill had lunch and then got on with revising for her exams.* |
| **get over** | recover from (an illness, etc): *It took Mary a long time to get over her illness.* |
| **get round to** | start (after planning to do sth for a long time): *When do you think you'll get round to fixing the bathroom door?* |
| **get through** | use all of, finish: *I can't believe we've got through ten pints of milk in a week!* |
| **get up to** | do; do sth you should not do: *My brother and I used to get up to lots of things our parents didn't know about when were young.* |
| **give away** | give free of charge: *Did you hear that they're giving away free tickets to the concert tonight?* |
| **give away** | reveal sth you are trying to hide: *I know you haven't seen the film yet so I won't give the ending away.* |
| **give in** | stop making an effort to achieve sth difficult: *I couldn't finish the crossword, so in the end I gave in and had a look at the answers.* |
| **give off** | produce sth such as heat or a smell: *The fridge gets hot next to the cooker because the cooker gives off a lot of heat.* |
| **give up** | stop doing sth you do regularly: *I gave the piano up about a year ago and started playing the guitar.* |

| | |
|---|---|
| **go away** | go on holiday: *We go away every summer, and this year we're thinking about Russia.* |
| **go down (as)** | be remembered for having done something: *Churchill went down as a great war-time leader.* |
| **go in for** | enter (a competition, etc): *You should go in for the talent contest they're holding at the youth club this weekend.* |
| **go in for** | like: *I could never go in for windsurfing. It's just not my kind of sport.* |
| **go into** | deal with sth in detail: *The head teacher asked me to go to the school to talk about Alexander's behaviour, but she wouldn't go into it on the phone.* |
| **go off** | be no longer fresh: *Milk goes off very quickly if you don't put it in the fridge.* |
| **go off** | explode; be fired (for a gun, usually accidentally): *A bomb went off outside the Syrian embassy in London today, injuring five people.* |
| **go off** | stop liking: *Will used to really like jazz music, but he's gone off it lately.* |
| **go on** | continue happening or doing sth: *Even though everyone said they had heard it, Carol went on telling the joke.* |
| **go on** | do sth after doing sth else: *He started by criticising me, and then went on to offer me promotion!* |
| **go over** | repeat or think about again in order to understand completely: *I'd like to begin by going over what we did in last week's lesson.* |
| **go/come round** | go/come to sb's house to visit them: *We were wondering if you'd like to come round for dinner one night this week.* |
| **grow on** | if sth grows on you, you start to like it more: *I didn't like reality TV at first, but it really grows on you after a while.* |
| **grow out of** | develop from: *My ambition to be a computer programmer grew out of playing computer games.* |
| **grow out of** | become too big for: *Tracy's grown out of her shoes so we'll have to buy her some new ones.* |
| **grow up** | become older: *I'd like to be a bus driver when I grow up.* |
| **hand down** | give something valuable to your children or grandchildren, usually when you die: *This necklace was handed down to me by my grandmother.* |
| **hand in** | give to a person in authority: *I took the wallet I had found and handed it in at the police station.* |
| **hand out** | give things to people in a group: *Johnnie, please hand these out to everyone in the class.* |
| **hold up** | rob while threatening violence: *Two men held up a security van today and then escaped on motorbikes.* |
| **hold up** | delay: *I was held up in a traffic jam.* |
| **join in** | participate, take part: *You'll feel much better if you join in, instead of just watching everyone else have fun.* |
| **keep on** | continue doing sth: *If you keep on being late for work, you're going to be in trouble with the manager.* |
| **keep up with** | stay at the same point/level as: *Gordon walks so fast that no one can keep up with him!* |
| **knock out** | defeat and remove from a competition: *Steve Wilson, the British number one, has been knocked out of the US Open tennis championship by Peter Collingwood.* |
| **knock out** | make unconscious: *When I fell off my bike, my head hit the ground and I was completely knocked out for about five minutes!* |
| **leave out** | not include: *If you don't like cinnamon, then simply leave it out and add sugar to the apples instead.* |
| **let down** | disappoint: *Voters feel really let down by the government.* |
| **let off** | give little or no punishment: *I can't believe that the teacher let Ben off with just a warning!* |
| **let off** | make a bomb, etc explode: *Be very careful if you're going to let off those fireworks.* |
| **line up** | get/put into lines: *The soldiers all lined up, ready to be inspected by the officer.* |
| **live on** | use as a source of money: *I wanted the job, but I wouldn't be able to live on the salary.* |
| **look after** | take care of: *Could you look after my cat while I'm on holiday?* |
| **look down on** | think that you are better than: *It annoys me the way Vera looks down on other people.* |
| **look into** | investigate: *Police are looking into the theft.* |
| **look out** | be careful: *Look out! You're going to fall!* |
| **look round** | examine (a place): *We looked round the house but decided that it was too expensive for us.* |
| **look up to** | admire and respect: *I've always looked up to my elder brother because he never gives up.* |
| **look up** | try to find information in a book or list, etc: *Just a second – I'll look Harry's number up in the phone book.* |
| **make off** | escape: *It seems that the burglars made off without being seen by dressing as postmen.* |
| **make out** | pretend that something is true: *Neil tried to make out that he'd won the lottery, but we all knew it wasn't true.* |
| **make out** | see, hear or understand sb or sth with difficulty: *Someone was waving at me in the distance but I couldn't make out who it was.* |
| **make out** | write all the necessary information on a cheque, etc: *Could you please make the cheque out to 'Eurofinance Limited'?* |

**make up** become friends again after an argument: *I had an argument with my best friend, but we soon made up.*

**make up** invent an explanation, excuse, etc: *As I got to school, I knew that I would have to make up an excuse for being late.*

**make up** create a story, poem, etc: *Leo made up a poem about the English teacher.*

**make up for** provide sth good, so that sth bad seems less important: *When the concert was cancelled, my dad took us to the cinema to make up for it.*

**make/head for** go in the direction of: *It started to rain so we made for a nearby farmhouse.*

**name after** give sb or sth the same name as sb or sth else: *My dad named his boat after his grandmother.*

**narrow down** reduce the number of possibilities: *I still haven't decided which university to go to, but I've narrowed it down to about four.*

**pass away** die: *I was sorry to hear that your grandfather passed away.*

**pass out** suddenly become unconscious: *It was so hot that several members of the crowd passed out and had to be taken to hospital.*

**pick on** keep treating someone badly or unfairly: *It's not fair when some of the bigger boys pick on the little ones.*

**pick up** stop in a vehicle to give someone a lift: *I'll pick you up from outside your house and we'll drive into town.*

**plug in** connect to the electricity supply: *I couldn't understand why the vacuum cleaner wasn't working and then I realised I hadn't plugged it in.*

**pop in(to)** visit quickly or for a short time: *Mum popped into the cake shop to get something for after dinner.*

**pull in** stop by the side of the road in a car: *Could you just pull in for a second so that I can buy some chewing gum?*

**pull out** stop being involved in an activity: *The other company pulled out of the deal at the last minute.*

**pull through** survive (a serious illness, etc): *The doctors were really worried about Simon, but in the end he pulled through.*

**put by** save an amount of money for the future: *I try to put a little by each month for emergencies.*

**put down** criticise, make someone feel stupid: *I wish you wouldn't keep putting me down in front of other people!*

**put down** kill (a sick/old animal): *We used to have a horse, but he fell and broke his leg so he had to be put down.*

**put down to** suggest that sth is the result of: *The minister put the recent economic problems down to the rise in oil prices.*

**put forward** suggest: *A number of suggestions were put forward during the meeting but none of them were very useful.*

**put off** delay, postpone: *Wendy told me that the wedding has been put off until next January.*

**put off** make sb not want to do or not like sth: *I've never tasted blue cheese because the smell has always put me off.*

**put on** gain (weight): *I put on so much weight over Christmas!*

**put on** hold, perform (a show, play, etc): *I read that they're putting* Macbeth *on at the Luvvies Theatre.*

**put out** make something stop burning: *I'm afraid you'll have to put your cigarette out before you enter the building.*

**put through** connect by phone: *I'll just put you through to the supervisor, Mrs Edwards.*

**put up with** tolerate: *You have to put up with a lot in this job, but it's worth it in the end.*

**run into** meet by chance: *You'll never guess who I ran into in town this afternoon!*

**run out of** not have any left: *I'm afraid we've run out of time, so I'd like to thank my guests and I hope we'll see you next week on 'Discussion Time'.*

**run over** hit with a car: *Andrea was run over outside her house and she's been taken to hospital.*

**sail through** do something or deal with something very easily: *With a little bit of revision, you should sail through the exam.*

**save up (for)** save money little by little (for a specific purpose): *I'm saving up for my holiday in India.*

**see off** go to a train station, etc to see someone leave: *We all went to the bus station to see Grandma off.*

**see through** recognise that sth is not true and not be tricked by it: *The guard saw through the woman's disguise and immediately arrested her.*

**see through (to)** continue (or help to continue) to the end of sth unpleasant or difficult: *I'm not enjoying my computer course any more, but I'll see it through to the end.*

**see to** deal with: *Could you answer the door while I see to the baby?*

**set in** start and be likely to continue for a while (for rain, winter, an economic depression, etc): *Many birds fly south before winter sets in.*

**set out** explain, describe or arrange sth in a clear and detailed way: *I liked your composition, but I think you need to set your ideas out more clearly by using paragraphs.*

**set out** start working on sth in order to achieve an aim: *In the beginning, we set out to build a successful company, but we never expected to become millionaires.*

| | |
|---|---|
| **set out/off** | start a journey: *As the sun rose, we took down our tents and set out across the desert.* |
| **set to** | start doing sth in a determined or enthusiastic way: *We only had a few hours to get the party ready so we set to work quickly.* |
| **set up** | start (a business, organisation, etc): *You're such a good cook that I think you should set up a restaurant.* |
| **settle down** | become calm after being upset, etc: *When his mum left him at school on the first day, Charlie was quite upset, but he soon settled down and started to enjoy himself.* |
| **settle down** | stay in one place or get married and live quietly: *She spent her twenties travelling round the world and then settled down in a quiet village in Sussex.* |
| **show (a)round** | take sb on a tour of a place: *Let me show you round the garden.* |
| **show off** | try to attract people's attention and make them admire you (usually used negatively): *My sister thinks she's a good singer and she's always showing off when people come to visit.* |
| **slow down** | decrease speed: *The train started to slow down as it approached the station.* |
| **speed up** | increase speed: *I realised that I might not have enough time to finish the exam so I started to speed up.* |
| **stand for** | represent (for abbreviations and symbols): *BBC stands for 'British Broadcasting Corporation'.* |
| **stand for** | put up with: *I wouldn't stand for it if someone spoke that rudely to me.* |
| **stand in for** | do sb's job for them while they are not available: *Mr Howard will be standing in for Mrs O'Connell while she's ill.* |
| **stand out** | be easy to see because of being different: *Molly has bright red hair, so she always stands out in a crowd!* |
| **stand up for** | support in an argument or fight: *I know that my best friend will always stand up for me.* |
| **take aback** | surprise (usually in passive voice): *We were all taken aback by the news.* |
| **take after** | look or behave like an older relative: *George really takes after his grandfather, doesn't he?* |
| **take down** | write down what someone says: *Could I just take down your details?* |
| **take in** | trick sb into believing sth that is not true: *The man at the door claimed to be a policeman, but the old woman wasn't taken in.* |
| **take off** | become successful or popular very fast: *The iPod has really taken off over the last couple of years.* |
| **take off** | leave the ground: *As the plane took off, I looked down at the houses below us.* |
| **take off** | remove (a piece of clothing): *Carl took off his coat and started to warm himself by the fire.* |
| **take on** | start to employ: *There's so much work to do in the office that maybe we should take on a secretary.* |
| **take on** | accept (work or responsibility): *I haven't got time to take on any more projects at the moment.* |
| **take over** | take control of (a business, etc): *When Mr Barker retired, his daughter took over the family business.* |
| **take to** | begin to like: *The class took to Mrs Openshaw straight away.* |
| **take to** | start (as a habit): *I've taken to going for a five-mile run every morning.* |
| **take up** | start (a hobby, sport, etc): *Why don't you take up a hobby, like collecting something?* |
| **take up** | fill an amount of space/time: *Studying takes up most of my time at the moment.* |
| **tear down** | destroy or remove (for buildings, statues, etc): *That beautiful old building was torn down to make way for a new supermarket.* |
| **tear up** | rip into pieces: *Robin suddenly grabbed the letter out of my hand and tore it up.* |
| **think over** | consider: *When I asked Theresa to marry me, she said she'd have to think it over.* |
| **throw away** | get rid of, discard: *The CD wouldn't play any more, so I threw it away.* |
| **try on** | put on (a piece of clothing) to see how it looks and whether it fits: *Debra took the skirt into the changing room to try it on.* |
| **try out** | experiment with: *England need to try out a few new players before the World Cup starts.* |
| **turn down** | not accept (an offer, request, etc): *I applied to join the Air Force, but they turned me down because of my eyesight.* |
| **turn into** | change into sth different: *It started as the holiday of a lifetime but soon turned into a nightmare.* |
| **turn off** | stop a machine working: *Would you please turn that stereo off and get your homework done?* |
| **turn out** | develop in a particular way or have a particular result: *I was late for the interview, but it turned out all right in the end and I got the job.* |
| **turn over** | turn a page so that the other side is towards you: *If you all turn over, you'll see a table that shows how sales have gone this year.* |
| **turn round** | go back in the opposite direction: *I realised I'd forgotten my phone so I turned round and went back to get it.* |
| **turn up** | appear unexpectedly or without making a firm arrangement: *Victor hadn't been invited to the party but he just turned up anyway.* |
| **wear off** | stop being effective (for a drug, etc): *My arm started to hurt again as the effects of the painkiller wore off.* |
| **wear out** | become old and unusable: *I had to get a new pair of trainers because my old pair had worn out.* |
| **work out** | find the solution to a problem, etc: *If you look at the context, maybe you can work out what the word means.* |

| | |
|---|---|
| **accident** | have an accident; be (involved) in an accident; do sth by accident |
| **account** | on account of; take into account; account for sth |
| **advance** | in advance; advance to/towards a place |
| **advantage** | take advantage of sth/sb; have an advantage over sth/sb; at an advantage; an/one/etc advantage (of sth) |
| **agreement** | come to/reach (an) agreement (on/about sth); in agreement (on/about/with) sth |
| **ahead** | go straight ahead; go ahead; ahead of sth/sb |
| **alternative** | alternative medicine/therapy; find an alternative (to sth) |
| **amount** | an amount of sth; in large/small/etc amounts; amount to |
| **appointment** | make/have/break an appointment |
| **approval** | show/give (your) approval of/for sth; meet with sb's approval |
| **argument** | have an argument (with sb) (about sth/doing); win/lose an argument |
| **arrangement** | make an arrangement (with/for sb) (to do); have an arrangement (with sb) (to do) |
| **art** | work of art; modern art; art gallery; art exhibition |
| **attempt** | make an attempt (at sth/doing/to do); attempt to do; in an attempt to do |
| **attention** | pay attention (to sth/sb); attract (sb's) attention; draw (sb's) attention to sth |
| **average** | on average |
| **bath** | have/take a bath; run a bath (for sb) |
| **beginning** | in the beginning; at the beginning (of sth); beginning with |
| **best** | make the best of sth; do your best; the best at sth/doing |
| **blame** | be to blame (for sth/doing); get/take the blame (for sth/doing); put the blame on sth/sb; blame sth (on sb); blame sb for sth/doing |
| **bottom** | at/on the bottom (of sth) |
| **break** | have/take a break (from sth/doing); lunch break; tea break; commercial break; give sb a break |
| **business** | do business (with sb); in business; go somewhere on business; business trip; small business; big business |
| **care** | take care (of sth/sb); care for/about sth/sb |
| **cause** | (be/find/look for/etc) the cause of sth |
| **chance** | have/take/get a chance to do; have a chance of doing; some/little/etc chance of (your) doing; the chances of (your) doing; take a chance (on sth); chance of a lifetime |
| **charge** | charge sb (an amount of money); pay a charge; take charge (of sth/doing); in charge (of sth/doing) |
| **clothes** | put on/try on/wear/take off clothes; clothes line; clothes peg; best clothes |
| **combination** | in combination with; combination of |
| **complaint** | have/make a complaint (about sth) (to sb); letter of complaint (to sb) (about sth) |
| **compliment** | pay sb a compliment; compliment sb on sth |
| **conclusion** | come to/reach the conclusion (that); in conclusion |
| **control** | in control (of sth); lose/take/have control (of sth); under control; under the control of sb; out of control |
| **cook** | a good/great/etc cook; cook a meal/chicken/etc; do the cooking |
| **courage** | have the courage to do; it takes courage to do |
| **damage** | do/cause damage (to sth) |

| | |
|---|---|
| **danger** | in danger; out of danger |
| **day** | have/take/get a day off; day job; day trip; day by day; the other/next day |
| **debt** | in debt (to sb); get in/into debt; clear a debt; owe sb a debt of gratitude |
| **decision** | make/take a decision (to do sth); come to/reach/make a decision (about sth) |
| **demand** | in demand; on demand; a demand for sth |
| **description** | give a description of sth/sb |
| **difference** | make a difference (to sth/sb); tell the difference (between); there's no/some/little/etc difference between |
| **direction** | a change of direction; in the direction of sth; in this/that direction |
| **discussion** | have a discussion (with sb) about/on sth/doing |
| **disguise** | in disguise; wear a disguise; disguise yourself; disguised as sth/sb |
| **dream** | have a dream (about sth/sb/doing); daydream; dream of/about doing |
| **drink** | make (sb) a drink; have a drink (of sth); drink sth; drink to sb; drink to sb's health; drink a toast to sb |
| **duty** | do one's duty; a sense of duty; on/off duty; have a duty to sb/to do |
| **effect** | have an effect (on sth/sb); take effect |
| **effort** | make an effort (to do); put effort into sth/doing |
| **end** | in the end; at the end (of sth); come to an end; come to/reach the end (of sth); happy ending |
| **enough** | have enough (of sth); have enough sth (to do); enough is enough |
| **exam** | take/do/have/pass/fail an exam; sit (for) an exam |
| **example** | be/set an example; an example of; for example; follow an/sb's example |
| **exercise** | do an exercise; do exercise; take/get (some) exercise |
| **expense** | at sb's/your own expense; go to the expense of; business expense; expense account |
| **experience** | have an experience; have/gain/get experience in/of sth/doing; experienced in/at sth/doing |
| **experiment** | do/perform/carry out an experiment (on sth); experiment with sth/doing |
| **fact** | in fact; the fact (of the matter) is (that); face the facts; as a matter of fact |
| **family** | have/start a family; nuclear family; extended family |
| **fashion** | in fashion; be/go out of fashion; follow fashion; fashion model/show |
| **fault** | at fault; find fault with sth/sb |
| **favour** | do/owe sb a favour; be in favour of |
| **feed** | feed an animal/etc; feed on sth |
| **fill** | fill sth (up); filled with sth; full of sth |
| **fit** | get/stay/keep/be fit; fit and healthy |
| **floor** | on the floor; on the ground/first/second/etc floor |
| **food** | make/prepare/cook/serve food; fast/junk food; pet food; health food |
| **fortune** | make/earn/win/spend a fortune; cost (you) a fortune; make your fortune |
| **friend** | make/become/be/stay friends (with sb); best friend |
| **fun** | have/be fun; make fun of sb |
| **funny** | find sth funny |
| **fuss** | make/cause a fuss (about sth/doing) |
| **go** | your go; have a go |
| **good** | do sb good; sth does you good; good for sb (to do) |
| **granted** | take sth/sb for granted |

| | |
|---|---|
| **hair** | cut/brush sb's hair; have/get a new hairdo/hairstyle; have a haircut; let your hair down |
| **head** | off the top of your head; head for/towards a place; head over heels (in love) |
| **health** | in good/bad/poor/etc health; health centre; health care |
| **height** | in height; afraid of heights; height of sth |
| **hold** | put/keep sb on hold; hold on (to sth); hold sth |
| **holiday** | go/be on holiday; have/take a holiday; bank holiday |
| **home** | make yourself at home; be/stay at home; go/get/leave home; make your way home |
| **homework** | do your homework; have homework (to do) |
| **idea** | question an idea; have an idea; bright idea; have no idea (about) |
| **impression** | give sb the impression; do an impression of sb; have the impression; make an impression (on sb) |
| **increase** | an increase in sth (of a certain amount); a wage/price increase |
| **influence** | influence sth/sb; have/be an influence on sth/sb |
| **injection** | have an injection (for/against sth); give sb an injection |
| **intention** | have the/no intention of doing |
| **interest** | have/take/express an interest in sth/doing; in your interest to do; earn/get/pay interest |
| **Internet** | on the Internet; over the Internet; surf the Internet |
| **interview** | have/go to/attend an interview; job interview |
| **introduction** | with the introduction of sth; an introduction to sth/sb |
| **job** | do a job; have a job (to do); apply for a job; take/get a job; in a job |
| **joke** | joke about sth/doing; joke with sb; tell/make/hear/get/understand a joke |
| **laugh** | laugh at/about sth/sb; laugh out loud; roar with laughter; have a laugh |
| **learn** | have a lot to learn about sth/doing; learn (how) to do |
| **least** | at least; at the very least; last but not least; to say the least |
| **left** | go/turn/etc left; on the left; on the left-hand side; in the left-hand corner; left-handed |
| **lesson** | go to/have a lesson; double lesson; learn a/your lesson; teach sb a lesson |
| **long** | (for) as long as; (for) a long time; take a long time (to do); long to do; long for sth (to do) |
| **look** | have/take a look at sth/sb; look like sth/sb; look at/for sth/sb |
| **love** | be/fall in love with sb |
| **mad** | mad about/on sth/sb/doing; go/become mad |
| **make-up** | put on/apply/wear/take off make-up |
| **meal** | make/cook/have a meal; go out for a meal |
| **medicine** | take/prescribe medicine; practise/study medicine; the best medicine; alternative medicine |
| **mess** | make a mess (of sth); in a mess |
| **mind** | make up your mind (about sth/doing); bear (sth) in mind; in two minds about sth/doing; change your mind (about sth/doing); cross your mind; to my mind; (not) mind if |
| **mistake** | make a mistake; a mistake (to do); mistake sb for sb; do sth by mistake |

| | |
|---|---|
| **money** | make/earn/win/save/have money; spend money (on sth/doing); short of money; do sth for the money |
| **mood** | in a good/bad mood; in the right/wrong mood; in the mood for sth |
| **necessary** | necessary (for sb) to do |
| **news** | in the news; on the news; hear the news; newsflash; newspaper |
| **note** | make/take/keep (a) note of sth; note sth (down) |
| **notice** | notice sb doing/do; take notice of sth; at short notice; give sb notice of |
| **occasion** | on this/that occasion; on occasion; on the occasion of sth; special occasion |
| **opinion** | in my opinion; give/express your/an opinion (of/about sth/doing); hold/have an opinion (of/about sth/doing) |
| **order** | in order; put sth in order; in order to do; give an order (to sb) (to do) |
| **part** | take part in sth/doing; be a part of sth; part with sth; have a part (in a play, etc) |
| **party** | have/throw a party (for sb); give sb a party; go to a party; dinner/birthday/etc party |
| **pass** | pass sth (over) to sb; pass an exam/test/etc; pass a building/etc |
| **pattern** | follow a pattern; a checked/striped/plain pattern |
| **permission** | give sb permission to do; ask (sb) for permission to do; have/ask for/get permission (from sb) to do |
| **phone call** | make/receive/get a phone call |
| **photo(graph)** | take a photo (of sth/sb) |
| **pity** | pity sb; take pity on sb; feel pity for sb; it's a pity (that) |
| **place** | take place; in place of; at a place |
| **play** | play a part/role (in sth); play with sth/sb; play sth; have a part/role to play (in sth); be/act/star in a play; watch/see a play |
| **pleasure** | take pleasure in sth/doing; gain/get pleasure from sth/doing |
| **point** | see/take sb's point (about sth/doing); (see) the point in/of sth/doing; there's no point in/sth/doing; make a point of doing |
| **popular** | popular with/among |
| **profit** | make a profit (from sth) |
| **promise** | promise to do; give/make sb a promise; break a/your promise |
| **purpose** | do sth on purpose; purpose of sth |
| **question** | ask/answer a question; question sth/sb; in question; question mark |
| **queue** | join a queue; in a queue; queue up; stand/wait in a queue |
| **reason** | reason why; reason for sth; reason with sb |
| **recipe** | follow a recipe; recipe book; recipe for disaster |
| **research** | carry out/do research (on/into sth) |
| **responsibility** | have/take (the) responsibility for sth/doing |
| **route** | plan your/a route; take a route |
| **save** | save money/time; save sth for later |
| **sense** | make sense of sth; it makes sense (to do); sense of humour/taste/sight/etc |
| **shape** | get in/into shape; stay/keep in shape; the shape of sth; in the shape of |
| **shopping** | do the shopping; go shopping; shopping centre; window shopping |
| **show** | put on a show; show appreciation (for sth/sb); show sth to sb; show sb sth; on show; steal the show; TV/radio/quiz/game show; show business |

| | |
|---|---|
| **shower** | take/have a shower; a rain shower; a light/heavy shower of rain |
| **side** | (on) the opposite side; (on) the far side; side with sb; on the winning/ losing side |
| **sight** | catch/lose sight of sth/sb; in sight of sth; at first sight |
| **sights** | see the sights |
| **sightseeing** | go sightseeing |
| **silence** | in silence |
| **solution** | have/find/think of/work out/come up with/figure out a solution (to sth) |
| **speed** | at (high/full/etc) speed; a burst of speed; speed limit |
| **spread** | spread sth; spread sth over/on sth; spread to a place |
| **style** | in style; be/go out of style; do sth/go somewhere in style; have style |
| **suggestion** | make/accept a suggestion |
| **table** | lay/set/clear the table; book/reserve a table |
| **talent** | have a talent (for sth/doing); talent contest |
| **taste** | have/show good/bad taste (in sth); in good/bad taste |
| **tendency** | have a tendency to do |
| **time** | on time; (just) in time; the whole time; high/about time; take your time (doing); take time to do; sth takes up (your) time; spend time doing; spend time on; at/for a certain time; time passes; find time to do; make/find time for; for the time being; have a good/nice time (doing); tell the time; free/spare/leisure time |
| **tour** | go on / take a tour of/(a)round somewhere; tour a place; tour guide |
| **trend** | a trend in sth; follow/set a trend |
| **trip** | business trip; school trip; go on a trip; take a trip (to a place) |
| **turn** | turn (a)round/away; turn sth over; in turn; take turns; take it in turn(s) (to do); your turn (to do) |
| **view** | have/hold/take a view; be sb's view that; in my view; in view of; look at/ see the view; view of sth; view from sth/swh |
| **voice** | in a low/deep/high/etc voice; have a good/ bad voice; voice an opinion (about sth); |
| **wash** | wash the dishes; wash one's hands; do the washing-up; dishwasher; washing machine |
| **waste** | a waste of time; waste your time; industrial/household waste |
| **watch** | watch sth/sb; watch (out) for sth/sb; keep watch |
| **way** | lose/make/find your way; in a way; on the way; go all the way (to sth/swh) |
| **weather** | weather forecast; under the weather |
| **work** | do some work; have work to do; go to work; at work; work hard; out of work; place of work |
| **world** | all over the world; around the world; throughout the world; the whole world; in the world; world record |
| **wrong** | do wrong; do the wrong thing; the wrong thing to do; go wrong; the wrong way up |

| | |
|---|---|
| **able** | to do |
| **absent** | from sth |
| **according** | to sb |
| **accuse** | sb of sth/doing |
| **addicted** | to sth |
| **admire** | sb (for sth/doing) |
| **advise** | sb to do; advise sb that; advise sb on/about sth; advise (sb) against sth/doing |
| **afford** | to do |
| **afraid** | of sth/sb/doing; afraid to do |
| **agree** | with/on/to sth; agree with sb; agree to do; agree that |
| **allow** | sb to do; allow sth |
| **announce** | sth (to sb); announce that |
| **anxious** | about sth/doing; anxious to do |
| **apologise** | (to sb) for sth/doing |
| **appear** | to be |
| **apply** | for sth; apply in writing |
| **approve** | of sth/doing; approve sth |
| **argue** | with sb; argue about sth/doing; argue that |
| **arrange** | sth (with sb); arrange for sb to do |
| **arrest** | sb for sth/doing |
| **arrive** | in/at a place; arrive here/there |
| **ask** | sb sth; ask sb to do sth (for you); ask about/for sth; ask if/whether |
| **associate** | sth/sb with sth/sb |
| **attach** | sth to sth; attached to sth |
| **attack** | sth; attack sb for sth/doing; an attack on sth/sb |
| **attempt** | to do |
| **avoid** | sth/sb/doing |
| **aware** | of sth; aware that |
| **ban** | sb from sth/doing; ban sth |
| **beg** | sb (for sth); beg sb to do |
| **begin** | doing/to do/sth; begin by doing |
| **believe** | sth; believe in sth; believe that; believe to be |
| **belong** | to sb/sth |
| **benefit** | from sth; a benefit of sth |
| **boast** | of/about sth/doing (to sb) |
| **borrow** | sth (from sb) |
| **bound** | to do |
| **capable** | of doing |
| **careful** | with/about/of sth |
| **cause** | sth (to do) |
| **charge** | sb with sth |
| **charge** | sb (for sth/doing) |
| **choose** | between; choose to do |
| **claim** | to be/do; claim that |
| **comment** | on sth; make a comment (to sb) about sth |
| **compete** | against/with sb; compete for/in sth |
| **complain** | (to sb) (about sth/sb/ doing); complain of sth |
| **compliment** | sb on sth |
| **concentrate** | on sth/doing |
| **confuse** | sth/sb with sth/sb; confused about/by sth/sb |
| **congratulate** | sb on sth/doing |
| **consider** | sth/doing; consider if/whether; consider sb for sth; consider it strange, etc (for sb to do) |
| **continue** | sth/doing; continue to do; continue with sth |
| **convince** | sb (of sth); convince sb to do; convince sb that |
| **cope** | with sth/doing |
| **correspond** | with sth/sb |
| **covered** | in/with sth |
| **criticise** | sb (for sth/doing) |
| **demand** | sth (from sb); demand that |
| **deny** | sth/doing |
| **depend** | on sth/sb |
| **describe** | sth/sb as; describe sth/sb to sb |
| **deserve** | sth/to do |
| **differ** | from sth/sb |
| **difficult** | to do; find sth difficult; find it difficult to do |
| **disappointed** | with/by sth; in sb |
| **discuss** | sth/doing (with sb) |
| **doubt** | sth; doubt that; doubt if/whether |
| **dream** | about/of sth/sb/doing |
| **enjoy** | yourself; enjoy sth/doing |
| **except** | (for) sth/doing; |
| **expect** | sth/sb (to do); expect that |
| **experienced** | in/at sth/doing |
| **explain** | that; explain sth (to sb) |
| **fail** | to do |
| **familiar** | with sth; familiar to sb |
| **famous** | for sth/doing |
| **fond** | of sth/sb/doing |
| **force** | sb to do sth; force sb into sth/doing |
| **forget** | to do; forget doing; forget about sth/doing; forget if/whether |
| **forgive** | sb for sth/doing |
| **free** | to do; free from/of sth; free for sth |
| **full** | of sth |
| **glance** | at sth/sb |
| **glimpse** | sth; catch a glimpse of sth |
| **good** | for sb (to do sth); good at sth/doing; good to sb |
| **guilty** | of sth/doing |
| **happy** | to do sth; happy for sb (to do sth); happy about sth/doing |
| **hard** | to do; hard doing |
| **hear** | sth/sb; hear about sth/sb; hear from sb |
| **hope** | to do; hope that |
| **independent** | of/from sth |
| **inform** | sb that; inform sb about/of sth |
| **inject** | sth into sth/sb |

| | |
|---|---|
| **insist** | on sth/doing; insist that |
| **instead** | of sth/doing |
| **intend** | to do/doing |
| **interested** | in sth/doing |
| **invite** | sb to do |
| **involve** | sth/doing; involved in sth/sb/doing |
| **keen** | to do; keen on sth/sb/doing |
| **know** | (about) sth/doing; know of sb; be known as sth |
| **lack** | sth; lack of sth; lacking in sth |
| **lead** | to sth/(your) doing |
| **learn** | about sth/doing; learn to do; learn by doing |
| **legal** | (for sb) to do |
| **lend** | sth to sb; lend sb sth |
| **let** | sb do sth |
| **like** | sth/doing; like to do; be like sth/doing; be like sb (to do) |
| **likely** | to do; it is (un)likely that |
| **listen** | to sth/sb |
| **live** | in/at a place; live on/for sth; live here/there |
| **look** | at/for sth/sb; look forward to sth/doing |
| **love** | sth/sb/doing; love to do |
| **make** | sb do; be made to do |
| **manage** | to do |
| **mean** | to do; it/this means that; it/this means sth/doing |
| **need** | to do; need doing; in need of; no need for |
| **object** | to sth/doing |
| **offer** | sb sth; offer sth (to sb); offer to do |
| **operate** | on sb/sth |
| **pay** | sb (for sth/doing); pay sth (to sb) |
| **persuade** | sb to do; persuade sb that; persuade sb of sth |
| **plan** | sth; plan to do |
| **plenty** | of sth; plenty more sth; plenty to do |
| **point** | (in) doing |
| **possible** | (for sb) to do; find sth possible; find it impossible to do |
| **prefer** | to do (rather than [to] do); prefer sth (rather than sth); prefer sth/doing (to sth/doing) |
| **prepare** | (sb) for sth; prepare to do |
| **pretend** | to be; pretend to do; pretend that |
| **prevent** | sth; prevent sb from doing; prevent sth from happening |
| **profit** | from sth/doing |
| **promise** | to do; promise sb (sth); promise that |
| **proud** | of sth/sb/doing; proud to do |
| **prove** | to do; prove sth (to sb) |
| **qualify** | as/in sth |
| **refer** | to sth; refer sb to sth |
| **refuse** | to do sth; refuse sth |
| **regard** | sb as (being) sth |
| **regret** | (not) doing; regret sth; regret to tell/inform you |
| **rely** | on sth/sb |
| **remember** | to do; remember sth/sb/doing; remember that |
| **respect** | sth; respect sb for sth/doing; have respect for sth/sb |
| **responsible** | for sth/doing |
| **result** | of sth/doing; result in sth; result in (your) doing; result from sth/doing; as a result of sth |
| **save** | sb from sth/doing; save sth (for sth/sb) |
| **say** | sth (to sb); say that |
| **seem** | to be; it seems that |
| **send** | sb sth; send sth (to sb) |
| **settle** | for/on sth |
| **short** | of sth; short on sth |
| **similar** | to sth/sb/ doing |
| **specialise** | in sth/doing |
| **spend** | sth (on sth/sb/doing) |
| **stare** | at sth/sb |
| **stop** | sth/doing; stop to do; stop sb from doing |
| **study** | sth; for sth |
| **succeed** | in sth/doing |
| **suffer** | from sth; suffer sth |
| **suggest** | sth/doing (to sb); suggest that |
| **suitable** | for sth/doing; suitable to do |
| **supposed** | to do |
| **sure/certain** | make/be sure/certain that; sure/certain to do; be sure/certain of sth |
| **surprise** | by surprise; surprised at/by sth |
| **talented** | at sth/doing |
| **tell** | sb sth; tell sb that; tell sb about sth/doing; tell sb (not) to do |
| **tend** | to do |
| **think** | of/about sth/sb/doing |
| **threaten** | to do, threaten sb with sth |
| **tired** | of sth/doing |
| **train** | to do |
| **try** | to do; try sth/sb/doing; try and do |
| **use** | sth (for sth/doing); use sth to do |
| **useful** | for sth/doing; useful to sb |
| **wait** | for sth/sb; wait (for sth) to do; wait and see |
| **warn** | sb about/against sth/doing; warn sb of sth; warn sb not to do; warn (sb) that |
| **willing** | to do |
| **wonder** | about sth/doing; wonder if/whether/why |
| **work** | as/at/in sth; work for sb |
| **worry** | about sth/sb doing; worried that; worried about/by |
| **worth** | sth/doing |
| **write** | about sth/sb/doing; write (sth) to sb; write sb sth; write sth down |

| | |
|---|---|
| **able** | unable, (in)ability, disabled, disability |
| **academy** | academic, academically |
| **accept** | acceptance, accepting, (un)acceptable, (un)acceptably |
| **accurate** | accurately, inaccurate(ly), (in)accuracy |
| **accuse** | accused, accusation |
| **achieve** | achievement |
| **act** | (in)active(ly), acting, actor, actress, action, (in)activity |
| **add** | added, addition, additional(ly) |
| **addict** | addicted, addictive, addiction |
| **advertise** | advertisement, ad(vert), advertising, advertiser |
| **allergy** | allergic |
| **allow** | disallow, allowance, allowable |
| **amuse** | (un)amusing(ly), amusement |
| **announce** | announcement, (un)announced |
| **anxious** | anxiously, anxiety |
| **appear** | appearance, apparently |
| **apply** | (in)applicable, applied, applicant, application |
| **appreciate** | (un)appreciative(ly), appreciation |
| **argue** | argument, argumentative |
| **arrange** | rearrange, arrangement |
| **arrive** | arrival |
| **assist** | assistance, assistant |
| **associate** | disassociate, association, (un)associated |
| **attend** | attention, (in)attentive(ly), attendance, attendant |
| **attract** | (un)attractive(ly), attraction |
| **aware** | unaware, awareness |
| **beauty** | beautiful(ly) |
| **behave** | behaviour |
| **belief** | disbelief, believe, (un)believable, (un)believably |
| **benefit** | beneficial |
| **bore** | boring(ly), bored, boredom |
| **broad** | breadth, broaden |
| **build** | builder, building |
| **care** | careful(ly), careless(ly), (un)caring |
| **certify** | certificate, certified |
| **comfort** | discomfort, (un)comfortable, (un)comfortably |
| **commerce** | commercial(ly) |
| **communicate** | communication, (un)communicative, communicator |
| **compete** | competition, competitor, competitive(ly) |
| **contain** | container, content(s) |
| **converse** | conversation |
| **convict** | convicted, conviction |
| **convince** | convinced, (un)convincing |
| **correspond** | correspondence |
| **create** | creative(ly), creation, creativity, creator |
| **crime** | criminal |
| **culture** | cultural(ly), (un)cultured |
| **current** | currently |
| **danger** | dangerous(ly); endanger; endangered |
| **day** | daily, everyday |
| **decide** | decision, (in)decisive(ly), undecided |
| **dedicate** | dedicated, dedication |

| | |
|---|---|
| **desire** | (un)desirable |
| **develop** | (un)developed, developing, developer, development |
| **differ** | different(ly), difference |
| **direct** | indirect, direction, director, (in)directly |
| **discover** | discovery |
| **discuss** | discussion |
| **disgust** | disgusting, disgusted |
| **distant** | distantly, distance |
| **economy** | economic, (un)economical(ly), economics, economist |
| **edit** | editor, editorial, edited |
| **educate** | education, educator, educational(ly) |
| **effect** | (in)effective(ly) |
| **emphasis** | emphasise, emphatic |
| **employ** | (un)employed, (un)employable, (un)employment, employer, employee |
| **end** | endless(ly), ending, unending |
| **enjoy** | enjoyment, enjoyable |
| **enter** | entrance |
| **entertain** | entertaining, entertainment, entertainer |
| **enthuse** | (un)enthusiastic(ally), enthusiasm, enthusiast |
| **environment** | environmental(ly), environmentalist |
| **equip** | equipment, equipped |
| **evident** | evidence, evidently |
| **excite** | (un)exciting, excited(ly), excitement |
| **expect** | (un)expected(ly), expectation, expectancy |
| **expense** | (in)expensive(ly), expenses |
| **explain** | explanation |
| **extreme** | extremely, extremity, extremist |
| **fail** | failure, failing |
| **fame** | (in)famous(ly) |
| **fashion** | (un)fashionable, (un)fashionably |
| **finance** | financial(ly), finances |
| **fit** | unfit, fitness |
| **forge** | forgery, forger |
| **fortune** | misfortune, (un)fortunate(ly) |
| **freeze** | froze, frozen, freezing, freezer |
| **friend** | friendship, (un)friendly |
| **globe** | global(ly) |
| **great** | greatly, greatness, |
| **grow** | growth, grown-up, growing, grown, home-grown, grower |
| **happy** | unhappy, (un)happiness, (un)happily |
| **harm** | harmful(ly), harmless(ly), (un)harmed |
| **help** | (un)helpful(ly), helpless(ly), helping, helper |
| **honest** | dishonest, (dis)honesty, (dis)honestly |
| **humour** | humorous, humourless |
| **ill** | illness |
| **important** | unimportant, importance, importantly |
| **improve** | improvement, improved |
| **industry** | industrial(ly), industrious(ly) |
| **inform** | information, (un)informed, (un)informative |
| **inhabit** | inhabitant |
| **inject** | injection |
| **injure** | injury, injuries |
| **intense** | intensity, intensify, intensely |

| | |
|---|---|
| **interest** | (un)interesting(ly) |
| **introduce** | introduction, introductory |
| **invent** | inventor, invention |
| **invest** | investment, investor |
| **investigate** | investigative, investigation, investigator |
| **involve** | (un)involved, involvement |
| **jealous** | jealousy, jealously |
| **journal** | journalist, journalism, journalistic |
| **kind** | unkind, (un)kindness, kindly |
| **know** | knowledge, (un)knowledgeable |
| **law** | lawyer, (un)lawful |
| **like** | alike, dislike, unlike, likeness, (un)likeable, liking |
| **likely** | unlikely, likelihood |
| **literate** | illiterate, (il)literacy, literature |
| **lose** | lost, loss |
| **low** | lower, lowness |
| **luxury** | luxuries, luxurious(ly) |
| **machine** | machinery |
| **maintain** | maintenance |
| **manage** | managing, management, manager |
| **marry** | marriage, (un)married |
| **medal** | medallist, medallion |
| **meet** | met, meeting |
| **mix** | mixed, mixture, mixer |
| **murder** | murderer |
| **nature** | (un)natural(ly) |
| **neighbour** | neighbourly, neighbouring, neighbourhood |
| **nerve** | nervous(ly), nervousness |
| **obey** | disobey, (dis)obedient(ly), (dis)obedience |
| **observe** | observer, observation |
| **offence** | offensive, offend, offender |
| **operate** | operation, operator, operating, cooperate, cooperation, (un)cooperative |
| **oppose** | opposition, opponent, opposite, opposing |
| **origin** | (un)original(ly), originate, originator |
| **pay** | paid, payment, payable |
| **perform** | performing, performance, performer |
| **person** | (im)personal(ly), personality |
| **photograph** | photography, photographer, photographic |
| **poison** | poisonous, poisoning |
| **polite** | impolite, (im)politely, (im)politeness |
| **politics** | political(ly), politician |
| **pollute** | (un)polluted, pollution, pollutant |
| **poor** | poorly, poverty |
| **popular** | unpopular, popular(ly), popularity |
| **possible** | impossible, (im)possibility, (im)possibly |
| **power** | powerful(ly), powerless(ly), empower |
| **practice** | practise, (im)practical(ly) |
| **prepare** | preparation, preparatory, (un)prepared |
| **prison** | prisoner, imprison(ed), imprisonment |
| **produce** | product, producer, production, (un)productive(ly) |
| **profession** | (un)professional(ly) |
| **prove** | proof, (un)proven, disprove |
| **psychology** | psychologist, psychological(ly) |

| | |
|---|---|
| **qualify** | (un)qualified, qualifying, qualification |
| **real** | unreal, really, realise, realisation, reality, realistical(ly) |
| **reason** | (un)reasonable, (un)reasonably, reasoning |
| **recognise** | (un)recognisable, recognition |
| **recover** | recovery |
| **relate** | relative(ly), relation, relationship |
| **research** | researcher |
| **reside** | residential, resident, residence |
| **responsible** | irresponsible, (ir)responsibly, (ir)responsibility |
| **revise** | revision, revised |
| **revolution** | revolutionary |
| **ridicule** | ridiculous(ly), ridiculousness |
| **rob** | robbery, robber |
| **safe** | unsafe, (un)safely, save, safety, saviour, saver |
| **say** | saying |
| **scholar** | scholarship, scholarly, scholastic |
| **science** | scientist, (un)scientific(ally) |
| **second** | secondly, secondary |
| **secure** | insecure, (in)security |
| **similar** | dissimilar(ly), similarity |
| **solve** | solution, (un)solvable |
| **strong** | strength, strengthen, strongly |
| **study** | student, studies, studious |
| **style** | (un)stylish(ly), stylist, stylishness |
| **succeed** | success, (un)successful(ly) |
| **suggest** | suggested, suggestive(ly), suggestion |
| **sun** | sunny, sunshine |
| **supervise** | supervision, supervisor |
| **surgery** | surgeon, surgical(ly) |
| **surprise** | (un)surprising(ly), surprised |
| **sweet** | sweetly, sweetener, sweetness |
| **teach** | teacher, taught |
| **technology** | technological(ly), technical(ly), technician, technique |
| **theft** | thief |
| **think** | thought, (un)thinkable, thoughtful, thoughtless |
| **thorough** | thoroughly, thoroughness |
| **time** | timetable |
| **tour** | tourism, tourist |
| **train** | retrain, trainer |
| **treat** | treatment |
| **understand** | (mis)understanding, (mis)understood, understandable, understandably |
| **use** | usage, useful(ly), useless(ly), user, (un)usable |
| **value** | (in)valuable, (in)valuably, valueless, valuation |
| **vary** | (in)variable, (in)variably, varying, varied, various(ly), variation, variety |
| **wealth** | wealthy |
| **willing** | unwilling, (un)willingness, (un)willingly |
| **wood** | wooden |
| **work** | working, (un)workable, worker, works |
| **world** | worldwide |
| **write** | writer, writing, wrote, (un)written |

| US English | UK English | US English | UK English |
|---|---|---|---|
| **Travel and transport** | | **Food and drink** | |
| airplane | aeroplane | burner | hob |
| gas(oline) | petrol | can (eg of beans) | tin |
| highway, freeway | main road, motorway | candy | sweets |
| one-way (ticket) | single | (potato) chips | crisps |
| parking lot | car park | cookie | biscuit |
| pavement | road surface | French fries | chips, French fries |
| railroad | railway | silverware | cutlery |
| sidewalk | pavement | stove | cooker |
| subway | underground | take out | takeaway |
| tire | tyre | | |
| trailer | caravan | | |
| truck | van, lorry, truck | | |
| vacation | holiday | | |
| windshield | windscreen | | |
| **Hobbies, sport and games** | | **Education and learning** | |
| football | American football | elementary/junior high/ senior high school | primary/secondary school |
| soccer | football, soccer | eraser | rubber, eraser |
| sneakers | trainers | grade | mark, grade |
| to practice | to practise | principal | head, headteacher, headmaster, headmistress |
| track and field | athletics | quiz (at school) | test |
| | | recess | break |
| | | school ( = university) | university |
| **Science and technology** | | **Weather and the environment** | |
| aluminum | aluminium | downtown | town/city centre |
| antenna | aerial | fall, autumn | autumn |
| cell phone | mobile phone | garbage can, trash can | dustbin, (rubbish/litter) bin |
| elevator | lift | garbage, trash | rubbish |
| faucet, tap | tap | neighbor | neighbour |
| flashlight | torch | neighborhood | neighbourhood |
| zero | nought, zero | yard | garden |
| **The media** | | **Money and shopping** | |
| talk show | chat show, talk show | check | cheque |
| TV program | TV programme | check, bill (in a restaurant) | bill |
| | | realtor | estate agent |
| | | sales clerk | shop assistant |
| | | store, shop | shop |
| **People and society** | | **Entertainment** | |
| apartment | flat, apartment | humor | humour |
| crazy ( = insane) | mad, crazy | movie | film |
| diaper | nappy | movie theater | cinema |
| line | queue, line | theater | theatre |
| mad | angry | | |
| mean ( = unpleasant, rude) | nasty | | |
| stingy ( = not generous) | mean, stingy | | |
| **The law and crime** | | **Fashion and design** | |
| attorney, lawyer | barrister, solicitor, lawyer | closet | wardrobe, cupboard |
| jail | prison | color | colour |
| license | licence | cuffs (on trousers) | turn-ups |
| offense | offence | modeling | modelling |
| | | pants, slacks | trousers |
| | | sweater | jumper, jersey, sweater |
| | | vest | waistcoat |
| | | zipper | zip |
| **Health and fitness** | | **Work and business** | |
| doctor's office | (doctor's) surgery | desk clerk | receptionist |
| drug store, pharmacy | chemist('s) | labor | labour |
| restroom | (public) toilet/lavatory | raise | pay rise, raise |
| | | two weeks | fortnight, two weeks |